T0115173

Dreams Are Reality

Reprogram Your Subconscious
And Obtain Your Dreams

Vanaja Ananda MA; MS

And
All The People Who Joined Together As One To Bring
Our Planet Back To Its Utopian Beginnings

Cover Design by Ishwar Suthar

BALBOA.
PRESS

A DIVISION OF HAY HOUSE

Cover art copyright© 2012 by Ishwar Suthar

Balboa Press books may be ordered through booksellers or by contacting:

Balboa Press
A Division of Hay House
1663 Liberty Drive
Bloomington, IN 47403
www.balboapress.com
1-(877) 407-4847

ISBN: 978-1-4525-5412-9 (sc)
ISBN: 978-1-4525-5413-6 (e)

Because of the dynamic nature of the Internet, any web addresses or links contained in this book may have changed since publication and may no longer be valid. The views expressed in this work are solely those of the author and do not necessarily reflect the views of the publisher, and the publisher hereby disclaims any responsibility for them.

The author of this book does not dispense medical advice or prescribe the use of any technique as a form of treatment for physical, emotional, or medical problems without the advice of a physician, either directly or indirectly. The intent of the author is only to offer information of a general nature to help you in your quest for emotional and spiritual well-being. In the event you use any of the information in this book for yourself, which is your constitutional right, the author and the publisher assume no responsibility for your actions.

Any people depicted in stock imagery provided by Thinkstock are models, and such images are being used for illustrative purposes only.
Certain stock imagery © Thinkstock.

Printed in the United States of America

Balboa Press rev. date: 08/01/2012

Dedication

Dreams Are Reality is for my dear friend Nachu. He exemplified the qualities of a true hero and a saint. His pure heart would not enable him to utter a single word of contempt or hostility to another human being; in the end, he chose death rather than hurting anybody's feelings. Nachu was perfect in every other way. He had dreams of going to college and being happy; these are traits most other people take for granted. This boy was deprived of living in a world free from physical pain since the age of 16. For two years, he endured chemotherapy, radiation, tons of medicine, body ailments, loss of his hair and so much more that I don't even understand. I was told by his close family members that he never complained. In the short week that I knew him, he radiated smiles and thoughts of unconditional love for all except himself. I believe this book never would have been published without Nachu because he gave me the strength to release my fear of name and fame. That fear seemed absolutely ludicrous compared to the fear he had to encounter in his last dying days. His story is included in this book so you could get a glimpse of a close to perfect soul and feel his energy through my words. Nachu is a tribute to the world and I bow down to him in reverence.

ACKNOWLEDGEMENTS

There are many people and beings I want to thank. My family is at the top of my agenda. Raquel, my angel, always supported me even when she had doubts. She also wrote on Nachu's Caring Bridge guestbook and told him he was going to live. Her undying love for me was amazing and I am so blessed to have a wonderful daughter. Raquel is an actress, singer and dancer. I just asked her this question . . . if she could have any dream, would she choose to be on Broadway, a TV show or the movies and which actor would she want to star with? She responded that she would love to be in a movie with Zac Effron or Channing Tatom. I bless her to achieve this dream. Raquel has already recognized her own power and the strength of the divine.

Kyle always thought I was crazy, but he always told me he loved me and those three words kept me moving forward on many occasions. Kyle is also an angel even though he doesn't realize it. He is sensitive, brilliant, and caring. Kyle shows his love for me constantly, but totally different than his sister. Kyle is also a blessing in my life. Kyle has natural acting ability like his sister, however he never had the confidence to pursue his dream to be in the movies. Kyle could tell you about any film in detail and his passion bubbles to a point of ecstasy when he speaks about movies and actors. I asked him yesterday this question . . . if he could have any dream, which actor would he want to star with? His answer was Daniel Day Louis. I bless Kyle to fulfill his dream and recognize the power he has inside.

Duane was my very best male friend who I shared my innermost secrets with and when we divorced, we became acquaintances. Now, we are friends, but it is not the same. My love for him is strong. He supported me through everything and I will always be grateful. Even when I thought he let me down, I was wrong because perception is so deceiving. Duane has always wanted to be a politician for as long as I could remember. A couple of weeks ago, he told me he was no longer interested in that career path because it was so corrupt. He was so right, but that is changing in 2012 and we need people with Duane's brilliance, passion and fortitude to help our country transition easily into the 4th and 5th dimension. I bless Duane to obtain the dream he held onto for most of his life! Also, I bless him and his girlfriend Elise with many years of happiness and joy together!

Glenn, Karen and Josh are my brother, sister-in-law and nephew. Their support came through their prayers. They weren't able to speak to me much through my transformation and I believe they thought I went insane the last three months. I could feel my brother's tears of worry and fear for me and my children. Their energy was transmitted directly to me and I thank them from the bottom of my heart. I want to release them right now for any guilt or remorse they may feel once they realize I was not crazy after all. I know they loved me through it all. I know Glenn's dream is to become a comedy writer and I can't wait to see his first film. He is hysterical! I am not sure what Karen and Josh's dreams are, but whatever they are, I bless all three of my beloved relatives to achieve them.

Heidi offered her home to me when I had nowhere to go. Also, her basement was my sanctuary and the energy in that room enabled me to write Dreams Are Reality. Heidi often made me delicious treats and I watched her blossom as she began to realize what she was capable of. She has been a great friend to me and showed me the power I possessed inside. I am eternally grateful to this magnificent soul. I bless her with financial prosperity because that is one of her major concerns.

Ralphie, like Raquel, stood by me and shared posts even if he wasn't sure about its contents. You will read about Ralphie in the book as well. I wanted Ralphie to know his support and love was so special to me. I bless Ralphie with his dream of becoming a major league baseball player or anything else he truly desires if this wish changed!

Michele always kept me laughing through all the turmoil. At times she totally believed me and at other times she thought I hit the deep end. She always gave me messages from the Divine in times of need. She is a beautiful soul. I really don't need to bless her because she could already manifest her desires. She manifested chocolate every single day for a week and was having so much fun; then she stopped because she thought I went nuts. I will bless her anyway to continue manifesting wonderful miracles into her life.

Jacqui is someone I became close with through her meditations and emails. It was her meditations that I played every single day for the last three months. I also played them for Nachu the last week of his life. Jacqui is a blessing to all of humanity. She could also manifest anything she desires, but I bless her anyway and thank her for everything she has done for me especially in the last 3 months.

My house was a great support to me. I spent many days in the last year in my room, the family room, dining room and kitchen. This house was my sanctuary. I treated my house poorly for many years. You will read the details. However, I knew my house always loved me. My house was a deity and I didn't even realize it. A deity is an energized intelligence and even though my house doesn't speak or breathe, I definitely feel its life form.

Swamiji's padukas, his energized slippers, helped me through many traumas along the way. These padukas brought me closer to God in so many forms. I love these beautiful slippers. In fact, I treasure them and treat them like the God they are. I was planning to give the padukas to Nachu to ensure the cancer never came back.

Swamiji, Jesus Christ, Buddha, Archangels, Angels and so many other divine beings guided me along a path. To be honest, I never knew where it was leading, but I always knew the outcome was spectacular! I totally trust every single divine being and I am so deeply grateful for all the blessings and abundance in my life. Swamiji carried me many times when I no longer had the strength or desire to persevere. I felt his presence every minute of every single day. Without Swamiji, this book would not exist. Swamiji is the greatest blessing for all beings on this earth. My goal was to emulate his love and compassion for all of God's creations. I feel I have gotten to that point and it is only because of him. There is nothing I could bless him with since he is able to download anything he wants from the cosmos. His wish is to have 10,000 people at the Bidadi Ashram on December 12, 2012. I now realize this could mean physically at the Ashram or tuning in live through en-tv. Please help me make his dream come true. He has given so much to humanity. Let's give something back to him!

I have to mention the banyan tree separately. This tree stands tall at the Bidadi Ashram in India; Swamiji Nithyananda's Ashram. The banyan tree offers healing whenever you go near it. You could hug it, sit against it or be anywhere in its physical presence and you will immediately feel its healing powers. The banyan tree comes to me in dreams and meditations as well. I love that tree so much!

Marcy was the only person who invited me to her house for Easter and she also offered me her home after I left Heidi's. Although Marcy and I haven't seen eye to eye on a lot of things, I have always loved her even though she was downright mean at times. Marcy has a heart of gold and is extremely talented in so many arenas. I have spent many days at Marcy' house because she lives near the beach. I slept in a room with a huge picture of Jesus hanging above the bedpost. I believe sleeping in that room connected me to Jesus. I am eternally grateful to Marcy for showing me that the God in the cosmos exists in so many forms. I bless Marcy with perfect health!

Shelly sent the Dreams Are Reality passages and a written letter to Louise Hay by certified mail. I lost contact with Shelly from November 2011 to April 2012 so she never knew what was transpiring. In addition, she doesn't have a computer or internet connection so she was unable to receive any emails from me. When I explained the contents of the book, she didn't understand it. However, she somehow knew that I was speaking the truth. She never judged me and only asked how she could help spread the word. I bless Shelly with prosperity, perfect health and her passion to help people self-heal.

My beloved little angel Champie . . . . You will read about him throughout the entire book. He was my best friend and savior at the same time! I miss him so much! Without him, I would never have been able to endure and overcome the suffering of the past two years. In form or outside of form, my Champie is my guiding angel.

Fluffy is my cat who helped me through so many difficult times, especially when Champ left us. You will read about Fluffy as well. I bless Fluffy to release any fears he may have, enjoy life in his new home and become friends with his new friend Roxy.

Ishtar designed the cover for Dreams Are Reality. He always believed everything I had to say and shared all my links with his friends. I bless him with any dream he desires.

I met Jas and Wael (Mohesh) through facebook. I felt a close connection with both of them. They are beautiful souls and I could feel the sadness in their hearts. I bless them both to release any sadness and enjoy life to its fullest. I am also hoping they will be married one day, but of course that is their choice, not mine!

ABCPEACE and True Potential curriculum were developed for the sole purpose of changing the educational paradigm. Currently, I believe the educational system is failing the majority of our students. I have given ABCPEACE curriculum to one school and that school is Bright Beginnings in Sparta, New Jersey. I also gave part of True Potential curriculum for the kindergarten and first grade students to Bright Beginnings because I thought that was an extension from the preschool ABCPEACE curriculum. I recently found out a different curriculum is being used at my baby Bright Beginnings or ABCPEACE is being used under a different name. Either way, that is unacceptable to me. If this is true, the curriculums I have given to Bright Beginnings will not benefit that school in any way because it is no longer the Bright Beginnings that was formed with tender, loving hands 17 years ago that originated out of the basement of my home. If I am mistaken, and the owner is using ABCPEACE and True Potential the way it was intended, then Bright Beginnings will soar to success beyond belief.

I want to bless all the Bright Beginnings children who were under my leadership from the genesis of the school in September 1994 to the time I sold the facility in December 2010. I love each and every one of you. You have all brought me immense joy for so many years through your smiles, hugs, innocence and brilliance. I still remember the excitement when I came into your classroom or you came into my office to show me your latest milestone. I remember fingerpainting, building castles, watching volcanoes explode, dancing, recitals, and graduation. I remember movie nights, exploring nature and the Trike-a-Thon. I remember you painting the peace pole for "The Rhythm of Peace Festival." There is not a day that goes by that I don't remember my Bright Beginnings students. Please remember I am always with you and you could achieve any dream that you want. I bless you to be the leaders and movers and shakers of this world. Even though I changed my name, I am still the same Miss Pam except my love has transferred from loving children unconditionally to loving the entire planet and beings in other dimensions as well!

There are so many more people to thank. Some are mentioned in this book. However, I would never write anything negative about anybody so that is probably why you weren't mentioned if you were close to me. I thought long and hard about the next thing I am about to say. I wasn't sure if I would be able to forgive humanity for the injustices that society placed upon me. Today, a text came from Michele. It is dated April 8th at

12:27PM and I am writing this on the same day at 4:21PM. Here is what the text said "This just in. When u forgive others, you forgive yourself." I wasn't sure if I could forgive myself for what I did to Nacho's family, however now I am ready to forgive myself. The only way to do that is to forgive all of mankind. I guess I am being selfish right now.

I am releasing everybody from any negative mental pattern associated with Vanaja Ananda and the book Dreams Are Reality. If you feel you betrayed me, gossiped about me, crucified me or sent waves of negative energy toward me, I totally forgive you. I want you to think of yourself as heroes. Even though you didn't support me in any way, shape or form with group prayer, you allowed me to delve deep into the subconscious so I could share those findings with the world. Thank you so much and God bless you all!

TABLE OF CONTENTS

PART 1

Where the Negative Mental Patterns Originated

Introduction

It is difficult for me to remember a time when I was not intrigued by human emotions, self-esteem and stress. I had many major traumas in my early childhood years and throughout my life. At the time, I couldn't understand why these horrible situations were occurring to me. I repressed some events because they were too traumatic for a little girl's psyche to handle; it was revealed to me many years later. I will confide this secret among many other revelations later in the book.

I never felt I really belonged in this world. I always felt like an outsider looking in. Even my parents would talk about me, directly in my presence, as if I didn't exist. It was an extremely lonely existence. I related well with children younger than me and never seemed to have anything in common with peers my own age.

My teenage years were torture. My family moved three times in four years so I went to three different high schools. Each time, I thought it would be a great opportunity to meet new people who would truly accept me for who I am. At each school, the same scenario emerged. Group cliques were everywhere. There was the athletic group who included the cheerleaders. Since I was not coordinated and never played team sports, I

Vanaja Ananda MA, MS

was not invited to join this group. Moreover, I could barely do a somersault so splits to me meant 3 scoops of ice cream, hot fudge, whipped cream and a cherry. Oh, and a banana of course. Then, there were the popular kids. They had the perfect bodies, perfect clothes, perfect boyfriends, perfect everything! It was more like the Stepford Wives if you know what I mean. How is it possible to be so perfect I always wondered? I mean I was close to perfect . . . totally flat chested, skinny like a rail, awkward and my nickname was Olive Oil. So, as you can see, I wasn't invited into this group either. The nerds were another group. I didn't even make the nerd group because I didn't try hard in school so managed to just get by with B's and C's. The nerds wanted the straight A's. There was the theatre and singing group, but since my dog howled when I sang, I figured that artistic circle wouldn't appreciate me in their chorus. There was the musical instrument group of kids. I used to hide under the bed when the piano teacher rang our doorbell so that was out of the question as well.

As you could see, I didn't fit into any group. I was extremely introverted so nobody knew about my fun, bubbling personality. I was a loner. I had a couple of friends at each school. God forbid if they were in a different lunch period or they were sick because then I would have to eat alone! It was a major tragedy for me.

College years were definitely the best years of my life. However, the first semester was the absolute worst. I left high school a half year early because I had enough credits and I just moved to my 3rd new school. So, I started college in the spring semester which should have been the 2nd half of my senior year. Also, since my birthday was in late November, I just turned 17 years old. It was like a Doogie Howser episode, but somehow he always turned out to be the hero. I, on the other hand, got stuck with Robin Red Breast as my roommate. I think I was her third roommate and she just started in September . . . oy vey! As you could imagine, she received her nickname from the entire college baseball team! It was unbelievable! She was never in the room which was a Godsend. However, the entire suite was prejudice against whites. Guess what? You got it! Robin Red Breast and I were the only Caucasians in the suite of 8 girls. Since she was never there, I was constantly bullied although I can't for the life of me remember the details. Everyone at the school was already in cliques, so it was a difficult semester and I went home a lot on weekends.

I dealt with a lot of anxiety, stress and depression during my adult years as well. I ended up in the most unusual, scary circumstances. It is totally amazing I survived. The divine was always there to protect me even when I thought I was all alone.

Since research suggests emotional security is the foundation of a fulfilling and productive life, one could surmise it is the key ingredient of self-esteem and self-reliance. It is also the platform for academic performance, friendship, and solid core values for children. If a child experiences emotional bullying from peers, family members and/or teachers, it could potentially have an extremely detrimental effect on a person's self-worth throughout their lives. This statement was validated throughout my life up until a few years ago. If we could help people shift into a positive emotional state, they could self-heal and live a productive life in every realm—social, emotional, physical, cognitive and spiritual.

All of us have experienced traumas in our lives. I grew up believing that I was the only person who struggled in life. Now, I realize major tragedies occur in a person's life to bring him to a higher state of consciousness. I know this sounds crazy, but it is true. A person has to experience the pain, fear, worry, jealousy, greed and many other emotions in order to learn his karmic lesson. These incidences begin in early childhood and create negative mental patterns within our subconscious or bio-memory. Our subconscious remembers everything even though on a conscious level we may have no recollection. The only way to release these unwanted behaviors is to delve into the causation and the origination of that belief system. Believe me, it took me many years, but then I had an inner awakening that transformed my life which I will share in future chapters.

Since destructive thought patterns occur at an extremely young age, it is relevant to discuss children and the reader's inner child who is craving love and protection. The pages in this book can be used as a guide for people of any age. This book is a learning tool for a parent to help his child soar through life and reach his true potential. It is for the adolescent who relies on his peers and the media to guide him instead of his inner being. It is for the teenager who has to forego bullying, peer pressure and perfection. It is for the adult who lost his childhood due to fears and worries that emanated in his mind and became an inner chatter obsession. Also, the elder generation will delight in reading this book as he realizes the neuroplasticity of the brain allows him to build new neuronal pathways forever! In fact, some of the chapters in the book will give the techniques for anti-aging, releasing depression and enjoying life to its fullest

I am grateful for all the people who have entered my life and all the injustices that occurred. Now, I realize I brought these circumstances into my life so I could be liberated from them and enjoy life to the fullest. It is my desire and mission to bring love, peace, compassion, healing and joy to the world.

I am here to share all my stories, pain, hardship and self-realization. I do not love pain, believe me. I am hoping, by revealing the truth, it will help many people overcome obstacles quickly. I am here to show you life is worth living and it is truly a blessing from the divine. A great self-esteem is the key to a joyous, blissful life on earth.

This book focuses on the importance of a great self-esteem. It is a compilation of real-life experiences, the thought patterns that were created and the internal agony that ensued as a result of low self-esteem. Most important, it shows the reader how one could persevere through any situation when one is able to take responsibility for his actions. Let me tell you . . . we create every situation in our lives. Once we are aware and allow ourselves to dig under the surface for the answers, our thoughts can be expunged instantaneously.

The world is changing rapidly and we must embrace the metamorphosis of the planet. It will be easy for people who are confident, fearless, compassionate and peaceful. It is time to understand our mission in life. It is simple. If you love yourself unconditionally, then you could love every being in this world unconditionally. That love will expand to nature and you will be able to handle any situation that occurs with calmness and serenity. As a result, you will be able to make choices that will benefit you, your family and potentially mankind.

A Skeleton Exists In Every Family

I lived in an apartment in Brooklyn for the first 5 years of my life. I don't remember a lot about those early years. However, I had flashbacks when I was in my 30's of an incident that ended up affecting my life in multifarious ways. I repressed that emotion so deeply into my subconscious; it was only communicated to me when my inner being felt I could handle it. When the sordid secret was divulged, it appeared like a 5 second film. At first it seemed bizarre and unreal. Was my imagination playing tricks on me? I did have a creative mind. However, the flashes continued. As much as I wanted to deny this, my intuition told me it was real.

After several months playing games between my intuition and my cunning mind, I decided to go to a hypnotist. Hypnotism always intrigued me. Prior to this scheduled appointment, I had always enjoyed hypnotists and saw several shows where the mystics pulled people out of the audience to demonstrate their abilities. I thought it was entertaining, but fabricated. So, why did I go see a hypnotist? Sometimes you are guided by a force so strong and there is no turning back. I felt compelled to go. I took my ex-husband, Duane, with me because I didn't feel comfortable being alone with a complete stranger who was going to journey into my subconscious.

What I experienced was a nightmare beyond my wildest imagination. It really wasn't horrific, but the fact that I was reliving an episode that occurred so many years ago, was petrifying and difficult to absorb. I went to the hypnotist for over a year trying to deal with the guilt and shame I felt, but somehow it didn't get released during this time period. It only became exacerbated.

Here is the story. My cousin was 9 years older than me and we would go down into the deep recesses of the apartment building basement. I really loved my cousin and always looked up to him. It seemed to be a fun game. I was only 4 years old at the time. He would tell me to pull down my pants and he would ask me to lick his lollipop. I have to tell you I really enjoyed it. However, he said "don't tell a single person . . . even grandma because she will not love you." That is when the trauma started.

My grandma was my idol. We would do everything together. She was more like a mother to me. We baked, played cards, crocheted, watched television, walked and had so much fun together. Since her apartment was right above ours, I spent almost every waking moment with her. We were inseparable the first 5 years of my life. The thought that she would somehow admonish her love for me created an intense fear inside my inner being, I would never say a word to anybody about this exploratory act between my cousin and I, and the scenario which occurred many times became solidly embedded in my subconscious. On a conscious level, I had no recollection of the event.

The problem was I enjoyed the sensuous feeling, but knew it was a forbidden and clandestine activity. There was a little bit of excitement, adventure, pleasure, guilt, anger, fear and worry. You could imagine the tumultuous rupture of thoughts piercing through my mind. In order to protect me from having a nervous breakdown, my subconscious buried it. When something gets buried, a variety of negative behavior patterns will manifest. Over the years, these patterns have an adverse effect on our physiological and emotional well-being. Two mental patterns emerged: "if **you enjoy sex, nobody will love you" and "I am not good enough."**

To add salt on the wound, my parents decided to move to the New Jersey suburbs a few months before my fifth birthday. I was being whisked away from the only person I loved and trusted more than life itself. I withdrew into myself and formed a huge imaginary wall that no one would be able to knock down for many years. It was more like a blockade or the "Rock of Gibraltar." I felt if I didn't allow people to enter my heart, I wouldn't be hurt. Otherwise, the pain is paralyzing! Also, I felt there was no one to protect me, so I was forced to protect myself. The best way to do that was to keep SILENT!

At my new house, I had a difficult time adjusting. One day, I was caught in the quicksand. The grass hadn't grown yet in our front yard and I was slowly disappearing into the muddy earth. My brother came to the rescue and saved me. He became my hero, but my shield was still up, even with him.

My first day of kindergarten was a disaster! The teacher would yell at me so I refused to answer any of her questions for fear of repercussions. Her name was Mrs. Gomez. It is funny how you remember the negative events and people in your life. Mrs. Gomez told my parents I needed psychiatric help. In those days, psychologist was a taboo word. As a result, my parents ignored her accurate evaluation. I am not sure if the educator's intention was good or if it was done in malice. However, her intuition was surprisingly correct. I still wonder if my life would have been totally different if I received the psychological help I internally cried out for at that young age. I guess I'll never know, but I could surmise that my self-esteem would have been great! The third mental pattern that emerged was **"I must depend on myself because I can't rely on others."** Also, two more negative beliefs evolved: **"I don't want to communicate with authority figures"** and **"I feel abandoned."** At the ripe old age of 5 years old, I acquired five harmful thought patterns.

Let's go back a little bit in time. I don't remember the details; however my mother remembered the incident clearly. She said I was about 2 years old. As I told you before, we lived in an apartment complex. On the floor by the window was a heating unit. Since I was an inquisitive and active child, I climbed out of my crib and walked across the room. I apparently had no fear at that time. I walked directly onto the heating unit and frantically screamed and cried until my mother came to rescue me. My brain went into a state of fight or flight and I was in panic mode. The idea to simply walk off the heating unit escaped my mind. My body was frozen in shock. As a result, my toes never bent. I thought everybody's toes were the same as mine until I took yoga. Everybody was able to bend their toes except me in the class! At that point, I knew something was amiss with my feet. Throughout my life I experienced sharp, excruciating pain in my feet that seemed to last forever, although it was probably a couple of minutes. Until very recently, I didn't realize another pattern was stored within my bio-memory . . . **"I hate my feet."** I associated my feet with the awful sensation that constantly erupted through my body. There were times I wanted to chop off my feet from the rest of my body.

The pain was just a reminder from my inner child to remember this incident so one day I could be released from the physical torture. I will elaborate further in later chapters. For now, put this thought in your head. We could literally release *any pain or disease* anywhere in our body. Our intelligent inner being naturally reminds us there is a thought to be reprogrammed and released. Once we have awareness, our emotional, physical, cognitive or spiritual self-healing will occur!

Vanaja Ananda MA, MS

The Popcorn Fiasco

Second grade should be a wonderful time in a child's life. Maybe it would have been if I didn't already have that intense fear of authority figures. Visualize this image—a seven-year-old child sitting at her desk quietly and politely so the teacher's primary attention was focused on the gregarious students and the disciplinary problems in the classroom. That scenario was splendid for a few weeks, but then the public speaking assignment was given. When I heard the words we were going to speak in front of the class, my insides turned to jelly. I was literally petrified and the presentation wasn't due for 2 more weeks. I agonized over this project since the announcement and endured many nightmares during those 14 days. My mind was convinced it would be a disaster. It is the self fulfilling prophecy; whatever you think will happen, actually will, because the intensity behind the thought transmits energetic signals to the universe. Since, I had no clue about energy, thoughts and quantum physics, I was doomed.

My mind tried to escape from the situation so I prolonged the inevitable as long as I could. I was the last student to present. The activity I chose to demonstrate was making popcorn. It seems like an easy enough task since I had all the equipment readily available—popcorn maker, popcorn, and oil. However, when I went in front of the class, all the things I imagined and dreamed would happen, actually came to fruition. My palms started sweating, my voice cracked, and my knees started shaking. I was totally humiliated! If I thought things couldn't get any worse, I was totally wrong. Since my entire body was doing the vortex hula, the popcorn kernels spilled all over the floor and the kids started laughing hysterically. This event set a pattern for all of my school years and up until adulthood. I had an intense "fear of speaking in public."

Every time I spoke in public, whether in high school, college or business, my hands or knees started shaking and my voice cracked. I dreaded any presentations. The irony of this situation is that now I am an excellent motivational speaker. As I have mentioned before and I will reiterate many times in this book, once you are aware of the original manifestation of an idea, you could follow the pattern throughout your life and quickly eradicate it!

The Truth Is Too Painful, So Let's Ignore It

I would still visit my grandmother often since we were only an hour away. Every vacation I was with her. I idolized her and wanted to spend all my time with her. I would have chosen to live with her if I was given that option. The activity with my cousin continued until I was 9 years old. At least, that is the age my inner child has revealed thus far. It was the only secret I ever kept from my grandma and the clandestine meetings haunted me daily. There was so much guilt and fear, but it was intermingled with joy!

It is amazing that not one adult came to my rescue. I found out years later that a few adults knew, including my grandmother and my mother. This finding was a tremendous shock. How could they know and not do anything about it? It still perplexes me, but it no longer bothers me. It was just an experience that I am grateful helped bring me to higher consciousness.

There was a time I didn't see my grandma for a few weeks. She was in the hospital for some tests. I missed her terribly. She would speak to me on the phone though so that eased some of the loneliness. Finally, my parents said we were going to the hospital to bring grandma back to her home. I was elated. I remember holding her weakened hand in the car and cuddling up with her. She looked emaciated, but she was still gorgeous to me. I figured she had a bad flu and would recover quickly. When I left her house that night, I never realized it would be the last time I saw my grandma. My mom never told me the truth. My grandma had cancer!

When my grandma died a few days later, I just wouldn't and couldn't believe it! After all, the coffin was closed so there was no proof there was a body in there. Nothing would convince me this was real. I even wrote a letter to my grandma. I don't recall what I wrote, but the essence was I didn't believe she was dead. Apparently, my aunt who lived with her, opened the mail and told my parents I needed to see a psychologist. Once again, there was no therapy for me! Were my parents in total denial? I felt **abandoned** once again!

I was 11 years old when my grandma left her body. I was a gawky pre-teen. I lost the most important person in my entire life. There was nobody to help me. I pretended I was happy, but deep inside I was miserable. I withdrew further into myself and no one was going to be allowed inside my heart. It was extremely painful! I felt like 1,000 knives simultaneously engorged my body. There were times during the next several years I contemplated suicide so I could be back with my grandma. Also, I felt I was such an outcast and nobody really understood me. I thought of ways to end my life, but never had the courage to take the action to leave this planet. This just confirmed to me **I had to protect myself if I was to survive** since I was too cowardly to change the situation.

I was praying to God to help me. I always believed there was a God, but what was God anyway? Was he like a Genie in the sky who could grant any wish you had? Was he just a particle floating around the universe? I was convinced that God was a Genie and I envisioned him as a giant watching over us. The image I saw before me in my fantasy world was a handsome man of perfect physical stature who was kind, gentle, compassionate and loving. At times, I thought my imagination concocted this picture. However, now I realize our subconscious knows all about our divinity and it often gives us clues or glimpses of reality. If we pay attention to these signs, life would be so much more spontaneous and free flowing.

Unfortunately, in my pre-teen and teen years, I would never listen to my intuition. In fact, I would do the complete opposite and therefore end up learning lesson after lesson. Life at school during this time period was not fun. I only had a few friends. I had another abusive teacher who would scream and read our grades to the entire class . . . another humiliating experience. I would often think if I moved, then things would be better because there would be new kids and new surroundings. You have to be careful what you wish for because I ended up moving three times in four years. I went to three different high schools. They all contained different students and teachers, but similar situations arose and my self-esteem suffered immensely.

I was a late bloomer as they say and I am not talking about underpants either. I didn't start menstruating until I was 16 so I developed much later than the typical teen. While all these girls were getting hot boyfriends, I was stuck with guys I wasn't even attracted to. I even hid from one boy who would come to my doorstep and wait for me. I am not proud of that, but it is the truth.

I enjoyed reading romance novels and watching "chick flicks." I would fantasize about my knight in shining armor sweeping me away on his white horse. I was convinced this would happen one day. In addition, the media showcased gorgeous girls with magnificent bodies with hunks on their arms looking extremely happy. Although my being craved for this type of relationship, I never looked like a model. As I told you before I was called Olive Oil and that was far from a compliment. A mental pattern that was triggered again was "**I am not good enough**." One part of me felt I would have to settle and another part of me felt my prince would soon be arriving to whisk me away. There were constant arguments occurring internally. It reminds me of the cartoon where the devil is talking to the person on one side and the angel is on the other side. The person is completely confused.

Vanaja Ananda MA; MS

The Tatoo Knight On A Motorcycle

The summer before my senior year, I obtained employment at the boardwalk in Point Pleasant. I loved this job. At first, I worked on the kiddie rides. It was entertaining until a child vomited and I had to clean it up. Since many of the rides rotated in rapid circular motion, bile spewed often. I eventually graduated to the cotton candy counter. The sugar would always attach to my hair even with a ponytail. Cotton candy is definitely not my favorite food to eat.

The manager at the pavilion was nine years older than me. Sound familiar? He was my fantasy or so I thought. He was handsome, fun, adventurous and romantic. He owned a boat, motorcycle, and a house. His body had attractive animal tattoos. He was a Casanova, but I had no clue. I thought I was madly in love. When he asked me out, I was in heaven!

On our first date, he was a complete gentleman. He even came inside and met my parents. He told them he went to Princeton University. They saw right through him and knew he was trouble. I went on my date and had a fabulous time. When I got home, my parents forbid me from seeing him ever again. A girl in love banned from seeing her knight? I don't think so. I decided I was going to still date him. What my parents didn't know wouldn't bother them. I should have listened to my parents. After all, their life experiences offered them wisdom beyond my youthful years. I chose to learn my lesson and it was an extremely traumatic tutelage.

I was a virgin and I thought I was ready to have sex with tattoo man. We both got undressed and we were making out. My inner voice told me to stop and so I told him I wasn't ready to have intercourse. He told me it was fine and to relax. When my tense body became calm and de-stressed, he penetrated me. The excruciating pain caused me to scream in agony so he placed a pillow over my mouth. I felt like I was suffocating! I don't know how long it lasted. It felt like an extremely long time. When he was satisfied, he released me. I saw blood and I thought I was dying. Noone ever explained to me about rupturing your cherry so I felt I was cursed and going to die.

He took me home that night. He apologized for his behavior and told me he loved me. Believe it or not, I wanted to see him again. However, my parents found out I was still dating him because my brother spotted us together on the boardwalk. Even though they didn't know about the date rape (or at least never said anything), they suspected he was not suitable for their daughter. They contacted him and told him they would call the police if he came near me. I felt **betrayed** by my parents because I convinced myself I was in love with him. Low self-esteem brings horrible connections into our lives. You may say there was "no way" I could have created this scenario. You will find out later how our thinking brings people, events, and circumstances into our lives to teach us karmic lessons. Unfortunately, this was a huge karmic teaching I had to encounter continuously until I finally comprehended the message from the divine. The answers were right in front of me, but I chose to ignore them. Unless we are ready to see the truth, we will never admit to its identity. It is easier to live in illusion.

Vanaja Ananda MA, MS

Men Are Unpredictable

My father had a bad temper. He would never hit my brother or me, but his words were lethal and the sound of his voice was frightening. My brother and I were petrified of my father. It was like living with a time bomb. One minute he would be happy, smiling and singing. The next minute, he would be yelling and cursing. I felt like I was walking on egg shells and it wasn't a pleasant experience. The smallest things would ignite his fire. We would be traveling in the car to go to a restaurant. All of a sudden my mom may disagree with something he was saying. The next thing we knew he was screaming he wanted a divorce and she was a horrible wife. If we tried to defend our mother, he would start abusing us. Vacations were even worse. We would be so excited to be going to the Caribbean. However, once we were there, my dad would be complaining about money or screaming at us about something we did. It didn't just occur once; it occurred every single day in some manner. We never knew who would be the target of his vehemence.

He was emotionally abusive. His disparaging comments would make us cringe and coil into a ball in the hope of disappearing. Each word penetrated our subconscious where it remained dormant for decades. Adjectives used by my dad to describe our personage were lazy, bad, useless, stupid, bum . . . you get the picture. At this point, you may be thinking your own parents called you worse names. Or, those words don't seem too horrible. You are probably right in that sense. However, when one hears ridiculing and condescending remarks over and over again . . . maybe even 5 times or more per day . . . the idea gets permanently embedded in your bio-memory. It builds a mold inside that is laborious and virtually impossible to break.

I started believing I was those identities. A person who loves me was giving me those suggestions. How could I not believe it was the truth? In our younger years, our parents play a crucial role in our opinion of ourselves. We begin to judge ourselves based on the attitudes of those close to us. Furthermore, we attract external objects into our life to confirm what we believe to be true. For instance, if my perception is that I am useless, stupid and bad. I may befriend people who set me up for failure and convince me that "**I am not good enough.**" It may be as simple as losing at a board game and the winner gloating. This loss has triggered feelings of inadequacy and it is proof that I am useless and stupid. For every situation that brings up images of incompetency, the sentence "**I am not good enough**" repeats like a broken record in our head. Through our inner chatter, we declare to ourselves repetitively we are insufficient, weak and inept. We program ourselves for failure without even being aware.

Now, let's go back to my father. He loved to sing and joke, although he had a dry sense of humor. He played the saxophone in the Tommy Dorsey band. My dad could play any song after he heard it once; his ear was toned to perfection. He was the life of the party, and people were attracted to his jovial personality. His anger was usually restricted to his family members and he displayed a different persona to the rest of society. His mother died when he was a young child and his dad passed away when he was 16 years old. My father silenced his anger internally during his adolescent and teen years for the injustices that happened in his life. As an adult, he would release his hostility by exploding. It is understandable, but it didn't seem justifiable to abuse your family.

I was always craving affection from a male. My father found it awkward to hug or kiss us. I can't remember any times we cuddled. He had a loving heart, but he didn't know how to express any positive emotions such as love and compassion. Instead, it was more comfortable for him to express his uncontrollable bouts of anger and then be remorseful after. I equated love with anger. I figured first you have an argument and then kind words and emotional support would be granted.

And so, the pattern was created. I didn't receive emotional security from my male role model, so I was forced to seek it elsewhere. My male cousin offered me a tiny bit of affection during our rendezvous. It was just enough to be obsessed with desiring it. I continued searching for love. When I met tattoo man, he was extremely affectionate so I convinced myself I was in love with him. We all know how that turned out.

When I was 24 years old, I met Duane. He had so many characteristics of my father. I now find it uncanny. At the time, I never made the connection. Duane had a heart of gold. He was romantic, affectionate and fun. However, he had the same evil temper as my father and it was triggered instantaneously without warning. We enjoyed the beginning years of our marriage screaming at each other and then making up. By this age, I learned to strike back with vicious verbage as well. We were living in a war zone. However, we thrived on the adrenaline rush from our intense and insane outbursts. It seems a little sickening, but it is the truth. When

Vanaja Ananda MA, MS

I finally had some clarity 20 years later, I decided I was going to live in peace at all costs.

We actually choose our parents before we come down to this planet. There are a certain amount of samskaras, or karmas, we bring with us. Our contract with the cosmos is to learn these karmic lessons before we die. We go into a coma when we are born because the pain being forced through the uterus is unbearable. A state of unconsciousness during this trauma gives us some semblance of sanity. However, we forget what our purpose was on this planet. We are born as a blank slate ready to enjoy the world, but then society bestows its ideas upon us and we accumulate more karma. Incredible!

First, our thought patterns commence with the parents as I prefaced at the beginning of this chapter. Next, teachers have a huge impact on a child's psyche. I explained personality behaviors that emanated from the wrath of my kindergarten teacher and other teachers who followed in her footsteps. Neighbors also play a part. I used to hear my neighbors whispering about how shy I was. They would criticize my peer group. They felt I should be socializing with children my own age and not kids who were a few years younger. Once again, the belief **"I am not good enough"** emerged like a sore thumb. Everybody plays with kids their own age so there must be something wrong with me.

Children younger than me looked up to me as a role model. I enjoyed younger children and I am sure they felt that energy. Even today, I act much younger than my chronological age. I love being innocent and spontaneous. I treasure every moment of every day.

Adults are extraordinary at instilling biases. Parents buy treasure chests of dress up clothes for girls. Princess and fairy costumes embellished with matching jewelry, high heels and exotic dresses fill the bins. From toddler age, girls are encouraged to pretend and fantasize which is so healthy and a part of a human's innate nature. Boys, on the other hand, are given trucks, cars and weapons. Usually parents think it is not normal for boys to wear dresses and put make-up on. Children need to explore no matter what gender they chose for their body. By prohibiting fun and freedom of choice, an internal anger starts to build. The same could be said about the opposite gender. A girl who is athletic and may want to participate in sports like football or rugby will feel malice that is directed inside when she is told those activities are solely for boys.

We are taught to adhere to society's rules at all costs. Since, the anger can't be thwarted outside, it becomes self loathing inside. Children are unintentionally brainwashed to feel bad about themselves by adults who were conditioned when they were younger. It becomes an unending circuit from generation to generation. The mass population considers a female truck driver or male nurse to be inferior members of the community based on notions of gender bias. Some people are even ostracized from the area because they choose a different sexual orientation. Could you imagine growing up your entire life realizing that you don't fit into your gender identity? We are not here to judge and condemn people, but rather to love, help and have empathy and compassion for all beings.

The media can be poisonous as well. Beauty is a major focus in almost every advertisement. The product could be perfume, clothes, shoes, electronics, motorcycles, sports cars and more. The subliminal message suggests when you buy this product, the sexy woman or hunk comes with it. The perfect man or woman will land on your doorstep in a box complete with ribbon and bow once you pay for this product. How absurd is that? However, research shows instant flashes of messages will go directly into our subconscious without us being cognizant. Conceptualize the trickery the person faces when he buys the product, but the prize never arrives. He inadvertently turns the blame on himself and feels unworthy.

I just wanted to reiterate the causes of our anxiety, low self-esteem, and depression. Our family, teachers, peers, media, and neighbors all play a substantial role. Our world has become a place of fear and despair instead of contentment, faith and hope. This needs to be altered quickly in order for humanity to confront issues head-on and develop effective solutions. If kids are taught ways to look inside instead of outside for answers, they will become the enlightened beings God intended for them.

The universe is full of abundance waiting to shower us with whatever we desire. Our inner child knows exactly what our desires are. Some desires may be materialistic and that is alright. However, our true desires reflect our connection with all entities whether they are humans, animals, plants, rocks, trees or anything else. We are all made of energy. We see ourselves as individuals, but in reality we are all attached. Let's live in a world of cooperation, guidance and support for each and every member of society. Choose to see the divine in everything that surrounds you!

PART 2

Death In So Many Ways

Death Means More Than Leaving The Body

When we hear the word death, the first vision that enters our mind is a person in a coffin or ashes in an urn. We might conjure up images of people in our lives that passed away or a character in a book or movie that encountered death. We may envision soldiers at war dying. Usually, death means no longer existing in this world and that concept is extremely scary. The fear and shock your physical body endures when someone close to you dies puts us into a state of numbness, pain and paralysis. We sleep for hours or even days to escape from the torment of our reality. We may pretend everything is fine, but know deep down a part of our soul has been viciously ripped from our essence. The fun and entertainment we once enjoyed is no longer satisfying us. There is a magnanimous void in our lives and it takes a lot of courage and divine seeking to swim across these tidal waves until we are rescued by a small boat.

The person who crosses to the other side is definitely in a better place for it is a dimension of happiness and bliss. Hindus, Buddhists, Islamics, Asians and other nationalities are taught the cycle of birth and death. When one leaves the body, he takes another birth until he fulfills all his karmas and eventually becomes enlightened.

A lot of westerners understand this train of thought as well. By westerners, I am referring to people from the United States, Europe, and Canada. Eastern philosophy is now integrating with the western philosophy; it is a blessing for the beings who currently reside on our planet. Vedic and Asian methods are mystical, powerful and self-healing while the traditional Western civilization resorts to chemicals and stimulants for healing. Times are changing and as a result holistic practices are emerging all over the world at rapid speed.

There are multitudinous ways for death to happen in our lives. Death is more than just leaving our body. It could surface as the death of an idea, the death of our identity, the loss of a house or a business, the loss of a family during a divorce, the death of a relationship or the death of name and fame. The link that unites all these forms of death is the misery, anguish and suffering our body undertakes in all the scenarios mentioned. When our heart breaks into a million pieces, there is not enough glue in the universe to cement the fragments together.

It takes many years to recover unless we bring ourselves to higher consciousness and live in a place of peace and happiness. First, we need to take responsibility for everything in our lives and cease blaming external forces. I repeatedly echo that we are responsibility for every situation, person, or event we bring into our lives whether it is exciting, joyful or catastrophic.

Second, when we treat everyone with love and respect, we value them. Therefore, when a person, animal or material object leaves us physically, we know without a doubt their non-physical form is always there to guide us. We are still able to communicate with our beloved and receive answers by these energetic entities. So, the bottom line is we have guardian angels that will support, teach, love and nurture us even though we are unable to see them.

Third, we need to engage ourselves internally to comprehend the rationale for our depression. After all, the dying person is released from suffering in physical pain and we intuitively know the soul is liberated and joyful. Why do we continue to stay morose? Does a societal conviction impart us with the knowledge we must be upset and distraught when someone passes away or when we are faced with a deep loss. We must have the courage to look within for only we are aware of how to help ourselves heal completely.

Vanaja Ananda MA, MS

This section of the book will lead you through a variety of calamities I brought into my life. I didn't take responsibility at the time, but once I took responsibility the universe moved mountains to bless me with miracle upon miracle. I want you to be liberated from the bondages of illusion and transform quickly and as painlessly as possible. I created my own pain, withdrawal, solitude and unhappiness to the point where I wanted to be released from my body before my time. Every incident generated doubts about my value, capability and worthiness to society and existing on this planet. With a great self-esteem, you could conquer the world and fulfill any dream. It is as simple as that. Noone is any better than anyone else. They are just blessed to have the secret revealed to them. You will be able to sustain a beautiful life and help all those who come in contact with your presence.

Illness Prevails

As long as I could remember, my father was afflicted with some type of illness. He had meniere's disease. Meniere's is a pathological condition of the inner ear characterized by ringing in the ears and progressive loss of hearing. In addition, he had heart problems, diabetes and high blood pressure. Also, he had intermittent illnesses with kidney stones and ulcers.

I was living in California, attending school and raising a family. My parents still lived in New Jersey. I received a call from my mother that my father was going to the hospital for surgery. Hospitals petrified me since I correlated that word with death from the experience with my grandmother. I journeyed across country immediately after New Year's believing I would be back home by the end of the month. However, six surgeries within seven months made it impossible for me to join my family on the west coast so they all moved to New Jersey by the end of January. My ex was supportive during the entire time, never complaining about the sudden upheaval. Through God's grace, he landed a new job by the time his plane hit the ground.

Every day I would go to the hospital, sometimes my mother would accompany me. Some days, my mom would watch the kids. Almost simultaneously, my mother was diagnosed with lymphoma. I would go one day to the New York hospital to be with my dad and the next day to the Jersey shore hospital to visit with my mother. Meanwhile, the kids went to daycare. It was a traumatic experience for all involved. I was running on auto pilot.

During the seventh operation, my father's legs were amputated. His toes became gangrenous, filled with poison. Shortly after his surgery, he was relocated to a rehabilitation center to learn to walk with prosthetics. His health seemed to be improving so I returned to California to rent our home, move all our belongings and submit my assignments to college. We were gone about two weeks. When I returned, my father had dementia. It was the most horrifying circumstance to witness. A man who had vitality had withered away to a skeleton with considerable memory loss. Two weeks before he had all his faculties. I had tremendous guilt since I blamed myself for not being there. He must have felt abandoned and I knew exactly how that feels.

Vanaja Ananda MA, MS

The rehab facility released my father into my hands. We tried nursing him in our home. However, he had a feeding tube and would be incontinent. There were occasions he would throw his feces around the room. I had no choice but to put him in a nursing home since I was still taking my mom for chemotherapy treatments over an hour away. My entire life I promised him I would never put him in a nursing home and here I was driving him to his deathbed. I would visit him almost every day. It was difficult for my mother to see him that way so she often stayed home with the kids.

He didn't recognize me most of the time and would hang onto the curtain in fear. I think he was reliving his army days when he was stationed in Japan during World War II. The sentences he spoke no longer made any sense. He was alive in a body being fed through a tube, but the father I knew was no longer in existence. My mother and I fought to have the feeding tube removed. We won the case through an ombudsman, but the doctor still refused to remove the tube. He left his body a few days after the judge's decision.

There was no time to grieve because my mother was weak and she refused to take her medicine. I brought her to a psychologist and she convinced him she was perfectly fine. My mom was always one to smile and pretend everything was great, while internally she created a malignant tumor.

There were so many times during my life that I hated my father and wished he was dead. Hate is a strong word, but the emotion was strong with me. I have harbored a lot of guilt and shame about these strong feelings. It was a love/hate relationship between father and daughter. Although, when he became deathly ill, I couldn't and didn't want to leave his side. My inner child was always trying to protect me from his wrath, but my higher consciousness saw the divine within him and knew he needed love, compassion and care. I bless the God inside of me for helping me through this awful ordeal.

Our Mind Can Be Deceiving

There was another woman in my life. She was a female of poise, substance, and presence. Her smile radiated the room and she smiled often. She would live in a world of fantasy since nothing seemed to bother her. The worst fiasco can happen in her life and she gracefully slid right through the incident. This woman was my mom. I learned a lot from my mom because I thought she was always correct since in my eyes my dad was always wrong. The paradoxical effect was I grew up developing more negative beliefs.

My mom lived the Cinderella story. Her mother died at childbirth and her father blamed the baby for his wife's demise. My biological grandfather soon married another woman who became my mother's worst nightmare. I wouldn't wish her beginning years on anybody! In order for you to comprehend the pain and agony my mom endured, I will give you small flashes of the first 11 years of her life. Her stepmother and father referred to her as the "adopted monkey" and treated her accordingly. Actually, I think monkeys are handled much nicer.

My mother was locked out of the house when her parents and step-sisters weren't home. Inside, she was only allowed to visit certain rooms of the house, while the other inhabitants of the household were offered free reign to explore. They fed her meals to sustain her, but never any desserts or treats. She often was left alone for hours in the snow, rain and other inclement weather. Nowadays, DYFS would have been called. In those days, abuse was tolerated.

When she turned 13, my grandmother adopted her. She went from Cinderella to the princess. It was a fairytale. However, the embedded memories were already solidified in her subconscious, so even though she was living the life of a princess, her past always intruded on her happiness. Her protective shield as a child was passed down to the next generation.

On one side, I saw my mother as innocent, helpless, victimized and controlled. Contrarily, I witnessed happiness through her continuous smiles and the ability to live a stress free life. As a result, I associated the four negative elements with happiness. Little did I know, her smile was a mask to cover the terror and solitude she lived with her entire life. The mother I believed was superwoman, taught me lessons that were as damaging as my father's abusive pattern.

Vanaja Ananda, MA, MS

Throughout most of my life, I thought **men should be in control** and **avoid conflict whenever possible.** With my father, brother, cousin, tattoo man and even my ex-husband, I allowed myself to be controlled and helpless. It was easier to give in even if I didn't agree then to fight in an unending war. I would always smile and pretend everything was great, when in reality it was far from being even good. Today, I have a genuine smile and am happy almost all the time! It is a spectacular change!

I have told you about the emotional abuse so I don't want to belabor that point. I would like to tell you about financial issues that emerged as a result of my mother's inability to voice her opinion when external circumstances bothered her.

My father controlled all the money and he was frugal. My mom would have to beg for money to do anything. My brother and I also had to plead if we wanted to go to the movies or out to eat with friends. There were a lot of times my neighbors paid for me since I was afraid to ask my father. My mother would even give my father her entire paycheck. We always knew if we wanted money, we would need to ask my father.

"Money doesn't grow on trees," "rich people are arrogant," "the mafia has tons of money because they kill people," and other antidotes were recorded in my memory. Often I would hear "that is too expensive" or "I don't have enough money." Money became a word of fear and greed instead of joy and abundance. I witnessed two bankruptcies and many years of conflicting thoughts about money. For example, we would go on a beautiful vacation to a 4 star hotel, but then we would need to skip lunch because we didn't have enough money. Or we would go to dinner and not be able to get dessert for lack of money.

Money was a famous topic in our household and I chose to spend money quickly. My ex had control of our money and often I would beg him for money. It was humiliating. When I had money, I would spend it quickly. I somehow felt if I had too much money, people would think I am arrogant or conceited. I didn't take responsibility for finances until very recently. It was a hard habit to break. I love money now and realize when you have money, you could help so many more people. I believe in the law of attraction. The cosmos is full of abundance and I am a money magnet. I can easily attract money to me through my intense desires. When the energy vibration is the same at both an inner and outer level, the cosmos is able to give you what you want.

The bankruptcy experiences were painful. I saw my father crying on the verge of committing suicide, while my mother seemed to ignore the situation. I watched helplessly as the bank took our house. We were forced to sell most of my belongings for there was nowhere to store the vast amount of items. This was a different type of death. It was the death of our home that we lived in for 12 years and not knowing where we would be next. This loss created a fear of the unknown. The fear was unwarranted because my family lived in a hotel for a month and then moved to a beautiful townhouse.

Vanaja Ananda, MA, MS

A Little Girl Enters and Exits Our Lives

A year after our marriage, my ex and I moved to California. Shortly after our move, my mother-in-law came to visit and she brought my niece with her. I fell in love with that little girl. She was five-years-old when she arrived on our doorstep. We were told horror stories of her living conditions. Her father was a drug addict and her mother an alcoholic. She would only eat french fries and drink pepsi because she was given money daily to walk to the local store. My niece had one outfit—the one she was wearing. It was the first time I ever heard the word lice since it took several washings to remove those eggs from her hair.

My heart went out to her and I didn't want her to go back to those living conditions so she stayed with us. We were inseparable from the beginning. We had a beautiful family unit and enjoyed many wonderful experiences together. We also encountered some hardships.

She was a perfect child . . . too perfect. She would lie to your face and even though you knew it was a lie, you started believing it. She was that good at it. We took her to several psychologists and she even lied to them so that was useless. Her mantra from a very young age was lie, lie and lie some more! It was her sole source of protection. We never knew what went on in her studio apartment where a different man appeared every night as company to her drunken mother. We could only surmise that horror struck a little angel and she buried it deep within.

Even though we were so frustrated that we didn't know how to help her, she seemed happy; she was always smiling, had friends, loved swimming in the pool and learning new things. When we moved back to New Jersey during my parents illness, that all changed. She abhorred the move and being thrown into a new state, new school and a senior citizen development. I was overwhelmed with my parent's illness and had little energy for her and my little boy. She wanted to go live with her biological father because he was no longer on narcotics. She made life unbearable and we were fearful she would runaway, be murdered or become a prostitute. At eleven-years old, we put her on a plane to the west coast. From that day on, she stopped calling us mom and dad. It was heartbreaking! My dad died Christmas Eve, my mom died the following August and my daughter left us the following January. Three deaths practically in a row were too much for my fractured heart. And, if that wasn't enough, my dog that we adored, died one month later. I think I would have had a nervous breakdown. However, two weeks after my mom left her body, my second daughter was born. She was truly a blessing.

Vanaja Ananda MA, MS

The Car Jack

I was living in California and decided to go on a weekend journey to Virginia to inquire about a franchise opportunity in the early childhood industry. My family put me on the plane and I arrived at Dulles airport in Washington, DC around midnight. I went to the rental car agency to pick up my automobile and travel to the hotel. I paid for a compact car, but the agency had none left so they offered me a Lincoln Continental. I was thrilled!

I began my trek with my trusty map. My directional ability was not the best and it still isn't. I started driving and of course, got lost. I stopped at a gas station and finally found my way to the motel. It was approximately two in the morning. I went to the front lobby and registered at the desk. After I received the key to the room, I went outside to park my car. I was grabbing my luggage from the seat and as I was opening the door, a man came and whispered something to me which I couldn't hear. In a matter of moments, I was thrown onto the lap of another man who already entered the vehicle from the passenger side. He had a knife and the blade was aimed at my jugular. The original man jumped into the driver's seat and screamed at me to give him the key. I handed him the room key in a panic. He screamed at me and said if I gave him the key to the car, they would let me go. I actually believed them; that's how gullible I was.

When I finally gave him the key, he started driving away. The angels were there to rescue me once again. This is what transpired. If they drove left out of the parking lot, they would have been free and I probably would have been raped or murdered. However, they turned the vehicle right. In front of them were a closed iron gate and a dead end. I bit the man's arm that was holding me and managed to open the door. I ran screaming, pounding on the door until the guard came. It would have been easy for them to drag me back into the car since we were at the back entrance and it was the middle of the night. Luckily destiny interfered. The culprits became confused and alarmed about their predicament. They turned around as quickly as they could and tore out of the parking lot. They were caught three days later driving in the stolen vehicle. Unfortunately, they were minors and this was their first offense. I chose not to travel across country to press charges. I still wonder if that was mistake. I am sure justice will prevail in some form!

What type of death would this be? They sold all my belongings, most likely to purchase drugs. But, I believe there is something that infiltrates my system even deeper. It may be the death of my integrity because I felt helpless and disrobed even though they never touched one hair on my body. Or, it may be the death of being victimized. All of a sudden, I had the courage to bite the perpetrators arm while envisioning my children without their mother. Strong feats are performed under terroristic conditions. I became "superwoman" for those few seconds, enabling me to save my life!

Vanaja Ananda, MA, MS

The Marriage Is Over

My ex and I met at a nightclub. I remember "the Nerds" were playing that night and I was out with my girlfriend. He asked me to dance and we danced the whole night. There was definitely an energetic spark, but my intuition always told me something was missing. You know how well I listened to my intuition—not at all. We really enjoyed each other's company. He would write me poems and plan romantic getaways. I would reciprocate by cooking special meals or surprising him with little gifts. Intimacy between us was questionable. I was a virgin except for that date rape and I never felt that event counted. So, I considered myself a virgin when I met my ex. While I loved oral sex, intercourse wasn't enjoyable and at times painful. He could never understand why certain positions hurt because he tried to be gentle. I didn't understand why the physical act seemed like a chore and I would pray he would ejaculate so I could cuddle and watch television or go to sleep. I would pretend to have orgasm so he would finish quickly. After our divorce, I finally solved this dilemma that haunted me. Thank goodness because sex is actually awesome!

I should have been happy with my life, but for some reason I wasn't. I had a guy who adored me and I was blessed with healthy and bright children. I lived in a beautiful house. I had a great job. Any outsider would envy me for my perfect life. So, what could possibly be wrong? I would blame myself for endless hours for my unhappiness. It just didn't make any sense to me, but yet the feelings of melancholy existed. I was longing for something I didn't know existed, yet every cell in my body knew there was a missing link to my wholeness.

Finally, after 24 years of marriage, we mutually decided our contract was over. I encountered another grieving process for a couple of weeks. Denial, guilt, anger, and acceptance flooded my anatomy until I realized I was finally liberated to pursue my dreams.

The Loss of My Business

I founded and operated an early childhood education center. The business started out of the basement of my house with five children and skyrocketed to a student body of 120 within a 6,000 square foot state of the art facility. I always loved teaching and although my Bachelors Degree was in Marketing, my true passion was the educational field. When my first child was born, I took classes in the evening and a year after I gave birth to my second child, I opened my school. Even though it was a full day program in my house, I taught 2 classes every day. I always believed children are like a sponge and can absorb so much information. Playing with a purpose was always my goal and my motto was "where fun and learning go hand in hand."

After five years in my home, I was ready to close the business. My clientele adored me, but I felt devalued by the rest of society. I informed all the parents of my intentions a few months prior to the closing date so they had ample time to secure new childcare services. One of the families gave me a gift certificate for a massage the previous Christmas and I chose to use it shortly after my decision to leave. At the masseuse, the topic led to the closing of my school. She said the local church was looking to rent space and one of the options they were considering was a preschool. I couldn't believe my ears! The next day, I met with the minister and church devotees and we signed papers. The school moved from the basement to a church facility in August and its doors opened immediately after Labor Day.

Bright Beginnings was my baby. It was almost like I gave birth to this corporation. I loved every minute I spent there. I was only there a month when I was told the tax assessor was instituting an antiquated law that stated any business renting space from a church, must pay an accelerated tax to the state. In our case, it was $33,000 due by December 20th of that year. Of course, church authorities nor I could afford to pay that. This state mandate affected businesses within churches throughout the state of New Jersey, although we were the first to be notified. I contacted a lawyer to ascertain our rights. She said the only thing we could do was get the media involved. That is exactly what we did. Local and state newspapers wrote articles and television and radio stations broadcasted the injustices occurring at Bright Beginnings and soon to be other organizations housed in churches within the state. Also, we contacted local and state political leaders. As a result of these actions, a bill was fast tracked through the legislation the day before our deadline. It was a miracle!

After six years at the church, we outgrew these facilities and the new leadership wanted the church back for community events so they asked us to leave. Since the rent was inexpensive at the church, I wasn't able to find suitable space, so once again I thought Bright Beginnings would close. However, a friend of a friend was looking for tenants to rent spaces in the new building he was planning to construct. The best part was that the rent was a little more than my existing rent. The landlord's cousin was an architect so they were building to suit. The cosmos is incredible! I was ecstatic. The only caveat was it took the facility an extra year to be constructed and we had to temporarily move into a firehouse for a few months. Most parents were patient and followed us, but there were a handful of parents who didn't like the conditions at the firehouse. Personally, I thought the establishment had a lot of charm, but it definitely needed a lot of work. Suffice it to say, we have very fond memories of our adventures in the firehouse. We moved into the brand new building right after Labor Day and actually opened our doors as scheduled.

Our new building was everything I ever dreamed and more. I thanked God daily as I unlocked the door in the morning to enter the building. The school was a place of joy, bliss, education and healing. The teachers were great and it seemed like the people who were supposed to be there just walked in. Interviewing was easy, yet thorough. All staff members had the passion to help children be successful in all developmental areas of their life. I was truly blessed.

We organized multifarious community fundraisers and they were all a success. Bright Beginnings had an excellent reputation in the local area. The business got to a point where it was functioning on its own. The teachers were at the school for over 10 years and they knew the philosophy and mission to a T. They had outstanding classroom management skills. I constantly added innovative ideas to the curriculum, but I wasn't satisfied. I yearned to help more children and mainly those who were suffering in the current school system.

My intention was to be liberated from the school. I obsessed about it constantly. But how could I abandon the teachers, families and children who loved the school so much? I thought about it day and night. Be careful what your thoughts are unless you are positive that is what you want. I was in constant turmoil since Bright Beginnings was my baby. However, I felt it was time the baby survived without me leading it. I would pray to God to help me and he answered my prayer.

When I came back from India, the school was in financial distress. Being closed in the summer was always difficult, yet I managed every year to overcome that obstacle. The one monition I couldn't ignore was a lethal mistake that I believe occurred on a subconscious level since I was shocked and unprepared when I found out. The rent check for May was never cashed; the landlord decided to hold onto it for some unforeseen reason. As a result, May and September were due simultaneously. Since I was in India, I asked my friend who was managing the business to mail checks to creditors at the beginning of the month. When the second rent check was due, not including monthly property, taxes and condominium fees, it left the business in arrears. At my return from the Ashram at the end of October, it was impossible to pay the debt owed.

I thought I would have to close the school by the end of the month because the landlord threatened to put a lock on the door if rent wasn't paid immediately. There was no extra money either personally or from the business since we already declared personal bankruptcy the year before. Again, I felt like I was falling into an abyss and saw no way out. I wrote a letter to the parents and arranged an emergency meeting with the staff explaining the situation.

I never distributed the letter to the parents because the most amazing thing happened. I told all staff members to keep our conversation private until all the parents received the letter and they all agreed. One faculty member was unable to keep her mouth closed and immediately told a few parents. Lo and behold, I sold the school to one of the parents with the ability to pay off all debt and earn a profit. Though I abhor gossip and believe it is an extremely dangerous trait, this time it worked in my favor so I am deeply grateful. The divine has always come to my rescue.

We have come to all the major deaths in my life. Actually, there is one more whose death tore my heart physically out of my body. I will speak about this death in the section entitled awareness. This death transformed a major part of my being at such a great cost.

As you can tell, death materializes in a variety of ways. As described above, death occurred in the form of leaving the body, the loss of a house, a person leaving my life, bankruptcy, loss of a business, an imagined loss and divorce. Yes, even imagining in a state of panic convinces your mind that it is actually occurring. When I imagined I would never see my children if I didn't get out of the car, I was graced with super human strength beyond my belief. Without that thought, I wouldn't have had the courage to escape.

If you analyze your life, you will also notice death not only as the demise of a soul, but in a lot of formats. One goes through the grieving process of any death—denial, anger, bargaining, depression and acceptance. Going through this repetitively in your life, leaves you feeling unworthy, less than and insignificant! If we could embrace death as a natural occurrence in life and a lesson to be learned instead of fear, we will have eternal peace. That calmness will transmit to outer abundance through health, wealth, romance or anything your heart desires.

PART 3

The Importance Of A
Good Self-Esteem

What Is Self-Esteem

I have spoken about self worth and self esteem throughout this book. What is the definition of self esteem and why is it so important? In a nutshell, self esteem is how you value and think of yourself. Is a person who is constantly belittling themselves through internal voices (thoughts) or external voices (society) feeling good about themselves? Are these the leaders of the world?

Before we answer that question, let's identify the attributes of a good leader. A good leader listens to people and understands their point of view. Effective listening is a way of showing concern for others and builds trust. He consciously listens and repeats phrases to ensure his mind is not wandering off into daydream land. He stays in the present and if his mind does happen to float away, he sincerely lets the other person know so the statement is echoed again.

The speaker feels his voice is worth listening to.

In my opinion, ignoring, giving lip service or interrupting a person in the middle of a sentence is discourtesy and rude. I should know since I followed this pattern my entire life and still have to be reminded that I am not allowing people to finish their train of thought. I am already formulating a response in my head instead of letting it flow naturally from my mouth.

A good leader empowers people to accomplish tasks beyond their beliefs. He challenges them with assignments he knows they are capable of doing so they can understand their own abilities. He is there to foster their creativity, support them through the process and bring out their strengths.

A good leader knows he is no better than anybody else; he was taught by extraordinary leaders and wants to share that wisdom with all of mankind and not keep it secret. Some of our greatest minds such as Einstein, Lincoln, Disney, and Ford to name a few failed the first time and maybe even several times after that, but their perseverance and dedication enabled them to conquer the obstacles in their way and rise to success.

A good leader's sole mission is to help the world and elevate others to a high state of consciousness and as such embraces the talents and passions of all. For instance, a janitor's job conducted with love and passion emits a beautiful energy in the room where he washed the floors. A teacher instills the love of learning in her students when her lessons are taught with enthusiasm and excitement instead of boredom and dismay. A plumber fixing your toilet with a smile on his face shows he cares that you are unable to use the facilities in your house. A doctor's compassion for his patient escalates the healing practice. Everyone has a purpose on this earth and it is through their passion that great triumphs occur. Nobody and I echo nobody has the right to judge another human.

A good leader lives in the present in a relaxed and calm state so when problems occur, he could make rational as opposed to destructive decisions. He knows never to make a rash choice especially if there is any type of emotional charge associate with it. He welcomes the opinions and constructive criticism of others as long as there are solutions given. It is easy to complain, but when one needs to figure out the way to resolve the issue, he may realize his protest is unjustified.

A good leader honestly knows his subordinates well and understands their personal as well as business life. He shows empathy and compassion for afflictions that may occur in someone's life and offers techniques to help him resolve those issues so he is productive and happy both at the workforce and at home.

A good leader is an excellent role model. As such, he partakes in all activities and tasks, never thinking it is beneath him. For a true leader,

Vanaja Ananda, MA, MS

there is no such thing as identity like name and fame. Titles are irrelevant and everybody works together as a support system to live a stress-free life. Collaboration is key and others witnessing the camaraderie will have no option but to join the fun!

We are ready to answer the question set forth at the beginning of this chapter. Is a person with low self value a good leader? Let's evaluate each attribute and analyze instead of jumping to any conclusions. First, a good listener listens to people. Listening has many meanings so, of course, we could say a person with low self-esteem listens to others. Listening is a feature of the human composition. In the paragraph the word effective is added. Then we start wondering if a person feeling inadequate would be an effective listener. Effective could mean so many different things to so many individuals so we need to read further and determine what the writer means by the word effective. Here is the key sentence in the entire paragraph . . . he feels his voice is worth listening to. A person who does not value himself, obviously doesn't think his words are meaningful. We can conclude that a person with feelings of inadequacy and ineptitude would not be a good leader.

We could dissect every character trait that defines a good leader in the same fashion and chances are that a person believing he is undeserving of the gifts bestowed to us by our true nature, will most likely shy away from a leadership position. Instead, these people are followers often chasing a chemical to help them feel they belong in the world. I am referring to drugs, alcohol, cigarettes and other addictive behaviors. They could become womanizers or nail biters. When you are obsessed with an idea and you are unable to concentrate, that is considered an addiction. All addictions are negative whether they seem good or bad. For instance, drugs are definitely a bad addiction because it alters the neuronal pathways in the brain. A good addiction may be an obsession with exercise. It you think these things give you pleasure, but crave it every minute of every day, then it is an addiction and it is not healthy. When we look for outside sources to fulfill us, it will only translate to disaster.

Self esteem and self appreciation are the components to a healthy and happy lifestyle and I intend to show you how to improve your self esteem. It is not as hard as you think. When we are able to look inside and reprogram our beliefs, the cosmos will be showering our desires on us from the heavens above.

Vanaja Ananda, MA, MS

What Do Our Thought Patterns Create?

Motivational speaker and the author of "Biology of Belief" and "Spontaneous Evolution", Dr. Bruce Lipton, had an epiphany. This eye-opener changed his life forever. Dr. Lipton taught Medical Students in the United States and he also was in the research department at Stanford University. His lectures involved clinically based scientific evidence. He enjoyed the teaching profession, but was experiencing unrest that he couldn't explain. This unsettling feeling exacerbated and finally he acquiesced, resigned and took a position teaching Medical School students in the Caribbean. On that island, he had a mind blowing revelation. He realized that every cell in our body had its own intelligence, including its own central nervous system (CNS). In essence, he was saying every cell had its own brain, heart, and every organ that is in our human anatomy and physiology. Moreover, he ascertained our thought patterns contributed to the cell's health or disease. He actually linked science with spirituality and I applaud him for this service to humanity.

There are trillions of cells in our body. Each organ has cells. In the brain there are billions of cells called neurons. When neurons communicate with each other, they form neuronal pathways. These pathways build strong and healthy bodies because the connection between the central nervous system (brain and spinal cord) as well as the peripheral nervous system (anything outside the brain and spinal cord) is unblocked, therefore allowing information to travel easily through the anatomy. The nerves in the peripheral nervous system connect the central nervous system to sensory organs (such as the eye and ear), and other organs of the body, muscles, blood vessels and glands.

Neurons are similar to other cells in the human body in a number of ways. There is one main difference. Neurons are the only cells that transmit information through the body. Sensory neurons carry messages from the sensory receptor cells throughout the body to the brain and motor neurons transmit information from the brain to the muscles in the body. In other words, if your hand touches a burning stove, immediate responses go to the brain alerting danger and the brain reciprocates by sending messages to the hand to remove it quickly from the stove.

Let's see what transpires during the communication phase. The outside of a cell has a cell membrane which protects the cell from foreign inhabitants. Dendrites, long branches, are attached to the cell membrane.

These dendrites get information from sensory receptors and other cells, almost like a telephone line. When information comes into the cell, it goes through the cell membrane into the nucleus which is the control center of the cell and it is the place where genetic information is found. The nucleus is inside of the cell body or soma. At the end of the soma and the top of the axon is the axon hillock which controls the firing of the neuron. The axon hillock is similar to an accounting station. It adds up how many excitatory signals and inhibitory signals there are.

For instance, your brain receives the message your mother-in-law is coming for a visit. Your brain starts searching all the files stored inside the head for anything related to your mother-in-law. There may be wonderful excitatory files filled with family vacations on a tropical island, the smell of her baked cookies, or the dress she gave you for Christmas. There may also be some painful inhibitory memories stored like her death, her yelling at you in front of your children, similar traits to your first grade teacher whose personality didn't mesh with your own and so on and so forth. The axon hillock calculates the excitatory and inhibitory neurons. If there are more excitatory neurons, an action potential occurs. If there are more inhibitory neurons, nothing happens.

During an action potential, electrical impulses are released down to the end of the axon. The information must be transmitted through a synaptic gap to dendrites of an adjacent neuron. At the synapse, chemical messengers are released called neurotransmitters. The neurotransmitter process is similar to a lock and key because the chemical will only go to another neuron if it fits into the gap on the other neuron. Once this occurs, neuronal pathways are built. Neurons communicate with mass numbers of neurons simultaneously. In an enriched loving environment, pathways are built easily. However, when stress, anxiety and dissatisfaction occur, blockages begin in the neuronal pathways.

What effects do neurotransmitters have on the human body? These chemicals regulate numerous physical and emotional responses, therefore having an effect on health and well-being. When we are focused and motivated, we have a zest for life. Unfortunately, if neurotransmitter levels are inadequate, we feel more stressed, exhausted and anxious. That is why drugs are used to expedite the "feel good" adrenaline high. On the one side, the drugs have an immediate effect and help give us energy, focus and motivation. The downside is these chemicals are body invaders and don't fit into the lock and key pattern mentioned above. As a result, some of these substances leak to cells in other organs of the body where they are considered intruders, yet the cell body is forced to allow the foreign material in. This chemical leakage starts to create disease in that organ and it manifests in multifarious ways. Some side effects may include depression, insomnia, constipation, migraines and more. Then, more drugs are given to circumvent the ailments and the cycle continues. A patient could potentially be on 4 or 5 medications simultaneously!

What happens when disease or pharmaceuticals are used as a replacement to the natural chemicals in our body? I will mention a few of the major neurotransmitters and the disorders they are associated with. Endorphins are linked to emotions and pain. The body releases endorphins in response to fear or trauma. Instead of feeling the pain or stress which is expected by an injury or traumatic event, you would experience a temporary euphoria. However, if there is an endorphin deficiency, it is difficult to attain joy so increased stimulant dosages are required to obtain happiness. Also, you could become addicted to the event associated with the endorphin release. Pharmaceuticals become an obsession and people will do anything to achieve the state of ecstasy even if it is short-lived.

Dopamine is a neurotransmitter associated with motivation, interest and pleasure. It is linked with positive states such as being in love, exercising, listening to music and sex. When there is a depletion of dopamine, there is lack of motivation and completing tasks. There is a correlation between deficits in dopamine and schizophrenia or Parkinson's Disease. High dopamine levels are found in patients with Autism or ADHD.

Another neurotransmitter, epinephrine, also known as adrenaline, regulates attention, focus and cognition. When the body does not have enough adrenaline, the result is fatigue and lack of focus. High levels have been linked to sleep problems and ADHD.

What causes a lack of balance in the natural elements in our body? Our fast paced society which contributes to stress and anxiety reduces neurotransmitter levels. The fast food industry and our poor dietary habits create neurotransmitter imbalances. Since neurotransmitters are formed in the body from proteins, it is essential our diet includes enough protein, vitamins and minerals. Toxic substances such as pesticides, drugs, pollution and metals cause damage to the neurons. Excessive amounts of caffeine, alcohol, and nicotine reduce neurotransmitter levels. Supporting scientific evidence says stresses in the home, school, and work environment are detrimental to a person's optimal health and well being and significantly reduces neurotransmitter functioning.

What happens when we are under excessive stress? When we are anxious or experience intense stress, we function solely from the lower part of the brain called the brainstem. This is also known as the reptilian brain because all animals respond from this area in the brain. What distinguishes humans from other animals is our capacity to use the higher level, frontal lobe of the brain for decision making purposes. The innate response triggered in the brainstem is called "fight or flight." This response protects animals and humans from bodily harm. For instance, if a tiger is about to pounce on an animal, the "fight or flight" produces adrenaline so the animal fights or flees from the situation. Moreover, if a mother lifts a magnanimous weight off her child due to the surge of chemicals coursing through her body, she temporarily has superhuman strength. It is used as survival so in that sense it is good. However, when the body is in a constant state of fear, it is extremely detrimental.

So how does this work? When we are in fear the hypothalamus is stimulated. It starts many action potentials so chemicals can be released quickly and prepares the body for running or fighting. When the neurotransmitters are released into the bloodstream, our breathing rate increases, our awareness is strengthened and any thoughts of pain dissipate. We are in survival mode searching for the enemy. Anybody or anything can be perceived as a threat. The mind is not thinking rationally and we view our surroundings as harmful. We may overreact to a comment, strike out in anger or cower under the table. It is impossible to think clearly and all negative beliefs and thoughts from the subconscious are surfacing. Our life becomes one upset after another with no ending. In fact, we don't know how to handle calm moments and look for ways to sabotage our happiness. "Fight or flight" becomes a habitual way of existence and it could potentially lead us to a fast death.

Any technique that allows us to change our attitudes, beliefs and emotional reactions to events will help release us from habitual "fight or flight" response. If we exist in a peaceful and calm manner, the stressors that affect the majority of the population will not be a burden on us. We will handle any situation that comes our way with awareness, clarity and alertness. Students will be able to easily learn, remember and apply knowledge in "real life" situations. However, that is currently not the norm.

Vanaja Ananda, MA, MS

Stresses in the Classroom

In the adult world, when our "fight or flight" response is activated, we need to control it. As a result, it erupts into a rage because it is bottled up inside. Teachers are constantly in stress. Test scores on nationally standardized tests have become the primary focus in the educational realm. Educators are coerced to "teach to the tests" so that becomes the curriculum content. Creativity and innovation takes a back seat because test taking strategies and rote memory skills are at the forefront. Teaching to the test merely means students are adept at answering multiple choice questions correctly. The ones who are the higher level, problem solving thinkers are diagnosed with learning disabilities and placed in special groupings. Most teachers become frustrated and there is high turnover because of these government initiatives that require more paperwork, less origination and no imagination. In addition, disruptive pupils, constant changes and mass amounts of work create a less than desirable environment for these revered adults. Many feel like they are "putting out fires" instead of "creating a spark." It is called teacher burnout. It is a horrible situation for them, but it is even worse for the minors in their care.

We spoke about the "fight or flight" response earlier. When these teachers become stressed in the classroom, their students are punished. After all, the adult has control, right? Removing recess, going to the principal, detention and other forms of discipline are implemented continuously. These educators are operating from the lower brainstem because their fear of failure is too great. It is easier to blame the students than to take responsibility for their own behaviors. One would think, if a system is not working, it is time to find a solution. However, if a person is in a cloudy, fearful state 24/7, he cannot make good choices. Not only does the person suffer internally because it justifies the belief that has existed for so many years, but now innocent beings are subjected to this ridicule and humiliation. It is a vicious cycle that could be ceased once they are taught the secret.

Children, nowadays, are too smart to buy the propaganda that used to work for prior generations. The new generation of Indigo children doesn't sit quietly and conform to the school rules and regulations. Instead, they protest vehemently and they are considered behavioral problems and often diagnosed as learning disabled. Their brain is active and therefore they have difficulty sitting for long durations. Their hands and feet need to be moving frequently so their bio-memory absorbs the concepts being thrown at them. They came into this world ready to explore, experience and create, but they were reprimanded so often their spirit became diminished and subdued. It is their birthright to enjoy the wonders of nature; however teachers with low self-esteem spoil that dream for the Indigo children in their care.

These children have visions beyond our imagination and they have a strong mission for this planet. As a result, we have to liberate them from the chains that bind them. They have unbelievable ideas and intuition that they are able to tap into once their stress is released. We owe them, and our world, the right to share their viewpoints with support from all those around them as opposed to criticism and demoralization. We need to help them surpass the limiting beliefs infiltrating their soul which prevent them from demonstrating the power within. Let's embrace these children with a warm hug and see the God inside of them begging to be released. Let's worship them for bringing a new paradigm in the form of education, health, economy, environment and other major issues facing the world right now. They have the solutions and it is time that we are aware of their capabilities!

How does the United States school system compare with countries around the world? John Stossels from the news show 20/20, conducted a segment on public schools titled "Stupid in America." He analyzed schools across the nation. The criteria were standardized tests. The United States is one of the few in the nation who depend mainly on standardized tests as accountability measures to assess their students. Other nations use other performance based methods such as projects, "real life" experiences, debates and more. The amazing conclusion was even though the U.S. teaches to the test, other nations outperformed our country. Belgium had the highest scores. Poorer countries that spend less than the U.S. on education were ahead of our country as well. Poland, Czech Republic and South Korea beat the American students according to the report.

How is this possible? John Stossel says the problem lies with the monopoly in the school system. There is no choice where your child goes to school. If you live in a certain area, your child goes to the public school in that vicinity regardless if the curriculum meets his needs. The government funds public schools in America and that is exactly how the system works. As a result, mediocre teachers and administrators employ antiquated practices and innovation is tossed out the window. There is no bar to reach, so many teachers, already stressed as mentioned above do whatever they need to do to appease the school leaders and nothing more. Once they receive tenure, usually after three years, they are protected even from evils such as child molestation and emotional abuse. The teacher's union saves them at all costs. I don't want this to be misconstrued. There are many great teachers who have a passion for the field and advocate for their students and families. Unfortunately, there are many who also fit the other mold.

In other countries, the government allows the parents to choose the best school for their child. It is not based on academics. One of the principals in Belgium said she had to work hard to impress parents like leaders would be forced to do in any other business. She said to John Stossel, "If we don't offer them what they want for their child, they won't come to our school." She constantly improves the teaching saying, "You can't afford 10 teachers out of 160 that don't do their work, because the clients will know, and won't come to you again." This is a beautiful lesson for the educators of the United States to put to action. Competition has to be brought into the education system so there is an incentive to meet the needs of their clients, parents and students.

The voucher system was proposed a few years ago and the education union and politicians shot it down. Parents who chose to send their children to private schools would be allotted the tuition expenses by the government. In other words, it was "free choice." There has been much controversy over this issue. Next, charter schools were formed to accommodate children who had certain affinities. For instance, students with a passion for the environment, technology, sciences, math, history and other innovative ideas went to a charter school specifically geared toward their interest.

I was the lead founder of a charter school that went all the way to the final interview. At the final interview, the New Jersey Department of Education said the government cut the funding so we were obligated to obtain personal funding. There was no time for that, so to me it was a joke. When we were denied approval, I was not surprised, but extremely disappointed at the bureaucracy of our government. Ironically, the day after the refusal letter arrived, the department administrator asked me if I was planning to resubmit the proposal which was due a few days later. After careful deliberation, I decided not to apply again. Being in the midst of the bureaucracy, I could tell you firsthand that the public school administrators do not like charter schools because it takes money away from them so there is no collaboration among leaders of the public and private schools. Also, the decision makers have public school mentality so I am not convinced they are looking out for the best interests of families. In addition, they were focusing on schools in disadvantaged areas which I believe is wonderful. However, students from all geographical locations are subject to stressors and emotional problems. The funding should be equal for all since that is the premise of our constitution. As a reminder, we are all one and we are all divine so we all deserve a great life.

Now, I believe also that I may have sabotaged the granting of funds for the public school. At the time, I was still harboring the negative mental pattern that "I was not good enough." That thought permeates at a low vibrational level even though my conscious desire to open a charter school was at a high vibrational level. If an imbalance or conflict exists between the subconscious and conscious, the desire will never come to fruition because the cosmos doesn't really know what you want. Once the scale is equally balanced between the inner and outer self, the divine showers you with abundance in all forms.

It is an amazing lesson to learn because now I am able to manifest my true dreams and desires! I am thinking much bigger NOW and feel I already have it. Now, my wish is to change the educational paradigm starting at the early childhood level not only in the state or this country, but globally. That is just one of my mass desires to help mankind. I also plan to have Children Healing Centers around the world to help young people self-heal their neurological disorders. I have tons of other ideas too and I plan to implement them all. Life is a JOY full of FUN, SPONTANEITY and SURPRISES! I want your life and your children's lives to be filled with wonderful opportunities as well. The choice is yours, but I plan to help you if you want my assistance.

Vanaja Ananda, MA, MS

Stress in the Family

Parents are the first role models their children encounter. If parents are exhibiting behaviors related to stress, they are inadvertently passing on those thought patterns to their children. Due to economic hardships, in many families both parents work. Infants and toddlers are left with babysitters or day cares for extended periods of time. Sometimes, children are brought to the learning centers when they are sick; the parent gives the child Tylenol to mask the symptoms, at least temporarily, for fear their boss will terminate their employment.

Young adolescents and teens are often left at home unsupervised when they exit the school bus. Television and computer games become the babysitter and the youngsters start living in a two-dimensional world hypnotized by the television screen. Most of the senses are not activated, thereby pruning synapses and shortening connections between neurons. Subliminal messages leave the children feeling depressed and inadequate for they start comparing themselves to others.

Parents feel suffocated, not having a moment to themselves. Extra-curricular activities monopolize the afternoons, sports take over the weekends, and there is little time for pure family fun and togetherness. Children are rushed from one activity to another, barely able to digest food and usually they are forced to consume fast food or processed foods because there is no time to cook a healthy dinner. The parents are exhausted by the end of the day and very rarely have intimacy.

What happened to the days of the cohesive family? Grandparents and neighbors lived close by so the children felt secure and protected. Everybody in the neighborhood watched out for each other's children as if they were their own. It was a time when love and compassion for each other was prevalent. Children would go outside and enjoy nature. Rocks would be used as hidden forts and grass would be used as symbols for communication. Digging holes for hours in the dirt would unveil worms, spiders and other interesting creatures and rock formations. Imaginary skills became perfected naturally. Self-made games became the norm. Adolescents would put on performances and design outfits for their plays. The thought of being inside was sacrilegious. You may be thinking these events happened in the old days, maybe the 1920's or 30's. In reality, I am referring to the 70's, 80's and 90's.

46

The family unit has become disengaged. It is easy to get a divorce and people jump at the opportunity before trying to resolve issues. Families have become like the Brady Bunch; a few kids from one family and a few kids from another family living all together. The society of the 21st century is not working. There are more teenage suicides now than in any other decade. Mass amounts of people are taking drugs, alcohol and nicotine to hide their pain. Others are overeating, co-dependent and sexually ravenous. None of these addictive behaviors are healthy. In order to be satisfying and fulfilling, everything needs to be done in moderation.

Lust is not a substitute for divine love for when two souls merge together, you become one with the divine. It is way beyond the physical act. It involves mutual commitment at every level—emotional, physical, cognitive and spiritual. Nothing can describe it; you just have to experience it. Lust just leaves you dissatisfied feeling something is missing. Inhibitions about your body start emerging when overeating as pounds and body fat glob onto the skin in unforeseen places. Looking in the mirror makes you uncomfortable and furious at your body proportions. Co-dependency is an attention/need for another person. You obsess about the person and don't give him the space to breathe. All these addictions create stress and emotional ups and downs like a rollercoaster.

This is the world we are living in right now. Children are witnessing their parent's shortcomings on a daily basis. Moreover, tempers are flaring and punishments are ensued instead of consequences. There is a distinct difference between punishment and consequences. The former is a harsh disciplinary action based on power. The latter is a teaching experience where mistakes are considered learning opportunities. The latter needs to be employed more often, but the parents are in "fight or flight" in a constant survival mode. Financial burdens, relationship issues, family dynamics and work problems are the leading thoughts in their mind and there is no space for peace and relaxation.

A baby born pure and innocent is exposed to these conditions as an infant. Impoverished upbringings are subjected to more painful situations. These kids experience hunger, see knife fights and murders in front of their eyes and sometimes live in unsanitary conditions. No wonder so many children have a poor self-esteem which gets solidified every year until they are elderly and eventually leave the body or they change their thinking patterns.

Vanaja Ananda MA, MS

Stress in the Work Place

The economic downward decline has caused many companies to merge or declare bankruptcy. As a result, many people are finding themselves unemployed. With unemployment rates at an all time high, the middle age people are finding it difficult to secure a good job because the competition is fierce. Corporations are able to hand-pick from a bowl of extremely qualified applicants who may be happy to start at a low salary. The business person with a family suffers, finding it hard to make end's meat. If one is lucky to be employed, he sits on "pins and needles," wondering if he will be laid off soon. Employees feel they have to work longer hours with less benefits and pay. There is a lot of stress and tension in the work force.

Losing a job is similar to the death of an identity and creates self-loathing. This thought pattern creates physical illness, relationship strain, anxiety, depression and thoughts of suicide. It is especially worse for men because society expects men to be the "bread winners." Feelings of unworthiness and not being good enough germinate. It may manifest in the bedroom when mass amounts of Viagra are needed. It may manifest in emotional and/or physical abuse. Unethical behaviors, such as stealing, uncontrollable gambling and embezzling may occur because all hope and faith is diminished. Living in this type of household is not only detrimental to the head of household, but it is debilitating for the entire family.

Children may misbehave at school because there is no one to turn to for support. Undesirable peer groups may form because at least those kids resemble a close-knit family even though they are involved in unscrupulous behaviors. Teens feel helpless and will be seeking some form of relief from this agony of not knowing what to do. Hatred, disappointment, anger and blame dominate their minds. Rap music filled with sexual innuendos and perfunctory language play in their heads. They become destructive and are harmful to both themselves and society in general.

There are heart-wrenching articles in the news and in the newspapers about suicides. Pharmaceutical industries gain tons of wealth at the expense of our emotional and physical health. There are extraordinary amounts of commercials for medicines that will cure this ailment or that. Instead of using preventative measures to stop a disease from occurring, these corporations are relishing in the vast amount of depression, anxiety and suicide among our society. This needs to be stopped immediately. Through holistic measures, people can self-heal without any invasive chemicals entering their bloodstream. The time has come for drastic changes in our health system! I am not saying problems will not prevail. The distinguishing factor is we will be able to deal with any unwelcome surprises that come our way in a healthy manner. Therefore, it will be difficult, if not impossible for disease to encroach on the cells in our body.

Self Healing Techniques That Work!

I am the type of person who must experience results for myself before I could share them with others. I am a great communicator, but I only preach ideas that work! I was a skeptic for most of my life expecting every theory or hypothesis to be confirmed with scientific evidence. I realize that is nonsensical because there are things happening beyond our logic and it is real. It is much more powerful than anything that enters our imagination. But, we could tap into it and get a glimpse of the ultimate, once we could calm our bodies down. I am going to share how I was guided by the divine and my higher consciousness to help you.

I owned a preschool/kindergarten and the business was successful. I went to quite a few workshops and educational trainings because I always had the thirst for learning. I started going to esoteric workshops which made no sense to me, but I loved everything I was learning. It started with Neurofeedback and I became fascinated with the brain. Then I took a variety of brain gym classes and was intrigued by the results. I became a Reiki Master and a hypnotist. I was certified in The Listening Program. I learned a tactile integration program for children with sensory motor deprivation. Wellness Kinesiology taught me about reprogramming limiting beliefs. Finally, I was compelled to obtain another graduate degree; this time in Neuroscience and Education. I never knew why my path was leading me in this direction because I didn't see the connection with the school I owned and founded at the beginning of my learning crusade. One day, it all came together and I founded another business titled Educational Healing. The holistic teachings I acquired were nicely packaged to help children, teens and even adults with learning disabilities related to inattention, compulsivity and anxiety.

I look back at those days wondering why I was spending all my earnings on classes. Thank goodness my inner being was determined to show me my mission in life. It was such a powerful force; I followed without complaints. Healing is my adoration. The pleasure and tingles that radiate through my body when I see people becoming happier and having a zest for life is indescribable. I was initiated as a Nithya healer from an enlightened Master in India who I will talk about in depth later in the book. Being a pure vessel for the divine's energy to flow through is the greatest blessing. I absolutely love it! My mission is to bring peace, love, compassion, joy, and healing to the world. Once you realize it is our divine nature, there is no one exempt from this rule, including the hardened criminal. We are all divine and we are all connected, so when one succeeds, we all succeed!

Vanaja Ananda, MA, MS

The Importance of Positive Affirmations

We all use affirmations throughout the day because they are thoughts and desires. Most of them are negative and self-defeating. Can't and no are usually the first responses to questions proposed to us. It is a defensive reaction already set in place to circumvent any situation that arises without contemplation. Wouldn't it be amazing if the first thought that passed our lips were yes and can? Instead of a defeatist attitude, we would acquire a winner's mindset.

Dr. Wayne Topping, a world renowned author and motivational speaker, founded Wellness Kinesiology. It is based on his studies at the Biokinesiology University in Oregon. Through muscle testing, one is able to ascertain organ imbalances and be able to correct them through positive affirmations.

What is muscle testing? Dr. George Goodheart, a Chiropractor, developed muscle testing. He determined that the weakness or strength of a muscle is associated with an organ in the body and meridians. Meridians are energy centers in the body. When they are healthy, the energy flows easily and the organ is in balance. However, when stress emanates, some meridians have energy blockages creating disease in the organs.

Dr. Topping realized statements, both positive and negative, are correlated with deficiencies in our organs. When the correct statement is asked, the body responds with a weak or strong muscle. Once the statement is accepted by the subconscious in a yes or no format, illnesses can improve and sometimes disappear.

There are over 200 statements that are affiliated with organs and meridian points in our body. The inner child forms these beliefs as a protection to outside forces. Dr. Topping mentions in several of his books programming starts in utero. There is evidence to support these findings. If the mom is calm, relaxing music is played, mom talks to the unborn child and generally lives in a peaceful environment, the newborn arrives automatically on earth with self confidence. On the contrary, if the child in utero is subject to harsh voices, mom is anxious, mom has emotional setbacks and generally lives in a chaotic atmosphere, the newborn arrives with negative thought patterns.

In order to understand Wellness Kinesiology better, I am going to use negative mental patterns that developed in my early childhood years and the organs that became disease ridden as a result. The dominant belief was "I am not good enough". Dr. Topping explains in his books and lectures an essential benchmark. He says a disease does not develop in an organ if the belief remains. It is when the person starts going against the embedded belief, the body is thrown out of balance. Let's remember the belief originated as a self-protective entity so when one acts or thinks contrary to the belief, it creates an energetic imbalance and the result is disease.

The negative belief "I am not good enough" is linked to the posterior pituitary. The posterior pituitary gland is controlled by the hypothalamus. If you remember from the earlier discussion, the hypothalamus was responsible for the fight or flight syndrome. Briefly, the hypothalamus activates the nerves in the nervous system and releases adrenaline through the blood stream. This puts the body into attack mode. The pituitary gland secretes the neurotransmitter or chemical into the blood stream. If this gland is out of balance, it consistently secretes chemicals into the bloodstream putting the body into a perpetual state of panic and fear. As a result, learning disabilities occur.

I believed "I wasn't good enough" in my earlier years. But, through my childhood there were times I felt good enough and that I was capable of tasks. For instance, I always had the desire to speak in public because I felt the information I had to share was valuable. I would convince myself I could do this feat. As a result, I went against the protective shield and started the degeneration in my posterior pituitary gland. When I went to speak in the classroom, I immediately went into the "fight or flight" mode and panic. This would happen even if I raised my hand to participate in class." Another statement connected to the posterior pituitary gland is "people in authority haven't time for me." Furthermore, the belief "it is safer not to make friends" is equated with the hypothalamus. I was condemned to be in the "fight or flight" state for a long time. I had issues concentrating, organizing and problem solving. I wasn't able to think clearly and this happened throughout the day almost every day.

When I worried which was often, symptoms immediately expressed in my abdominal area. I had bouts of nausea, vomiting, diarrhea and stomach cramping. Little did I realize, my liver was thrown off kilter by the statements "I retreat from conflict at all costs" and "I need to be quiet." As I explained above, when I remained quiet or escaped into the recesses of my mind, my liver was quite healthy. Be that as it may be, the minute

I expressed my opinion or argued back in retaliation, toxins traveled to my liver.

Intercourse was painful for me because "I didn't totally accept my body." Can you blame me? This belief affects the clitoris. Intercourse, pain and suffocation were synonymous in my vocabulary.

My dad would sit in his favorite chair in the bedroom and the entire family would watch television together. Often, my dad would scream out in intense pain. His toes stiffened and he said the cramps in his leg were unbearable. I would have empathy watching his face wince in physical agony, but at the same time I would wonder if part of this show was an act. That is, until I experienced the same excruciating, shooting pain that makes standing or sitting nearly impossible. My tendency was to cry out in distress and pray the sensation would exit as quickly as it came. Now, I am cognizant of the fact both my dad and I shared the same limiting thought pattern "I must depend on myself because I can't rely on others'.

Every year I was ill with bronchitis. It became a ritual. I was so sick with high fevers and didn't want to leave the comfort of the bed for one or two weeks. At those times, my parents would cater to my needs so it wasn't bad to be sick. I received sympathy from family members, peers and teachers. I enjoyed those nuances. If I knew the thought process related to the illness, I wouldn't have relished the attention. Buried deep within me was hatred so deep it is terrifying even to write these words right now. "Violent people should be eliminated" was ringing in my subconscious to protect me! Our thoughts can be terroristic! Another thought that deprecated my soul was "I'm not worthy of anyone listening to me." Both are bronchial related.

I watched both my parents disintegrate into nothing. Their bodies were there at the end, but the people I grew up with no longer existed in those frames. My mother went through chemotherapy and radiation. My father endured surgery after surgery. Their bodies were alive for they were breathing and their heart beat, but their lives were full of misery once their illnesses consumed their physical forms. I told myself I would never go to a doctor and succumb to toxic chemicals injected into my body. I would rather die not knowing.

I developed a lump above my ankle. At first it was the size of a small pebble, but it developed into a golf size ball. I ignored it and denied its existence. Not really, my inner chatter was consumed with the growth above my left ankle. I mentioned it once to my doctor at a physical and he gave me a prescription to get an x-ray. Of course, I never went and the doctor never pursued it. I thought it may be cancerous and that concept was gargantuan to grasp. Once I took the Wellness Kinesiology course, I was convinced malignant cancerous cells grew and continued to grow inside my body. The belief that is associated with cancer is "not being able to express myself." Expressing myself was problematic for as long as I could remember. I prayed to God to release me from this cancer and a miracle happened! I am thrilled to say that growth has dissipated to a fraction of its size and it is almost non-existent. Self healing is miraculous and every being whether it is a human, animal, plant, tree, or rock has that ability.

These negative and devastating patterns can be reprogrammed through Wellness Kinesiolgy techniques. First, the facilitator determines the statement the body will accept through muscle testing. It is important to ask the body permission to reprogram the belief. If the body acquiesces, the muscles respond to questions. The body releases pent up emotions at various ages through the lifetime of the client where that belief persists. Eye movements along with statements and various other methods reprogram the existing thought. The client usually has homework to do saying these positive affirmations.

Next, recently Emotional Freedom Technique has been added to my repertoire for emotional self healing. A friend spent a night with me while we tapped to Brad Yates and other EFT specialists on you tube. From that moment on, I tapped every mental pattern left out of my entire system. The process was intriguing. Sometimes, I was nauseous or headaches developed. At other times, diarrhea eliminated toxins from my body. I could feel the energy traveling up my body from my feet to my legs and up my spinal cord, usually on the left side of the body. I knew it was effective and forever grateful this technique is shared with the population for free.

Emotional Freedom Technique (EFT) is an acupressure routine without the needles. The meridian points, mentioned in Wellness Kinesiology, are done with this treatment as well. You say positive affirmations while tapping with your fingertips onto meridians on your face, chest and underarms. The combination of saying the statements aloud while tapping on energy centers, releases emotional blocks and restores the body back to health. It is an excellent way to reprogram persisting unwanted thoughts. Medical practitioners are using this method with their patients all over the world because it works.

There are meridians also in your fingertips, so energy centers will be unblocked on multi-levels. The key to EFT is to acknowledge the problem and then allow your inner being to accept its existence. By thinking about the problem, the energy flow will be disrupted so you can clear it out. Brad Yates demonstrates EFT on you tube covering many topics. They are usually 9 minutes in length and extremely powerful. Fear, worry, surrender, belonging, money, and abandonment are some of the subjects. The method is simple, even children delight in performing these techniques. Brad has developed tapping strategies for children. There are other professionals who are on you tube, but I am drawn to Brad because his spirituality emanates from his personage. I believe he is committed to helping people. It shows in his face, demeanor and voice. Brad is the author of several books, including the acclaimed "Wizards Wish", a magical book introducing children to the world of EFT and miracles. He has received numerous accolades for this bestselling book. Brad also conducts workshops around the country.

Internationally renowned author Louise L. Hay is another one of my mentors. "Heal Your Body" provides a compilation of ailments and the healing affirmation. This is the book that introduced me to the world of affirmations. It is a goldmine. Everyone should have a copy to carry around in their purse or computer bag. In fact, you should have one in your bedroom at home and one inside your desk at work. It is an invaluable resource. Before you say any affirmation, you must ask for your inner soul's permission. By doing this, you take the responsibility for having the illness and allowing yourself to change the belief. Louis Hay tells you how to do this.

It's a Mind, Body and Spiritual Experience

Located directly above the hypothalamus is the amygdala. Stored in the amygdala is the "fear" factor. Neuroscientists have found that people shift their brainwaves from the amygdala to the frontal cortex through meditation. Specifically, over 500 studies have been conducted using Transcendental Meditation developed by Enlightened Master Maharishi Mahesh Yogi. Studies have proven the efficacy of using meditation in the classroom, workplace and in any societal situation. It reduces stress, improves health and cognition, enhances relationships and increases creativity. Meditation puts the inner chatter to rest and helps us achieve clarity.

I never learned TM so I cannot personally endorse this program. However, I am convinced it is effective because I saw how I metamorphosed using another meditation called Nithya Dhyann. Nithya Dhyann was developed by Enlightened Master Paramahamsa Nithyananda or Swamiji. Nithya Dhyann meditation consists of five parts. The first part involves the breath. Our breathing patterns are associated with our emotions and deep rooted beliefs. If you observe your breathing while intense emotions are displayed, you will notice variations in your breathing. By its nature, breathing is a normal function. While negative emotions cause irregular breathing activity, the positive emotions produce smooth, rhythmical patterns.

At the University in Amsterdam in the Department of Experimental Psychology, Frans Bolten and colleagues analyzed emotions and respiratory patterns. They concluded fast and deep breathing was related to excitement while slow and deep breathing occurred when people were in a relaxed resting state. Humans in a stressful mental state had fast and shallow breathing. Sit and observe your breathing patterns while angry, sad, happy, guilty, or surprised and you will notice rapid changes transpire within your respiratory system. Your suppressed emotions have actually trained your respiratory tract how to behave and it becomes a fixed pattern. The breathing technique in Nithya Dhyann brings the memories to the surface so it could be expunged.

The second part of the meditation involves humming. There is constant chatter in our minds; we are thinking about a million things at once. Humming helps reduce the inner chatter allowing the body to experience some peace.

Vanaja Ananda MA, MS

The third piece deals with the 7 main energy centers in the body or chakras. To reiterate, when an energy center is blocked, it creates disease in our body. The third part works on releasing the blockages to obtain optimal health. Each chakra is linked to a negative belief that blocks it and a positive belief that unblocks it. Once the chakras are clear, the divine energy is able to flow freely through the body. During this meditation practice, we focus on each chakra and envision light coming into that chakra.

At the base of the spine, the chakra is called the muladhara. The muladhara is blocked by fantasy and lust. The thought that unblocks this chakra is reality. Two inches above that chakra at the public area is the swadishtana chakra. This chakra is ruled by fear so courage will unblock this energy center. At the navel center is the manipuraka chakra which is the worry center. So please stop worrying and your abdominal issues will be healed. The anaharta is located at the heart. Attention and need throw this chakra off balance. Unconditional love brings it right back! The vishuddhi chakra is found at the throat. Jealousy is the culprit of the throat. Embracing our uniqueness clears the energy clog. At the third eye, situated between the two eyebrows is the ajna chakra. This is the seat of our intuition. Laziness throws this chakra off course and spontaneity opens it up. At the top of our head or crown is the sahasrara chakra. This energy chakra is unblocked when gratitude is expressed. Discontentment keeps it closely locked.

The fourth section of the Nithya Dhyann meditation is what Swamiji is renowned for. Unclutching is the key ingredient in all of his meditations. What does unclutching mean? We have so many thoughts circulating in our head that we are unaware that each thought is separate. There is a gap between thoughts. We ignore that gap and connect one thought to another until it creates indigestion, angst and terror in our human structure. Essentially, we allow past events to be triggered through the linkage of thoughts. For example, I see a dog outside my window. All of a sudden I remember my neighbor's dog that was ferocious and bit me. I recall the blood gushing from my leg as my alarmed parent rushes me to the hospital. At the hospital, men and women in white were probing me with needles that hurt worse than the bite. Thoughts occur of being strapped down to the gurney and so on and so forth. A simple thought was seeing a dog outside and I perceived it as a threat to my physical being and brought myself to the "fight or flight" model. If I watched each thought as if it was in a bubble going up into the air, there would be no anxiety attached. I would have the thought I see a dog. Since I am aware of that thought and allow the gap to separate that thought from the next idea which may be I am hungry, there is no stress.

This may sound a little ridiculous to you. Try this exercise for yourself. Write down every thought that comes into your mind without analysis for 3 minutes. At the end of 3 minutes, tell me what you observe? If you are like the thousands who have done this task, you will realize your thoughts have no meaning. They are all over the place. We jump from one idea to another within milliseconds. When we are in an unclutched state and in the present, it is like watching a movie and it is very entertaining!

The last part of the meditation is my favorite part because it allows you to thank the divine according to your beliefs. You give thanks to your family, friends, doctors, neighbors and so on. The final section is chanted in Sanskrit. Your inner being understands the language so it enters your inner soul without judgment. I found it is so much better to hear without interpretation because the only choice is to allow your mind to rest. Doing this meditation daily for 40 minutes helped transform my life.

There are meditations you could do with children that are so much fun. Twirling, dancing, flying, looking at the sky and more has similar effects, but these meditations keep their bodies moving at the speed students adore. Since meditation is sometimes difficult to do in the classroom, guided imagery could be used as a replacement.

Guided imagery techniques help students learn how to make relaxation a part of their daily lives. Thematic environment provides rich ground for enhancing imagination. Although visualization is used as an exercise of imagination that actually engages all of the senses, the mind believes it to be true. As children improve their ability to visualize, they see how their world may be different and better.

Mirror neurons are a type of brain cell that respond the same whether we perform an action or witness someone else performing the same action. Mirror neurons were discovered in the early 1990's during experiments with macaque monkeys. The researchers found brain waves fired when the monkey grabbed or watched another monkey grab an object. Guided imagery follows this same pedagogy.

I discovered yoga is more than an exercise for physical health; it is a connection between mind, body and spirit. Using the body and breath enables the person to understand his connection to himself and the universe. This craft of oneness was developed by a yogi in India thousands of years ago. Patanjali is the father of yoga and his sacred text is known as the Yoga Sutras. There are eight steps to yoga according to Patanjali. I will interpret these eight key components of yoga the way I perceive it.

Yama is universal morality. In other words, treat others the way you wanted to be treated; with respect, honesty, non-violence, compassion and love. **Niyama** is personal observances. This refers to the attitude we have about ourselves. These postures assist us in achieving love, self worth, and purity. **Asanas** are body postures. Postures have two purposes: to aid in flexibility, coordination, balance and health as well as quieting the mind. The physical exercise becomes a vessel to achieve meditation and centering which eventually leads us to union with our higher self. **Pranayama** are breathing exercises. Breathing helps the energy become unblocked and nourished back to heath. It allows the energy to flow easily so the chakras become balanced. **Pratyahara** is control of the senses. It removes our attachment to external objects and trains us to focus on ourselves. **Dharana** refers to inner awareness. Being totally absorbed on the position brings you immediately to the present moment. **Dhyana** is meditation and devotion to the divine. When you focus on your eyes in the mirror, you begin to see the divine in you and notice the light in those around you. **Samadhi** is union with the divine. In this state, the truth is revealed. Each step builds upon the prior one. When you have reached Samadhi, you are a yogi.

The yoga I just described is called Hatha Yoga. I have been doing yoga for only 3 years and the changes are incredible. One form of Hatha yoga that I chose to explore was Bikram yoga. The first three months of Bikram yoga, my daughter lost 25 pounds. We went every day and sometimes twice per day in intense 105 degree heat, but the results were worth it! She could be their poster child. Not only did she go down several dress sizes, but she has tremendous flexibility, coordination and grace. Her teachers wanted her to enter competitions and I believe she will be a yoga instructor along with all her other talents. There are many yoga programs on the market so choose the one that is best for you and your family.

Selfless service is called Siddha Yoga. The founder of this practice was Swami Muktananda and has now become popular around the world to help one achieve spiritual growth. Serving others without expecting anything in return is the best contribution we could make to ourselves and society as a whole. When you have a pure heart, your ego is automatically deflated and there is no room for greed, jealousy, envy, or revenge. The joy you experience when you help others expands your horizons to unheard of dimensions.

"If we are to reach real peace in the world we shall have to begin with children." These are the wise words of Gandhi. In order to live peacefully, we need to find ways to work out differences without hurting each other. Accepting self and others, communicating effectively, resolving conflicts and understanding diversity are necessary concepts for children to learn.

Make Your Dreams Come True

Neuroscience research has revealed the part of the brain responsible for awareness is called the reticular activating system (RAS). This area is a bridge between the brainstem and the higher level areas of the brain. Just to remind you, the fight or flight effect is initiated in the brainstem. The RAS empowers us to sieve through unnecessary external stimuli to focus on one element.

Research from Harvard Medical School suggests ADHD is partly caused by a deficiency in the reticular activating system. That is why children have struggles concentrating. In their world, their brain is unable to filter out information, so they witness everything in their environment at once and are unable to discern which object is most important. For instance, the teacher will be lecturing in front of the class. At the same time there is an unusual bug on the floor, the gardening people are mowing the lawn outside the window and the person behind the child is whispering to his friend while the student is playing with the eraser on the pencil. The child doesn't know where to focus his attention. It creates distress, disturbance and agitation so the child usually loses self-control and we know where that leads.

There are simple ways to increase the neural connections in the RAS so it is operating at maximum capacity: the vision board, the Divine box and writing powerful words. "The Secret" was a documentary a few years back that explained "The Law of Attraction." The well-known speakers and leaders featured in the film talked about achieving dreams through beliefs. If you believe you have something, then it will appear. It sounded easy enough, but my manifestations never just seemed to appear. The reason was my subconscious was relaying conflicting messages to the universe without my approval. One of the experts from "The Secret" spoke about a vision board. I thought to myself that is a fantastic idea. Then, I waited about five years to design a vision board. My mind was self-sabotaging without my awareness.

Finally, one day I decided enough was enough. I have a lot of desires and I want them to come to fruition. It was time to speed up the process. By this time, the universe was totally confused with me; the Gods, angels, and existential energy were wondering if there was any hope for me and I was conjecturing that identical thought. Once I announced to my children

I was constructing this dream board, it happened in 2 days. I had so much fun; I was unable to stop until I was finished!

How did I create this board? I found pictures of everything I wanted on google images. First I started with romance because every cell of my body yearned for my lifelong partner. Now, this is the tricky part. It is necessary to be specific so the universe knows exactly what you want. I always liked men with dark hair, brown eyes, shoulder length hair, physically fit and so on and so forth. I looked for male actors or models that I found attractive. I chose Hugh Jackman and there is one particular picture of him that I fell in love with. I put him all over my vision board with me in different scenarios: at the beach, romantic dinners, pillow fights, snowball fights, whitewater rafting . . . you get the picture. Now, the exterior physical part was taken care of. But, I wanted so much more. I wanted a relationship that is mutually satisfying emotionally, physically, spiritually, sexually, and cognitively so I wrote those exact words. I want a romantic guy who loves children and animals. I wanted a confident guy who likes to play and is lots of fun. I wanted a man who loves yoga, meditation and adores my guru as much as me. I wanted a sexy man who writes music and poetry. I want it all and I know it is coming!

The next section had to do with my future plans. I wrote the names of books that I authored. Remember, you design this board as if these things already exist; everything is written in the present. I found a picture of a Children's Healing Center and underneath I wrote Dr. Vanaja heals children with neurological disorders. I found a picture of Oprah Winfrey and put me in the picture with her since I plan to be on her show. I put a head shot of Hugh Jackman and me and wrote "my lifelong partner and I travel around the world helping to change the educational paradigm."

I had a billionaire and enlightenment section. I put a picture of a beachfront house with massive windows looking out to the beautiful ocean. I found a picture of a convertible. I put lots of money pictures all over it. I had a chauffeur, a chef, personal shopper, masseuse and more. Are you beginning to see the joy you will have when you manifest your desires through this board.

On the last area of this board I put all the places I wanted to travel with my lifelong partner complete with pictures of us! I had pictures of the hanging bridge in Costa Rica, the huts in the middle of water in the South Pacific, Sedona, Mount Shasta, India, Greek Islands and numerous spiritual cities. Underneath the travel section I wrote "my partner and I help orphans around the world." Orphans, in particular, have grown up devoid of loving arms protecting and comforting them. I want to bring back the joy these children have so long ago forgotten. So, wherever I venture, I want to locate an orphanage and give these children hugs and healing.

Just in case Hugh Jackman and his wife are reading this book, I want to put your mind at ease. I don't want to break up your marriage; I want someone who resembles Hugh Jackman physically, but I am looking for so many other traits too and I choose to live in reality and actually know the person I fall in love with. I have lived in the fantasy world in regard to relationships for way too long. You will hear about those adventures soon.

Once you have produced your vision board, put it in the bedroom where you will see it the minute you wake up and the minute you go to sleep. As I mentioned previously, the mirror neurons in your brain are unable to differentiate between real and imagination so it is interpreted as real and goes straight to your bio-memory. Brilliant! Thank you so much the creators of "The Secret." You could also write out a check to any amount you want to yourself and tape it to the ceiling. Then, you have two vision boards.

Alongside the vision board is the divine box. You could call it the God, Buddha, Jesus Christ, Swamiji, tree, rock, cosmos, existential energy, or whatever your heart desires for it goes to the same energy. Listen to how straightforward this activity is. You write down desires and/or habits you want to be released from. For instance, you could complement your desires from the vision board and write out each idea on a separate piece of paper and then place it in a box. Or, you could ask to be released from fear, worry, and anger and give specifics. Please release me from my fear of public speaking is an example. Then close the box and put it somewhere special in your room. Don't open it! This box is surrendering to the divine and showing your trust. Once you put the papers in the box, the rest is up to God and you could relax and forget about it. The angels have heard your prayers and they are doing their part. Just be aware to do your part as well which is reprogramming your subconscious.

I just want to mention one thing. For these desires to become a reality there must be intensity within your inner being and outer being. These desires must be things you are passionate about.

A good idea to help you focus on the positive is something I learned at a Harv Ecker's "Millionaire's Mind" workshop. Every night before you go to sleep, write down five accomplishments you achieved that day and ignore any disappointments that may have transpired. By doing this practice daily, you will create a healthy mind.

I had body issues for most of my life; there were parts of my body I just didn't like. I would want my stomach flatter, my toes shorter and pushed together, my boobs fuller, and lots more. I would critique my body so carefully and it wasn't complementary. I was taught how to love my body, every square inch of it. In the shower, I would clean every part of my anatomy and as I did this ritual I would tell each ligament I loved it. I would say "I love you feet," "I love you flat stomach," "I love you knees." It sounds absurd, but your body reacts to this love because it is composed of energy. You could change any body type. Another hint that works is to choose a weight you think would be perfect. Put that number on a sheet of paper and tape it to your scale so every single time you weigh yourself, you will be that weight. Your body responds! It is the quick weight loss solution! If you don't believe me, try it. I love skeptics since I was one myself.

Gratitude is the foundation for living. It is the principal tenet for creating abundance, whether you are seeking prosperity, great relationships, optimum health, materialistic objects, inner peace or anything. Before going to sleep, thank God or whoever you want to thank for all the blessings and abundance in your life. Prayers should be filled with appreciation and thankfulness. At night, you are given the opportunity to look at your life and say thanks. I never realized how much I had until I started doing this exercise because the greedy part of me always asked for more. I am not saying desires aren't important; they are extremely essential and you deserve it. However, prayers should be a time when you give something back to the cosmos. Shower yourself, your family, friends, neighbors, colleagues and even people you have never met with love. That is the only gift you could truly give to the universe.

I want to end this section with a short you tube clip my friend sent me today http://www.youtube.com/watch_popup?v=Hzgzim5m7oU&vq=medium. It put everything into perspective. A blind man was sitting outside with a money can and a sign that said "I'm Blind, Please Help." A few people would drop some change into his container. A woman walks by, looks at the man and changes the sign. The man didn't know what she wrote, but he felt her shoes as she scribbled the message. Almost everyone who walked by the man from that point on gave the man money. He knew when the woman appeared again because his sense of touch was so keen and he touched her shoes. He asked what she did that changed his luck. She picked up the sign and told him. It said "It's a Beautiful Day and I Can't See It." Tears sprung to my eyes and I knew I was guided to include this video in this passage. The power of words is effectual.

PART 5

Trust And Faith In The Divine

My Inner Awakening

My soul always longed for something beyond my comprehension and just out of the range of my fingertips. Depression became my mantra. It was funny. I could function perfectly in the outside world, at least on a superficial level. On the inside, I convinced myself I was not happy. On weekends, I didn't want to get out of bed. I would perform activities mechanically when I wasn't working. Life was not fun at all. I felt trapped in every aspect of my life and didn't know how to become exonerated. There were moments I wanted to commit suicide to be free from the burdens of my existence. In societies eyes my life was perfect, but I was extremely unhappy nonetheless which made the feeling even worse. I would criticize and berate myself often, and at times despise myself, for these lugubrious reactions.

One day, a poem arrived in my email box from a dear friend. This prose was thought-provoking and I started looking at life different. A seed has to rupture before it could turn into a beautiful tree. In essence, I was the seed suffocating inside the shell and even though I was watered and fed daily, I ensconced myself in weeds. So, the seed remains a seed and only experiences dirt, ants and worms. However, the seed that has the courage to break out of its outer protection and transform into a

89

budding flower witnesses the sun, the moon, the sky, flying insects, and eventually becomes the tree where animals build their home. I chose to be the budding flower.

Now that I made the choice to explore the wonders of the universe, how was I expecting to accomplish this? It didn't take long to find out. The same friend went to a conference in California and brought back a DVD. She lent it to me and I immediately watched it. I was entranced. I viewed it over and over because this Indian man was so brilliant; his concepts were ingenious and it made so much sense. This man is Paramahamsa Nithyananda or Swamiji. From that moment on, my life became one of happiness, hope and faith. The day I saw him in person was the day I realized I found what I was seeking my entire life and probably thousands of lifetimes.

I went to volunteer for Swamiji in Ohio at a program titled Yoga Spurana. I hadn't met him yet, but I knew there was a connection there. Prior to seeing him, I went to a couple of workshops with his senior disciple Swami Bhaktananda whom I also adore. The minute I laid eyes on Swamiji as he gracefully walked or floated into the room, my eyes welled up with tears and my body began to shake. There was no rhyme or reason. It just happened that way.

Swamiji smiles often and he is hysterical. He explains ideas so the general population is able to comprehend. He has the patience of a saint and the love and compassion of Mother Theresa. He is stoic, altruistic and charming. There are so many more adjectives to describe him, but it would fill up an entire book. When you meet him, you are blessed thousand fold. The program was phenomenal; it was the best program I have attended in my entire life and I have taken multifarious classes, conferences, trainings and workshops over the span of my life.

Here comes the most unbelievable part. After one of his darshans, something beyond my interpretation happened to me. Darshan is when an enlightened Master infuses his energy directly into your body. Yes, Swamiji is an enlightened Master and more which I will explain in detail later in this chapter. During darshan, he puts his bio-memory inside of you. As I was saying, I was dancing and extremely blissful in the energetic room. When I went back to my room, I began to develop a headache. The headache persisted till it turned into a migraine. I had a couple of migraines in my life so I knew you go to sleep immediately. This happened to be the worst migraine I ever had. All of a sudden, it felt like I was in the

"Magic School Bus" on a trip to the brain. I literally was flying around the inside of my brain. I traveled from one lobe to another, swam in the cerebrospinal fluid and walked across the corpus callosum. I actually saw the blockages and disease in my neuronal pathways which was the cause of the head tics I encountered for years. It was a mind blowing venture and even though I was in tremendous pain, it was a titillating adventure I will never forget! That is the day I decided I wanted to help heal children with neurological disorders!

A month later, I was at the Inner Awakening program in India. It followed the old adage "when the student is ready, the teacher appears." Inner Awakening was a 21 day program in the energy field of Swamiji. He was with us daily. I was totally transformed in every dimension after this process . . . emotionally, physically, cognitively, and spiritually. I never realized the power of this guru until I experienced miracle upon miracle. To be honest, before my friend showed me that DVD, I had no clue what a guru even was.

Vanaja Ananda MA, MS

Be Careful What You Ask For Because
It May Come True

I began changing a few years before I met Swamiji. As I mentioned before, I became a Reiki Master and became certified in numerous holistic modalities. As a result, my entire being evolved. When you go up for darshan, you are allowed to ask Swamiji for anything and if you find it difficult to speak because of his intense energy, you could write it on a note to give to him. I chose to write the note. I felt I changed so much and wasn't the person my ex-husband originally married. I asked Swamiji to find him a soul mate since he didn't change one iota. Swamiji never answered me so I was perplexed. In fact, he talked about the sanctity of marriage for the remaining 20 days. I figured that was my answer; by the end of the Inner Awakening program, I was convinced and determined to make the marriage work.

As I was flying home on the airplane, I was excited my marriage was going to remain intact and we would be happy together. I told myself I would do everything for the marriage except take my mala off. The mala is a necklace filled with rudraksha beads. When you meditate, the energy goes into these beads and when obstacles occur in daily life, the energy from the beads support you. Three times in the past, he forced me to remove this necklace and I unwillingly acquiesced to keep peace in the family. This time, I was determined to set a precedent so it would no longer be an issue.

My family picked me up at the airport and we went home for dinner. Tension was amidst in the air since my ex apparently had been brooding about the trip the entire time I was gone. My children suffered from his negativity. At dinner, he immediately noticed I had the mala on and told me to take it off. I refused and so he said he wanted a divorce and I said OK. It was a civil, calm conversation. Afterwards, I was in a state of shock. How was I going to support myself and the kids? Maybe, I really do love him. I was supposed to make this work. I went into a total panic and felt I made the worst mistake of my entire life, but I didn't know how to remedy the situation. For two weeks, I remained in a state of shock thinking I really didn't want this divorce.

After the two weeks, the veil lifted and I felt liberated. In the past, I was walking on eggshells in my house for fear a time bomb would explode; he was living in the basement and we hardly saw each other and quiet was golden. My teenagers enjoyed the peace as well. For the time being, he was paying all the bills so I was still financially secure. Our dog that I absolutely adored and he was jealous of was now able to sleep on our bed. I realized two weeks of this surgery is not bad after all! I can definitely handle the fear, worry and distress for that short time because the rewards are astounding.

Three months later he met his soul mate. She reminds me of his mom in so many ways and she has a beautiful heart. Also, she treats my teens well. They are extremely happy and that is all I ever wanted for him. Slowly, we are becoming friends again; he was my best friend for 24 years! If you ask the divine for something with intensity, it will definitely happen. Apparently, my subconscious wanted to be free as much as my conscious.

Three years prior to this major altercation in my life, my ex-husband also went into a deep depression. I wanted to separate because I was miserable. He did everything in his power to keep our marriage together, but I was adamant. I didn't date the entire 8 months because my intuition told me we were getting back together and I didn't want to hurt anybody new in the process. He dated, but it became a chore for him instead of pleasure. Eight months later we were back together because I thought he was going to have a nervous breakdown.

During those three years, his business was falling apart and he was in total denial. He had little motivation to look for a new job or sell the business, so many of his days consisted of sleeping on the couch to escape. My business allowed me to pay the school bills and the profits enabled me to buy the kids clothes and miscellaneous items they desired. I was never responsible with home finances and I take full responsibility for this error. As a result, we went bankrupt shortly after I came back from India. That too was a shock to my system, but I was able to handle it so well; it even surprised me. It was a blessing in disguise because we were no longer tormented by collectors and worrying endlessly about finances. The slate was wiped clean and we were given a chance to learn from our past mistakes. It was time to be responsible and treat money with respect.

If you recall, I mentioned how my toes never bent as a result of that traumatic episode when I was two years old. I am thrilled to tell you, my toes bend easily now. The growth on my ankle started dissipating after the Inner Awakening program and now it is practically gone. Through my youth, whenever I became ill, a cold sore or fever blister would form. They lasted for weeks and were humiliating. It was impossible to cover up these huge canker blisters. After IA, I never had another cold sore. The head tics that consumed my life started disappearing as well.

Bright Beginnings during the summer goes into financial distress because we are closed and we still have to pay all the bills including rent which is substantial. The landlord always allowed me to pay partial payments, but then I had to pay double at the beginning of the school year so it was a catch 22. When I came back from Inner Awakening (IA), Bright Beginnings was in its typical hole which is usually easy to bounce back from. With the economy taking a nose dive so did Bright Beginnings. This was the first time I thought I would have to close Bright Beginnings. I prayed and prayed to Swamiji. Guess what happened? I was in turmoil for about two weeks again. Then, one of the parents offered to give me a loan. Not only did I pay that money back in full with interest, I paid every single bill and made a profit. What I didn't realize was the landlord didn't cash the last check so in reality I didn't make a profit, but every single bill was paid! I was proud and so deeply grateful for that miracle!

My intuition became superior. I kept thinking everything was a coincidence. I could see through everybody's deceit which was a little unnerving at first. I love it now because nobody could fool me anymore. In the old days, I was gullible and believe everything. I still see the divine in every one and believe people are inherently good, but I also recognize when people are dishonest. The consuming issue for me is how to handle each situation knowing the truth behind the motive of the individual. It took me about a year after IA to have the courage to confront uncomfortable circumstances.

Traumatic incidences from my past no longer bothered me. I was able to speak about them with ease. Problems come and go, but I am able to handle them easily with clarity and good acumen. I am truly happy almost all of the time and enjoy life to its fullest! The most difficult area for me which is my biggest engraved memory has to do with romance and fantasy!

Three Strikes And You Are OUT!

Most people seem to learn the first or the second time or at least the third time. Is it possible to be thrown out into the dugout every single time up at bat and still go back for more humiliation praying for a different outcome. Wouldn't it be better to change your strategy in some way? Maybe stand a different way, hold the bat differently or maybe even learn from your colleagues who get on base almost all the time. Logically, this makes perfect sense. However, I was craving my knight in shining armor for my entire existence and so my fantasy monopolized my mind at every waking moment. Plus, after IA, I was convinced God was showering me with the man of my dreams. You would think I would learn, but every time I was overcome with emotions so deep that no one could persuade me he wasn't a gift from the divine.

Once I was liberated, I was so excited about dating. I subscribed to my first dating site. Immediately, I had two people interested. They both fulfilled all my dreams. In fact, both were helping orphans in Africa. One of the men seemed a little dishonest, so after 2 days of being on the site I chose Anthony. I went off the site after the third day and didn't even pay for my subscription because it was a 3 day free trial. I thought I have been blessed, blessed, and blessed some more. When I first started talking to Anthony, he supposedly lived in New York. A few days later he was working on his engineering project for the African orphans. We spoke to each other and chatted through yahoo every day. I fell in love with him even though I never met him face to face. This may be difficult to understand, but he had every character trait I dreamed about my entire life and he looked like a model. After ten weeks, he was coming home. I was so excited. He wanted me to pick him up at Kennedy airport, at that time I had a fear of driving into Queens so I told him I would take the bus into the city to meet him the day after he arrived. I believe my higher consciousness was trying to tell me something because I would have done anything for him. I even wired him $500 because he fabricated a story and I trusted him.

He never arrived on the plane and I never heard from him again. My intuition told me to google his number. Our inner being will tell us exactly what to do if we allow. Right before my eyes was his number and name with about 20 complaints against him. He was a scammer and apparently

Vanaja Ananda, MA, MS

collected thousands from women who fell for his charisma. My heart shattered and I cried for a couple of weeks. It was devastating.

Two weeks later, I was on a different site. I was courted by two guys almost immediately again. One man I actually met and eventually dated for six months. However, I started out being good friends with Bill. The one I fell madly in love with was George. It was almost an identical scenario as Anthony, except I didn't express money oversees. I spoke to him for about the same amount of time. He was coming home for Christmas and I remember buying him the gifts I thought he would adore; I put so much thought and love into choosing those gifts. He called me a few days before Christmas and told me he was beat up and in the hospital in Africa. I trusted him. I felt I learned my lesson with Anthony so George was definitely a blessing from the divine. As you could imagine, he never showed up. I wanted the kids to have a good Christmas so I pretended I was happy for a couple of days. Then I cried uncontrollably for a couple. This time Bill was there to comfort me thank goodness, I don't know if I would be sane right now if it wasn't for Bill.

Bill was so much fun, spiritual, adventurous and free-spirited. I really liked him, but always felt something was missing. I would constantly tell him I wanted to date other people, especially because he lived three hours away and worked weekends. However, the times we were together were magical. One time, we made love every two hours for three days straight, eating, doing yoga, meditation and wrestling in between. He showed me that intercourse is phenomenal. I am sure my inner child believed I wasn't supposed to enjoy sex and six months later he cheated on me. His infidelity was my fault although I didn't understand that when it happened. I felt totally betrayed once again. The pattern was right before my eyes and I chose to ignore it and play the victim. My friends gave me tons of sympathy, but honestly what did that do for me. It confirmed to me that men were not to be trusted. In reality, it was my own fault.

After Bill, I went on four dating sites and I went on about five meets a week. I call them meets because at the beginning of the month I actually went on dates. Since I have a kind heart, I would struggle through the dinner. It seemed like every male I met wanted to go to bed with me instantly. They also lied about their age and pictures were over 10 years old. I know, now, that was the energy I was emitting; to attract men who only wanted sex. After all, it was imperative that I was right no matter what.

Ludicrous! Also, I met people who I became friends with and assisted with their self-healing so there were positives as well.

I was a serial dater for one month and then slowed things down, but my new occupation was online dating. After work, I would be on the computer for hours. It became an obsession and an addiction. Then I met bachelor number 3. Keith was a mute, looked like a model and seemed to have a heart of gold. We communicated mainly through email. However, he had a machine that connected to the phone so we sometimes spoke through that contraption. We continued daily communication for three months and we were supposed to meet. The bottom line is we never met and once again my heart was crushed. I think Keith was real, but he was afraid to meet me. So many times, I told him Swamiji could heal him and he would be able to talk again. I never even asked him if he wanted to speak. He probably thought if he wasn't healed, I wouldn't want to be with him. That definitely wasn't the case. Even though I live in my fantasy world, my emotions were so real. My brain interpreted our virtual love affair as reality because I had an amazing imagination. Anthony and George never spoke about sex, but Keith definitely did and it was extremely erotic.

After Keith, I was back on the dating sites in full swing. In fact, once I sold Bright Beginnings, dating sites became my full time job. I got so bored with it, but needed it more and more. It was like I was on drugs. I was extremely picky who I dated since I was searching for "the one." I would meet, meet, meet, but not date, date, date. One day, I had a brilliant idea. Why waste precious time going out to meet these people, when I could see what they look like through skype? I did not expect the first guy I skyped to disrobe in front of my eyes so that idea lasted about 2 minutes. The dating sites became my fixation. Night and day I was on the computer. I prayed for God to release me from this obsession because I knew it was unhealthy, but I wasn't able to control myself. I would find men whose profile meshed my ideals and I would scare them away with my ranting about how the divine has matched us and I feel a connection. Oh boy! I am surprised they didn't ship me to the loony bin.

One Sunday, I went to the beach because that was my favorite destination. I had a wonderful day! I opened the door at home and was surprised my dog, Champ, wasn't there to greet me. I figured the kids let him outside. I opened the sliding glass door to call him, but he was nowhere in sight so I thought he was playing with the deer. I went in my room and went to go on my dating sites and noticed some of the keys had fallen off the keyboard. I called my son and daughter to see if they knew where Champ was and to ask them what happened to the computer. Neither one of them answered. My daughter called back about two minutes later and while I was asking her the question, I turned around and saw Champ's body under the bed. I knew immediately he was dead and I let out a blood curdling scream. I stared at the body of my beloved best friend and wasn't able to touch him. I don't know how long it took, but finally I pulled him out from under the bed. I held him in my arms screaming and crying for hours. My son and his friend dug a hole in the backyard. I was told the room permeated with a foul odor and I had to bury my little angel Champie.

Champ's death was worse than any death I ever experienced. This animal who offered me the unconditional love from the moment our eyes met was gone from my life. This was the soul I chose over my ex when he gave me an ultimatum. This was the dog I drove 3 ¾ hours each way in one day because my daughter and I fell in love with him through the internet. This was the companion who followed me everywhere I went, offering me lots of love and millions of kisses. Champ had the most beautiful soul; I would look into his eyes and wonder why he wasn't human because he possessed every human trait. His death was such a tragedy and it was all because of me. I asked Swamiji during IA to allow Champ to be reborn as a human, never anticipating the horror that bestowed my life. I am not kidding when I say be careful what you ask for because it comes true.

Champie hated the computer so much because my addiction averted attention away from him. He wanted to destroy it. Also, he witnessed the pain and anguish I encountered with my fantasies and Champ blamed the computer for my angst. Champ choked on the keys and died. His body looked perfect with his eyes open, but there was no heartbeat. Champ gave up his life to cure me from my dating addiction and I will never forget that act of pure selfless love and devotion. I know Champ would have to agree before Swamiji would take him because of the cosmos law. It is the divine law to not interfere with any being. If an entity wants something from the divine, he must ask with intensity. Champ must have been praying with intensity because he understood every inch of my being; I talked to Champ about everything! From that day onward, I removed myself from every dating site except Spiritual Singles because I never dated anyone from that site so it didn't really matter.

My Baby Boy

My pregnancy with Kyle was quite good except for a small bout with morning sickness. The delivery was another story. We decided to go to a birthing center so the birth process was natural. All was going swimmingly. In fact, the room was spectacular, similar to a 5 star hotel and I was looking forward to the lobster dinner they promised the day after delivery. Even though it was a natural birth, I was induced because Kyle was two weeks late and showed no signs of leaving the warmth of my uterus. The nurse thought I was totally dilated and I wasn't so she had me pushing for hours. This intense pushing put Kyle into distress and he swallowed the myocardium fluid. We had no idea till a few weeks later.

Since I was pushing for so long, the delivery lasted forever and the pain was unbearable, I didn't even want to see Kyle when he was born. I blamed him for all the agony I just endured. The nurse immediately put him in my arms and I distinctly remember the anger I directed toward my innocent baby. I started him on a path of **"not being good enough"** and **"not being wanted."** Our thoughts are that powerful and I take full responsibility for the insecurity my son learned from me from the day he was born.

Kyle was rushed across the street to the hospital and that was the beginning of our horror. It was at that moment, I realized I loved Kyle so much, but the poison was already injected by my intense vehemence. The hospital across the street in California was unable to locate Kyle's veins so he was rushed to Stanford Medical. The doctor told us every worst case scenario that Kyle could be afflicted with. He was in ICU for three weeks and I was there night and day; I practically lived at the hospital. Thank God, Kyle had pneumonia as opposed to so many other diseases and was released three weeks later.

I adored Kyle and still do of course. His mental pattern was already set and I helped put it there. He grew up extremely insecure and never feeling that he was good enough. He had a lot of my negative emotions, never feeling like he belonged on this planet. Why should he when his own mother rejected him? Since he held the learning disability belief, he developed chemical imbalances and was diagnosed with ADHD in the fourth grade. We put him on Ritalin and it didn't work. He was smart and hated the mind altering medication so he was titrated off of the prescription. I took him to Neurofeedback and many other holistic

Vanaja Ananda MA; MS

treatments. He was energetic and bright, but didn't really respect authority and that created problems within the classroom.

He became addicted to marijuana. He wasn't eating and he was operating in a fog most of the time. He was hanging out with a different group of kids because his close friends abandoned him when he became addicted even though they introduced him to the stimulant. My ex and I were very concerned.

I asked Swamiji to help Kyle and he blessed him. It took about two years because Kyle didn't want to give up the drug that offered him some happiness in this crazy world. I am now happy to report he gave it up one day without looking back and now helps others who are addicted to any drug. He is successfully enrolled in college and achieving great grades. Deep gratitude goes out to Swamiji Nithyananda. Even through those days of adversity, Kyle managed to obtain the highest rank in Boy Scouts—the Eagle Scout. Kyle is an Indigo child and a mover and shaker of the world. Expect to see and hear about Kyle in the future because he will be helping mankind magnanimously.

An Angel Arrives In Our Lives

Raquel was due to be born the day before my mother passed away. She was two weeks late and induced just like her brother. My children preferred the safety of my womb to the outside chaos. Do you blame them? I requested an epidural months before the delivery and reminded the doctor at every appointment thereafter. He assured me I would have one. The day Raquel was induced; there was a huge traffic accident. The anesthesiologist was needed in the emergency room and I was left with no epidural. Could you believe that? Raquel's delivery was much easier than Kyle's. Her cherubic face caused everyone to stare at this divine creation. She was truly a Godsend. I took her to my good friend's wedding two days later and all the people were attracted to Raquel like a magnet; they would comment she was someone special.

Raquel has taught me so much throughout my life. She always smiles and brings joy to those around her. Unfortunately, she has negative mental patterns, similar to the rest of her family. Her biggest issue in life was her weight. **"I must please everyone"** is the statement that is associated with being overweight. Raquel always felt she had to please everyone to keep peace and maintain her angelic personality. To circumvent her desire to please, she would gorge pizza down her throat without even tasting the bites. She ate super fast as well. I have to say we ate a lot of junk food and that didn't help the matter. I would delicately tell her to exercise and eat less, but she would become defiant. She realized on her own one day she was unhappy with her body proportions. She tried diets, hula hooping and aerobics, but her weight remained the same give or take a few pounds.

Raquel was not obese by any means, but those extra pounds really affected her self image. I knew Raquel wanted to lose weight so bad and I didn't know how to help her. At IA, I asked Swamiji to help Raquel with her weight problem. He blessed her. When I came back from IA, I was horrified to see Raquel gained more weight because her father was furious during my absence even though he gave me the frequent flyer points to go. Apparently, he complained daily.

Shortly after my return, Raquel and I found Bikram Yoga. We both did the 30 day challenge which turned into 60 days and 90 consecutive days. We both absolutely loved Bikram and still do. Raquel lost 25 pounds in two months and continued to lose weight over the course of a year.

She went from a size 12 to a size 2 and that is the truth! She became a vegetarian and did Bikram. Those were the only changes in her life that produced the miracle that helped her self-esteem soar. By the way, she no longer pleases everyone either which is a shock to her father!

You Never Know Who is a Messenger from God

Duane's business was falling apart and every interview he went on was a rejection. He was extremely depressed. He no longer believed in God. He was raised a Mormon and his mother asked the priest to read her the last rites and the minister refused because she wasn't baptized. At that moment, Duane lost faith in God. His belief was demolished instantly. I always believed in God, but I was never religious so Duane's religious beliefs didn't concern me until I realized he had nobody to turn to in his hours of terror and fear. My heart went out to him and I wanted him to have some spirituality. I asked Swamiji to help bring Duane closer to the divine.

One day, a few months after my return from IA, Duane went on an interview. When he came out, there was a maintenance man in the parking lot. The maintenance man went up to Duane and asked him how the interview went? Duane was surprised and said it went well, but how did he know. The man replied, "You are dressed up and you look like you were going on an interview." The two of them talked for a couple of minutes exchanging pleasantries. At the end, the man said "You seem like a nice family man and I bless you to get that job." Duane immediately called and told me the story. Listen to this! He told me he thought the man was his guardian angel." I nearly dropped the phone and fell on the floor.

He was offered that job a few weeks later. He is now in international sales and guess where he happened to travel on business? You are absolutely right! He traveled to India and visited the Taj Mahal. India is the spiritual incubator of the world. The energy is so intense throughout the country and many enlightened Masters took birth there. When you visit there, it opens your path to spirituality exponentially. I guess Duane is becoming closer to the divine after all.

My brother, friends and people I come in contact with have benefited by my Inner Awakening experience. The grace of Swamiji transmits to all those around me. Since there is no distance between time and space, people even feel the energy through the telephone. It is beyond logic and I don't even try to understand it; I am so deeply grateful for all the fun, joy and happiness in my life.

Inner Awakening is an incredible program involving yoga, breathing and intense meditations. It is not a retreat. It awakens your inner being. Swamiji digs out the roots of your negative mental patterns instead of the branches. This means beliefs from past lives are being uprooted. When they come to the surface, you face them head on. You can choose to escape from them and continue the pattern over and over again. Or, you could delve into them so the root cause could be expunged, eliminated, persecuted and massacred. I chose the long route unfortunately. But, it is a good thing because now I could help people remove the toxins quickly. The toxins must be released in some way; that is the only way for it to exit the body. Diarrhea, vomiting, headaches and flu like symptoms are common. Even though there is some discomfort, the rewards are tremendous! IA is the best gift you could ever give yourself and your family! EnGenius is the IA program for children up to age 15 that begins and ends the same time as the adult program. If you want an enlightened child, don't miss En Genius!

PART 6

Messages Come In Many Ways

The Divine in The Cosmos

You probably think I am promoting Swamiji Nithyananda. I am here to tell you that thought is absolutely correct! I only share the best and Swamiji is truly the best. He is on FREE everynight live from India teaching, offering blessings through "Dial An Avatar," and initiating the world into kriyas. Swamiji developed breathing exercises along with yoga asanas (positions) to cure many diseases humans encounter in the lifetime; these processes are called kriyas. He spends endless hours in the gym to formulate the precise prescription for removing the ailments; then he shows us during his morning discourse every single day. Swamiji is full of love and compassion for all of humanity. Go to www.nithyananda.org/en-tv. It usually starts 9:45PM Eastern Standard Time. Moreover, the Inner Awakening gets to the core of our being. He is the only avatar I know who is available to the public in his physical form every day.

What do I mean by the word Avatar? Many of you have most likely seen the movie Avatar and reality is not far from that artistic film. I am going to explain my interpretation of an Avatar to the best of my ability because it still remains beyond my science of reasoning. We are all made of energy and everything in nature is made of energy . . . a flower, rock, spider, snake, cloud, ocean and so on and so forth. God or divine or

Vanaja Ananda MA, MS

whatever you want to call this energy is everywhere, in a form and without. The energy without form is the most powerful energy because that is the all consuming universe, cosmos or existential energy. The angels, fairies, Archangels, Gods, stars, planets and more reside outside of our bodies. They are the ones answering our prayers and protecting us. They supply whatever our thoughts project to them; thoughts are communicated to the cosmos through an electrical surge. Whatever is paramount in your mind, will broadcast to the higher realms. In return, the cosmos renders your wish. The cosmos never judges so it is always your choice. There is no such thing as good or bad in the universe; it just is!

Now that we appreciate the vastness of this lesson, we could literally manifest anything. The Secret, The Living Matrix and What the Bleep Do We Know are documentaries that explain this premise in detail. The element I am adding to these fabulous, well-known films is the act of reprogramming our thoughts so we can achieve abundance from the cosmos. The cosmos enjoys giving; we need to enjoy receiving. Once our thoughts are reprogrammed, we will relish in the miracles that occur constantly and unexpectedly. It is the ultimate. Anyone can do it! It is our God given talent!

In short, if we often conjecture we are not good enough, we will lose competitions, promotions, finances, health, and relationships. The cosmos is answering our prayer. Even though we may be praying for a job, for instance, the billions of thoughts permeating our mind are contradictory. Thoughts like I don't have enough money to buy this tells the universe you are lacking so you miss opportunities right in front of you to make money because your inner child is programmed to believe you are not good enough because the job of your dreams is right in front of you. You had two great interviews and everybody from the President on down loved you. They said they would call you the following week. You are thrilled. However, the entire week your thoughts start germinating in other directions. Is the pay enough? Maybe I won't like sitting in the office? Maybe I should wait to see what happens with this other company? You know, that one person looked a little suspicious; that could be a sign it is not a good company for me. By the end of the week, your subconscious talked you out of the job of your dreams. Guess what happens next. The company never calls you even to say you didn't get the job. This is exactly what happened to me . . . not once, but twice. Your mind could be very cunning and sabotage your biggest dreams if you allow it. It is time to reprogram those beliefs that are no longer supportive and beneficial. As you can see, the cosmos gives you exactly what you want.

I went off on a little tangent just to explain the power of our thoughts. I will explain what an Avatar is now that you understand the significance of the cosmos. An Avatar is formless outside of the body. When the planet is in a state of distress or forthcoming disaster, the Avatar arrives on the planet in body form. It is not mandatory for him to come because every entity has choices even in the cosmos. He comes out of the goodness of his heart and the unconditional love he has for humanity. He downloads whatever he needs from the cosmos to help him with his mission which is to restore humanity back to its peace loving constitution. In essence, when an Avatar arrives on this planet, remove every obstacle blocking you from meeting him because it doesn't happen in every lifetime. Avatars also took many births before they finally had a totally pure consciousness; no negative mental patterns. As our role models, they pave the road so we could transform and potentially transform into an Avatar as well. Nothing is beyond our possibility and all is well within our reach once we are aware. One must be initiated by an Avatar to achieve such great feats. An Avatar is a guide, teacher, friend, mother or father. His love is so real and unconditional love is a human craving.

That being said, I believe there is a hierarchy in the universe among the enlightened beings. I could only surmise since I haven't left my body yet. Gods are at the top and they come in many shapes and forms. Jesus Christ, Buddha, Shiva, Parvati, Ganesha, Ghandi, Allah, and so many more are all God in different forms and the ultimate Gods. Then, I believe there are Gods like Moses, Abraham, and Dhali Llama just to name a few. Archangel Michael, Raphael, Gabriel, Uriel, Jophiel, Haniel, Metatron and Sandolphan come next. The layer underneath are regular angels and below them are fairies that bring messages to humans in the form of signs. Signs can come through other people, non-animate objects like a billboard, animals or songs. They come in many other ways too. Dreams, for example, are powerful vehicles for messages. Listening to our intuition is the best because the ideas are emanating from our higher consciousness; the divine inside ourselves.

Although I believe Swamiji is at the highest of the hierarchy alive in the body today, there are many gurus, Avatars and angels existing among us right now. Every single one of them is a gift to mankind. Whenever you feel the presence of an enlightened being in any form, get a blessing.

Mountains, rivers, oceans, songs also give out this darshan or blessing. If you feel good doing something, chances are you are getting blessings from the cosmos through some form. The feeling is indescribable almost like an adrenaline high that only dissipates when you leave the source. That is the reason no one wants to leave an Avatar's side.

What is enlightenment? One definition that comes to mind is you are happy and content all the time. In order to obtain the feeling of constant restful awareness, all karmic lessons need to be learned and changed. The karmic lessons I am referring to are the negative mental patterns. In addition, when one achieves the ultimate state, he is no longer required to take birth as a human again. Only a pure soul would take birth as a human because when they arrive, their memory is vaporized so they encounter the same societal judgment as all mortals.

There are many enlightened beings on the planet right now whose sole purpose is to help mankind. I have encountered quite a few enlightened beings and I am drawn to them as well. I have learned a lot from them and am blessed to be in their energy field. All of them have helped me on my journey. Even though I love Swamiji's human form, his energy reverberates in all beings. The enlightened beings I will tell you about are Amma Karunamayi, Ammaji, Mother Meera, and Braco. They all contributed to my spiritual renewal.

When Amma Karunamayi came to town, I heard she was the incarnation of Saraswati. Saraswati is the Goddess of knowledge and creativity. She has come down to this planet to share her wisdom. I followed her from Philadelphia to New Jersey and New York. She was in this area for two weeks and I was in the audience every day the entire time. I had no idea why I was traveling hours to see her; I followed my heart. She performed chanting ceremonies, gave darshan and led homas. A homa is a sacred fire ceremony in which various forms of the Divine are invoked in a sacred fire. It brings powerful healing and spiritual healing. Special food, jewelry and clothing offerings are made into the fire while Sanskrit mantras are chanted. It is part of the Vedic tradition. Kyle and Raquel came on one of the days as my Mother's Day present. They were blessed with the Saraswati diksha which inspires students to do well. Both teens are doing extremely well in school. Amma Karunamayi addresses everyone as her baby whether you are an infant or 90 years old. Her melodious voice repetitively says "I love you my babies." You just want to cry when you hear those words for it is the voice of protection. Her website is www.karunamayi.org.

I love hugging and getting hugs so much! Children offer hugs easily. Usually, I will ask children permission to give them a hug. After all, we are all individuals and some people do not like the human touch and I must respect that. Some adults are suspicious about hugs so I usually could read their energy and know when it is appropriate or not to put my arms around them. The hugging saint was coming to New York and I was ecstatic to say the least. Even before I met Amma, I knew I was going to Boston for her four day retreat. I sat, ate or walked around the energy field for hours before I finally went up to get the special hug. It was a magnificent hug, filled with intense love. The smell from her being was intoxicating. She radiates the taintlessness of the divine. After my hugging darshan, I stayed in the room until the wee hours of the morning. I was present the entire time she was in New York and Boston. Her website is www.amma.org.

Mother Meera is another Avatar. She brings the Paramatman light to people. This light is the essence of the divine. It is the white light that contains love and energy. When I went to visit Mother Meera, the people in the room were in complete silence. This experience was so different than the other gurus I encountered. I went up and received darshan and the energy was mighty and omnipotent. I enjoyed the silence because I was able to connect with my inner source freely. Read about Mother Meera at www.mmdarshanamerica.com.

All of these gurus donate so much love, compassion and peace to the world. Their meditations are excellent. Moreover, most of their profits go toward building hospitals, improving the educational system, feeding the poor, rehabilitating criminals, and more. Their websites explain a fraction of what they do. They sleep a few hours per night in a state called Samaddhi; that is the only rest their bodies require. They spend endless hours developing new meditations, kriyas, and discourses to bring people to an enlightened frame of mind. Living enlightenment is the goal. They tirelessly give darshans to thousands of people without taking breaks. Their love for the population is authentic, genuine and different than any type of human love emotion. There are no expectations of reward by accolades or prestige; they provide this service to society selflessly. They have helped innumerable amounts of people heal from fatal illnesses. They have brought innovative ideas and techniques to the public, far in advance of 21st century thinking. They are helping to change the world dramatically because our planet needs a major overhaul.

I came across an angel on earth also. His name is Braco and he radiates goodness. Braco is from Croatia, but I met him in New Jersey. I saw a picture of him on a flyer and the next thing I knew I was volunteering for the entire four days of his program. He is different than the Avatars, yet the same. He chooses to give darshan in a dissimilar fashion. In fact, he says he is not a guru. He does not speak in public. He prefers not to have notoriety, but when you are a pure vessel for the divine, it is impossible to have anonymity. He offers his gift to society through eye gazing. Angelika Whitecliff talks about her experiences with Braco over a 21 day period so I won't go into the details. Her book is titled "21 Days with Braco" and it is a must read. Braco's powers are uncanny and magical. There are bountiful testimonials from people all over the world who have been healed by his eyes. Briefly, he comes onto the stage and you look into his eyes for 7 minutes. Children under 18 are not allowed to be present, because the energy is too strong. However, a person whose photo is placed over the heart of an adult who watches Braco will feel the same effects. Braco also does live streaming through the web and the effect is cogent. Divine energy channels across countries. We are all connected through energy so this statement is plausible. Whether it is conceivable or not, it just happens and that is all there is to it. Trust and have faith and there will be miracles abound in your lives. Furthermore, Braco has perfected his voice and usually in his last session of the tour day, he blesses you with both eye gazing and "The Voice." The Voice is done in Croatian, but the sound of the words goes directly to your inner being and you feel the tingling sensation through your body. Sometimes, The Voice is better than the gaze because you don't need to interpret the meaning because you don't know the language so it immediately puts your body in surrender mode. Many miracles happen through The Voice. To learn more about Braco, peruse his site at www.braco.net.

I love children and miss all the Bright Beginnings children immensely, but there were a handful of kids that will be close to my heart forever. They were the original Bright Beginnings students when the school was based out of my home. Kerry, Courtney, Ralphie, Jeff, Zachary, Amanda, Ryan, Erin, Luke, Kelly, Maya and Nikko were my surrogate kids. I became friends with all their parents and we went on many outings together. Ralphie was extremely energetic and often was blamed by adults and peers. I always protected him because I knew he felt misplaced in this world. Ralphie was challenging, but had a heart of gold. He grew up

Vanaja Ananda MA; MS

not really believing in God or an existential force. That is why I was so surprised when he allowed me to do a healing on his nose he broke in basketball. He was ready to have an operation and I begged him to let me try energy healing and he acquiesced. As a result, he didn't need the operation. The night before I went to volunteer at Braco's event, I received a text from Ralphie. He asked me to please do my magic and get him a car. I told him we would both pray to the divine and see what happens. He asked me what was the divine and I explained. I told him he had the divine inside of him; we all did. I think he thought I was from Mars! Anyway, I brought his picture with me and prayed for Ralphie to have a good self-esteem and release the anger he harbored against his mother. The last few seconds I said "by the way it would be great if Ralphie could get a car." Driving home that night, I received a text from Ralphie saying a car just became available and it was in his price range. The magic is fun, but the crucial part is that Ralphie is starting to become spiritual and believe in miracles!

Even though these Masters can create miracles in your life, for the result to stay permanently it is imperative to reprogram your limiting beliefs. Otherwise, the same old patterns will emerge and you will be tempted to blame God. The person you really need to blame is yourself. Blame is not the right word since these beliefs were designed for your protection. The correct word is awareness because when you are aware, then you realize you are responsible for all the events and people who have come into your life. It is not a time to blame, but an opportunity to rejoice and celebrate because now you could become the power that has always been inside, but fearful to come out.

Vanaja Ananda MA, MS

The Significance of a Deity

All of these gurus or Avatars I mentioned are from the Vedic tradition. You probably think I was born a Hindu or at least have ancestry from the Indian heritage. I wonder the same thing. I was born a Jew and my heritage is Russian and Romanian. I have a light complexion, blue eyes and dark hair. My name is the only component that signifies my Vedic roots. Maybe if I delve into my past, I will disclose Indian genealogy; even Native American Indian would explain my infatuation with the Vedic tradition. However, I believe it has nothing to do with race, but more with the brilliance behind the Vedic heritage. I now consider myself a Hinjew. I must confess I stole the title Hinjew from a friend so I need to give credit to Shelly for this magnificent term to describe my spirituality. I do embrace Buddhism and many other traditions as well so maybe I'll come up with an even better name than Hinjew. The diversity of the people in this world allows us to express our individuality, but at the same time we are all connected by our one energy source. Source is not described by race, creed or religion so it is nonsensical to have wars and destruction over these topics.

What is so special about the Vedic tradition? Deities, mantras, Sanskrit, yoga and Siddha medicine all derive from the Vedic culture. I already explained yoga in detail so you could visit that chapter to refresh your memory. I will spell out the influence deities, mantras, Sanskrit and Siddha medicine have on our civilization.

What is a deity? A deity is a sacred form that is energized by a Master, guru or Avatar. When I use Master in these passages, the term is synonymous with Avatar. A deity could be anything . . . a rock, mountain, tree, table and more. Once it is energized, the object has its own intelligence and by praying to these deities, one can receive darshan and miracles galore. The deities I will be expounding upon are statues of ascended Masters, specifically in the Hindu tradition. Ascended Masters infers they are not presently in human form. However, their energy is incredibly powerful. When a living Master infuses a sculpture with his own energy, the carving becomes alive. It may not be alive in the description you are accustomed to because it does not breathe. However, deities have been known to walk, open and close eyes and conduct other paranormal activities; it is not for us to judge if they breathe or not. All I could tell you is their energy is soothing and calming. When you are with a deity, you are with the Master who energizes it!

Shiva, Brahma and Vishnu are the head of the entire cosmos. Brahma is the creator, Vishnu is the preserver and Shiva is the destroyer. I am referring to ego when I mention destroyer. The ego forces us to do things contrary to the desires of our higher consciousness and the divine. It is the manipulator. The ego is the one who conforms to fear, greed, jealousy, and worry. If we listen to our heart, our "I am consciousness" will tell us what direction to follow. Instead, we allow our controlling imagination to run our lives. "I am that" relates to the God inside of us. Deities of these forms are revered in all Hindu temples. Some people have these statues in their homes and execute daily pujas to express deep gratitude to these enlightened beings. A puja is a ritual creating sacred space and honoring the divinity within each person and the Ascended Masters.

Devi is the female counterpart of Shiva in all her divine forms. Lakshmi is the Goddess of Wealth, Saraswati is the Goddess of Knowledge and Creativity and Kali is the Goddess who destroys the ego. In the Hindu tradition, female energy supersedes male energy.

Ganesha is the son of Shiva and Devi. He has an elephant head with a human body. Ganesha removes all obstacles. Also, he is playful and loves sweets. He is a boy I definitely could relate to. Ganesha is the deity most people are connected to.

There are so many Ascended Masters; I hit upon a few only to explain my point. There is a wealth of information on deities at temples or on websites if you wish to learn more. Deities have power beyond the typical human because they are a conduit for divine energy. Unlike humans, these inanimate objects accept the energy and enable the electrical current to flow easily within its entire structure. Contrarily, humans fabricate a wall making it challenging for the energy to flow through the human anatomy.

There is a banyan tree at the Nithyananda Ashram that has tremendous healing powers. Hugging that tree, sitting against its trunk or branches, or lying in the near vicinity of that humungous tree generates mass amounts of healing matter. Also, there is a mountain in India named the Arunachala that was energized by Shiva. Many Masters took birth at the Arunachala Mountain.

"India is the spiritual incubator of the world." What does Swamiji mean by this? Let's look at the definition of an incubator that is used to house premature infants. Preemies are put in an incubator because they are unable to sustain life on their own. They depend on the warmth of the electric box to supply them with oxygen. Also, incubators protect premature babies from infection, noise and light. Similarly, the temples and Ashrams in India are a place of protection for those seeking spirituality. We enter as premature infants, not understanding why we traveled across the world to be there, yet when we arrive believing it is our true home. It is a place we have been searching for our entire life without realizing it. When in India, it is like having a shield or bubble around your body at all times preserving your true nature while teaching the principals our higher consciousness knows and is begging to reveal. Little by little, the facts are divulged and our inner child is pressured to examine evidence. At first, it repels in defiance and fear for it is against every fiber of its being. However, our inner child eventually sees the light and realizes it is a prisoner inside its own body. The initiation of the Master and the energy field of India is the only way to awaken our inner being and make the dramatic changes required for happiness and ultimate fulfillment while existing on this planet.

Osho puts it beautifully, "*India is not just a geography or history. It is not only a nation, a country, a mere piece of land. It is something more: it is a metaphor, poetry, something invisible but very tangible. It is vibrating with certain energy fields that no other country can claim.*"

Mantras are omnipotent, all-powerful and have unlimited power. A mantra is a word or sound that is repeated to help with meditation. Sounds have major effects on our physiology. The sound of the ocean waves crashing against the shore calms our nerves, while the loud roar of a lion is terrifying.

Several researchers and doctors studied the importance of sound and vibration. Dr. Hans Jenny, a Swiss medical doctor and scientist, discovered sound influences matter. Briefly, Dr. Jenny put sand and various powders on metal plates and placed a speaker next to them. The sound from the speakers produced beautiful designs in each of the tactile substances. When the sound ceased, the design was no longer there. This study demonstrated that sound actually creates form. Another pioneer study in the field of sound was conducted by Dr. Emoto, Japanese scientist and author of "Messages From Water." He used music to observe its effects on water. The results were astonishing. When classical music was played, the ice crystals formed designs, but when heavy metal played the geometric patterns collapsed. In another experiment, words were used in replacement of music. When words of love and encouragement were recited, the ice crystals formed a pretty pattern. However, words of hate and disdain caused the particles to break apart. Moreover, Dr. Emoto found prayer had the ability to heal large bodies of polluted water. Dr. Emoto is featured in the film "What the Bleep Do We Know." Dr. Emoto states, "the vibrational energy projected by humans in the form of thoughts, words, ideas, intentions, and sounds has the power to alter water's molecular structure." Since the human body is composed of 70% water, these studies are profound. Our thoughts, words and beliefs affect the cells of our body; they have the capacity to bring healing or disease to our organs. Prayer, healing sound and vibrations provide an outlet to connect with the divine and internal peace.

Mantras in the Vedic tradition are associated with a guru. The guru through the form of meditation or intuition tests the sounds and develops the best vibrational arrangement to help treat anxiety and as a preventative measure for diseases on the rise. There is a direct relationship between mantras and chakras, the seven major energy centers in the body which was discussed in an earlier chapter. Using mantras consistently can reverse stored thoughts in your subconscious. The efficiency of mantras is more effectual when done with devotion and faith. Hindu mantras are composed of Sanskrit words.

Sanskrit is often referred to as the language of the Gods. It is the oldest language and it produces immediate effects whether you speak it or listen to it. When you listen to Sanskrit, you are uplifted by the beauty of the sound and the high energy vibration. It transforms the mind as it communicates directly with your inner child. As a result, you will perform better in all aspects of your life. Columbia, Cornell, Brown, Harvard, John Hopkins, University of Pennsylvania and Yale have a major element in common. These elite Universities have esteemed professors teaching Sanskrit to their student base. Sanskrit needs to be integrated in schools from preschool age through high school as well.

Siddha medicine is the oldest and most relevant medical system because it incorporates spiritual wisdom and complete knowledge of the human anatomy and physiology. Shiva, the leader of the universe has phenomenal powers and passed down his knowledge to his other son Subramanian. In return, the wisdom was taught to Agasthya, a disciple of Subramanian and was soon translated to humans in their language. Siddhas are enlightened Masters which means they only see the truth; there is no "maya" or illusion. Siddha means perfected one. Siddhas have siddhis or power. Patanjali, the father of yoga, was a Siddhar or physician. The Siddhars achieved

Vanaja Ananda MA; MS

the indestructible body and extended their lifespan exponentially. Siddha medicine acts at the atomic level, moving molecules for long time healing. Siddhas believe one should be an expert in all specialties of medicine because all the body parts together make unique wholeness of life. They probe into the cause and age of the disease.

According to the Siddhars, there are five states of matter: air, water, fire, space, and earth. Our body is composed mostly of the earth element and the location of the body is in the space element. The water element is found in the abdomen and connected to the brain, blood, uterus, marrow, and urine. The fire element is found in the chest and deals with digestion and the conversion of sugars into energy. The prana, breath or air element is located in the neck and helps with running, sitting, standing or walking. The space element is detected in the head and it struggles with lust, anger, greed and want. Most disorders start in the air element, travel to the fire element and end at the water element. Since plants contain all five elements, they are used to restore balance in our system. They bring people to optimal health with no side effects

Siddha Medicine Masters currently residing in Malaysia expounded upon the following. The sage's words are copied verbatim so as not to misrepresent what they have to say. "A common question asked of Siddha Vaidya physicians by modern medical practitioners is about scientific trials. Remedies in Siddha Vaidya have for thousands of years undergone trials and retrials, mostly using human subjects. All possible outcomes of therapies and herbal combinations have been observed and recorded. Siddha Vaidya remedies are formulated so as to reduce the incidence of adverse reactions to an absolute minimum, while promoting the therapeutic effects to the maximum."

Mankind is currently in an upheaval experiencing a lot of emotional and physiological anguish. The holistic solution is the new age medicine. I am amused. I asked numerous Masters to provide me with a means to view pathology inside the anatomy and physiology. At the time, it was my intense desire, dream and passion never believing it could actually come to fruition. The Malaysian Masters have devised a three year program to accomplish exactly what I prayed for. Nothing surprises me anymore and I have learned to go with the flow of the universe instead of the control of my mind and ego. It is another miracle.

Friends Are There To Help If You Let Them

The divine sends messages through people, animals, and nature in general. If your eyes are opened wide and your mind is focused in the present, the signs will appear. It may be in the form of a song that you are listening to on the radio. It could be buried in a poem someone sent you via email. The source can be a beggar on the street. You never know how it will materialize, but be open to the possibilities. These revelations will add spice to your life.

My first friend arrived by the name of Carter Volz. He was teaching a Reiki class at the local college. At that time, I knew nothing about Reiki or energy healing for that matter. I was drawn to the class probably because the description emphasized self healing and I had a list of ailments to mend. I immediately took a liking to him and was intrigued by his stories. The one that sticks in my mind involves his paralysis that ensued after being mugged on the streets of New York. One side of his body was totally immobile and he was forced to stay in bed most of the time. I believe it was for over a year, but please don't quote me on that. Dogs are a man's best friend is no longer a cliché; it is a fact. Carter had a dog who would sit by his side and lick his nerveless side day and night. The unconditional love offered from his dog was remarkable. As a result, Carter healed himself. I was flabbergasted by the contents of this event, yet believed it to be true. From that point on, anything Carter suggested we practice, I followed to a T. He said the symbols from Usui, the Master who founded Reiki, were extremely powerful. I had no clue what that meant, but I was determined to find out. Every day in the shower I would write these symbols on both hands and feet with my fingers while intonating the name of the picture. I did this for several years because I was led to another practice after becoming a Reiki Master.

One day, Carter was teaching how to do distance healing. He had us put the palms of our hands together and slowly separate them so we understood the concept of energy. When you move your hands away from each other, you could feel tingling sensations. I was shocked! I decided I was going to attempt to heal a chicken. Bright Beginnings incubated chicken eggs as a fun, educational lesson. Students had permission to bring the baby chicks home for play dates providing they took good care of them. To make a long story short, a cat attacked the chick's legs. The people at the zoo where we bring them after a month planned to feed him to the snakes. One of the teachers rescued him and brought him home. After my distance healing, I went home with lots of doubts. The next day I was told the chick's leg and foot healed and he was walking normally. It was incredulous! There wasn't scientific data to support my findings, yet the evidence couldn't be clearer. Carter introduced me into the world of mysticism.

Carter was a God send in another way as well. Raquel had a traumatic accident; she was bitten by a dog on a diet who wanted her cookie. The normally gentle canine went into attack mode. He momentarily became manic and bit Raquel four times on the face. She had plastic surgery in the emergency room and we dormed in the hospital for two weeks. During this time frame, Carter did Reiki on Raquel's face. While he had his hands on her face, he told her to envision her face before the mishap and repeat the words "I am more beautiful than before." Let me tell you she is gorgeous and you will probably watch her on television, the movies or Broadway. She also was blessed with an amazing voice.

My friend Lena introduced me to Swamiji and his senior disciple Swami Bhaktinanda. I remember internally announcing to myself there was no way I was bowing to anybody. Who does he think he is anyway? God? I had a huge ego! I found myself bowing against my will and relishing in the feelings that emerged after being touched by him. Little did I know, it was really the omnipotent, omniscient and omnipresent being in the flesh!

My best friend from college, who still remains my best friend even though we don't see each other often, opened the path to the existence of God; prior to meeting Nancy, I continuously questioned if God was a figment of my imagination. Nancy would pray about everything and she was extremely religious. I would query her faith and trust; even though I believed in God, tragedy upon tragedy happened in my life. In Nancy's life, one miracle after another seemed to manifest. I never understood since I felt I was a good human as well, or wasn't I subconsciously. I would observe her religious behavior and sometimes try to emulate it, but religion was never my true nature. Without realizing it, Nancy brought me into the realms of spirituality through her undying devotion to the unknown entity. About a year ago, she asked me to watch her children so she and her husband could go on a business trip to Hawaii. I planned to do a 21 day meditation for peace in New Jersey at the same time. I was in a quandary because she was my best friend. At the same time, I could be helping the mass population. I chose to help the world and Nancy's mom's plans changed so she was able to fly to upstate New York from Florida to be with her grandchildren. Nancy never criticized me for my decision. In fact, she supported it even though she was uncertain her husband would be able to go on the trip. Now you know why she is my best friend.

Michele seems to have a lot of answers whenever questions arise. She often goes on retreats and visits healers from around the globe, including John of God. She remembers her dreams and her imageries are fascinating. After all, our dreams are our reality. As hard as I try, I rarely remember my dreams. Michele not only elicits her dreams in living color with full detail, a lot of the time they had messages for me. We are all joined together so it is perfectly logical. Sometimes, I just think about Michele and the phone rings and it is her or she feels extra energy when I am praying for her. Michele is currently writing songs and I am assuming she will be teaming up with Train soon since that "Soul Sister" group is ensconced in every waking and sleeping moment. Michele is indubitably my soul sister. The divine is definitely sending Michele a message.

Duane was my very best male friend and that has been the most difficult part of our divorce; the loss of our close friendship. I owe Duane so much. Bright Beginnings and the educational system was originally his vision and it eventually became my passion. I was thwarted with so many negative emotions; I was unable to clearly see my path. In reality, Bright Beginnings was born due to his determination and perseverance. More important, even though Duane profusely loved me, he offered me liberation. It was the most selfless service of all of humanity. There is a poem that goes something like this "if you love somebody set them free and if they come back to you, you know it was real; otherwise it wasn't meant to be." I know we were soul mates and we helped each other with our karmas. The first half of my life, we were definitely meant to be together. However, his lessons gave me the strength to find my true calling. I am eternally grateful to Duane. Once I was free, I was able to delve into my subconscious and focus on my spirituality. I blamed him for almost everything that went wrong throughout our marriage and I realized I was responsible in so many ways because I had a guard up. I realized he was a beautiful human, who made mistakes like all of us, but I was not receptive to looking at his positive attributes; I only focused on the negative. Many times these habits that I abhorred were reflections of myself; I just didn't want to admit that to myself. I didn't give him the unconditional love he deserved. By unconditional I mean loving someone regardless of their imperfections and always looking for the divine in that person. My marriage could have been saved if I chose to see his soul through my heart instead of my head.

My brother Glenn and I were extremely close growing up. We protected each other through the trials and tribulations of our lives. However, when he got married, his new family dominated his life and we drifted apart. I had a lot of anger and resentment toward my brother and felt abandoned. I should have been able to understand this. But, my subconscious kept highlighting the word abandonment in my vision. The observed disappearance of Glenn in my life enabled me to reprogram the abandonment thought pattern. I can now handle the desertion because love always prevails. I am as much to blame as he. It takes two you know. Our unconditional love for each other never died. We perceive beliefs that aren't true, yet we are convinced it is the truth. From his perception, we all had busy lives and it is arduous fitting the normal tasks into our daily lives without adding a two hour drive each way. Physical presence is not necessary to have an excellent connection. That valuable lesson was an epiphany.

Jill came into my life through satsungs, group gatherings where we watch Swamiji live from India on two-way viewing; this means Swamiji sees our physical forms and we could see his physical form as if we teleported to India. Jill patiently taught me about the Vedic tradition. She and I would go on long excursions exploring new temples. She has a wealth of information about the Vedic philosophy and I believe she knows more than some of the Hindu priests we encountered. She started organizing pilgrimages to temples around the area and I joined the bandwagon. The deities (statues) at the temples have an intelligence of their own and I was drawn to their energy field. In every temple we visited, I would feel energy coursing through my body and transversing disease ridden matter in order to perform its healing magic. Hindu temples are healing. Soon, Jill will be leading pilgrimages to vortex spots and temples around the world. A vortex is a whirling mass of energy that boosts our higher spiritual consciousness. Having Jill as a spiritual director at the vortex spots will enhance your exhilarating travels.

Jill was also with me the day Champ sent a dog to cheer me up. Jill and I went to the beach on a beautiful, sunny summer day. The beach and ocean invoke serenity and peace so I travel there often. While walking along the shore, I started reminiscing about Champ. My eyes started to well up so we decided to sit down in the sand. All of a sudden, a dog came out of the ocean and sat right at my feet. The dog remained there for about a half hour. He gave me kisses and warmth. He had a beautiful disposition and I was overjoyed to feel his fur next to my skin. My angel Champ sent me a blessing that day! Jill's dog Neela also seems to be an amazing conduit for the divine. That little baby has met sages all over the world; Jill brings her everywhere and she is small enough to be hidden when she is not welcome. Neela always cheers me when I am missing an animal in my life.

Jacqueline introduced me to fairy and angel cards. I guess you call it Tarot. I have known Jacqueline for years; both her kids went to my school. Her little girl Kelly believed in fairies and still does as a teen. I always thought it was a fantasy and adorable. Kelly had porcelain angel and fairy figurines around her house. Never, in my wildest imagination did I think fairies were real. However, when I was trapped in the middle of a situation and couldn't think clearly, Jacqueline would come over with her fairy and angel cards to the rescue. Whenever we asked a question to these sacred cards, the answers were given and they were accurate. As a child I believed in fairies and angels, but society tarnished those ideas. I am back to believing in those winged apparitions and I am convinced beyond any doubt they are real. I owe a lot to Jacqueline for allowing opportunities to float in as a result of these readings.

MaryAnn is an excellent healer and has learned techniques from many experts. Her meditations are dynamic. She helped me release blockages when I was in a panic. She has taken many courses throughout her life and her meditations are outstanding. MaryAnn actually sent me angels. The concept is based on the movie "Pay It Forward." A young boy from an abusive family receives an assignment from his teacher. The homework was to think of something to change the world and actually make it happen. After careful deliberation, the boy decided to implement a new idea. Instead of paying a favor back which is typical, he decided to pay it forward. He did selfless service for three new people. Then these people did good deeds for three more people and so on and so forth. While this seems like such a simple idea, it inspired people to do positive actions for strangers. So MaryAnn paid it forward to me and I in return sent the angels to three more people.

I had a list of instructions to follow for the arrival of my three angels. I made an altar for the three visitors with a candle and white flowers; two envelopes were on the altar as well. One envelope contained three wishes and enclosed in the other envelope were the names and addresses of the three blessed people. Raquel and I were so excited to welcome the divine beings into our home. We opened the door at a specific time and said a special prayer. At this point, Raquel thought I was losing my marbles. However, we both saw a big black shadow and the front door closed by itself as we ended our prayer. We both looked at each other and laughed. I talked to the angels the entire week. One of the angels drove with me wherever I went. The air in the house was fragrant and stimulating. Friends came often during that week. It was a mystifying event and one I will always remember. I want to thank the angels for visiting my home and my family. If someone sends you angels, don't hesitate to accept the offer with deep gratitude.

I met Jacqui through email. Jill sent a message that a friend needed help. She asked me to please support Jacqui and sign up for a reading. The half hour session was $22. I figured I would help this person and since it was so cheap, I assumed the reading would probably be inaccurate. This was my second reading within a month and I was even skeptical about the first person. It sounded esoteric. Jacqui and I confirmed an appointment and she asked me what I wanted to ask. I was so new to this, but I began telling her about Champ for some unknown reason. Jacqui mentioned she was a channeler so we decided to channel Champ. A person who channels allows the cosmos to enter her body and the divine actually speaks through the person. Champ spoke to me through Jacqui and I thought it was so cute; I thought she was a great actress. During the session, Champ said I was a great mom and he loved me. Part of me wanted to believe it was him, but the cantankerous part insisted it was a scam. Michele also had a reading from Jacqui and she liked hers. Then, she had another reading with Jacqui and something Michele said unleashed the Champ channeling which luckily was recorded in my subconscious. All of a sudden, I wanted to talk to Jacqui again, not really understanding why.

During our next telephone encounter, Jacqui took me on a meditation to other dimensions of our galaxy. I now believe I left my body while in this trance and I also know I was speaking to Champ that night. All of us leave our body every night in our deep sleep without realizing it. I would like to learn how to astral travel in the awake state. That would definitely be an accomplishment for me. Jacqui opened me up to the world of parallel universes and other dimensions. If you want a lightworker who is connected to other dimensions, look at Jacqui's website at www.goddessofdivinity.com.

Fluffy was from a litter of eight. Jacqueline's family and my family traveled together to see these baby kittens. Jacqueline bought two kittens and she named them Fluffy and Shadow. We bought two kittens as well and named them Tonka and Brio. Tonka didn't enjoy our family and Fluffy wasn't happy at Jacqueline's house, so we switched. Fluffy loved Duane; he wouldn't leave Duane's side. He also liked Kyle, but he really didn't appreciate Raquel or me. Champ hung with the girls and Fluffy was with the boys. Brio seemed to like all family members. Brio, Tonka and Shadow had kidney failure within a year of each other and Fluffy was the lone survivor. When Duane moved out of our house, Fluffy started playing with Raquel and me although Champ sometimes became territorial. Fluffy would sleep on my forehead every night. He and Champ started to like each other; the animals and I would watch Swamiji every night and meditate. I called them the spiritual animals. When Champ left, Fluffy helped me survive. Fluffy started to greet me at the door; it is the strangest thing, but true. I began to adore Fluffy. I planned to volunteer at the Ashram in India and then I was going off to college for three years, so Fluffy went to live with Jacqueline. When I came back from India, I went to visit Jacqueline and Fluffy wouldn't come near me. I was heartbroken. I felt replaced once again.

I delved back a little into my life and had many replacement situations. It started with my first true love who preferred the radio station to me. My brother and I were inseparable and yet when his wife came along, he easily replaced me with her. No more vacations together, phone calls were shortened, and we saw each other rarely. The day April left, she stopped calling me mom and referred to me by my first name. Although I prayed for Fluffy to handle the separation and transition well, it traumatized me when I was easily replaced with Jacqueline. The teachers, kids and parents at Bright Beginnings have replaced me easily as well. Duane replaced me with a new girlfriend within three months. The most recent and earth shattering experience happened when my best friend Shamadu replaced me as his friend.

Shamadu was my very best male friend after Duane. I could tell Shamadu anything and he never judged me. His girlfriends were jealous of me even though they never met me. Instead of explaining our deep friend connection, he allowed his girlfriends to dictate when we were allowed to speak, email or text. Our friendship, which meant the world to me, was treated as something dirty which we had to sneak around to maintain. One day, his girlfriend forbade him from having any communication with me and I'll tell you why in a moment. I spent many weeks in torment trying to dissolve this limiting belief, but I believe I am finally free from this thought pattern.

Here is the story . . .

There was a day in November where you could invoke Shiva and whatever you asked for was granted. I asked Shiva to go inside my mind and remove anything that needed to be destroyed so I could surrender to the divine. My main purpose was to go to the Ashram the following week and do selfless service without expecting rewards. A couple of hours after this request, a turkey vulture walked across the deck and stared at me through the window. At first I thought it was a turkey and my friend said that it meant great blessings. However, my intuition realized it was a turkey vulture and I knew that meant death. I wasn't sure if it meant death of the ego or a physiological death. Shamadu called 2 o'clock in the morning that same night and asked if he could drive the three hours to see me because he had a fight with his girlfriend. He arrived around 5AM. He crawled into bed with me and we just slept cuddling.

When we awoke, we went on a nature hike. Shamadu and I were drawn to a rock that was about 12 feet high. He climbed the rock easily and gently helped me get to the top. The view from the top was breath taking! All of a sudden, I realized I had to get down and that is when the intense panic hit me. I started my descent, but all of a sudden became paralyzed with fear. I remembered the story when Swamiji was trapped by hyenas. He let out a blood curdling scream and the hyenas disappeared when he opened his eyes. I screamed and closed my eyes;

Vanaja Ananda MA; MS

somehow thinking Swamiji would come and carry me down to the ground. When I opened my eyes, I was in the same predicament. Shamadu slowly helped me down part of the rock formation, but then he had to transcend to the bottom and I was left by myself. Suddenly, I thought of the turkey vulture and knew I was about to die. I was petrified. The funny thing was I was only 6 feet off the ground, but to me it was like 100 feet. I was totally convinced I was going to die and couldn't move off the ledge to jump into Shamadu's arms waiting to embrace and protect me. I sat there for awhile, scared, tense and crying. Then, Shamadu said "you are no longer Pam Warehime; you are Vanaja Ananda and you could do it." From that moment, I became calm, my posture became erect and I was able to jump into his arms easily. This was a major breakthrough for me and I felt blessed to have Shamadu in my life and I thanked Swamiji for bringing Shamadu into my world.

But the story doesn't end there. We went back to my house and had dinner, talked and watched a movie. It was an amazing day and I was so relieved I wasn't going to die and my ego was going to be massacred. Shamadu told me he was breaking up with his girlfriend.

We went to sleep in the same bed again. We woke up in the middle of the night and this time we fooled around a little, but no intercourse. A couple of months later, he told his girlfriend about his infidelity and that was the end of our friendship. I am not proud of hurting his girlfriend and I take half the responsibility. I apparently brought that situation into my life for an excellent reason. After this traumatic incident, I was able to release emotions involving replacement and abandonment. I still miss Shamadu in my life and will definitely welcome him back.

Vanaja Ananda MA; MS

As you can see, messages arrive through people, animals or even inanimate objects like deities or padukas. Always treat all of nature with love and see the God within because each object has many lessons to teach when you are listening. I am finally opening up my heart and soul to the wonders of the universe.

Unity Among All

I collaborated with many non-profit organizations through my school. I was on the phone with the Director of Pass It Along, an institution that empowers teens to become leaders of the community. Diane needed a big fundraising activity and a vision came to me almost immediately. Initially, it involved preserving our environment, but skyrocketed into a huge community event called "The Rhythm of Peace Festival." In addition, what began as an idea to help Pass It Along, was graciously handed over to another organization called Hands on the World Global. Rachel, the founder of Hands on the World Global, brings in water wells to villages in Africa, Haiti and the United Kingdom. In these underprivileged areas, natives walk miles to get water. Moreover, the water is found at the bottom of holes in the ground. Rachel needed to bring water wells into the orphanages in Haiti after the earthquake, so the profits from the Rhythm of Peace Festival went toward this cause.

The premise of the Rhythm of Peace Festival was to create conscious awareness about the environment and help promote peace globally. The event was developed to serve several purposes. The main one was just described to you. In addition, an educational lesson for students and their families was essential for the function to be a success. Also, acceptance of cultural diversity and helping strangers in need was paramount. Furthermore, I wanted to build local community relationships. Now that I knew the receiving organization and the big picture, I needed a venue and lots of help! You ask and you receive. The event became a great festival and all components were fulfilled.

My friend Betsy told me about the Unitarian Church. I was not religious and was disillusioned by the bureaucracy of the religious community so it took a lot of convincing to get me to go with her. One Sunday, Raquel and I went to church with Betsy. From that day on, we didn't miss a single service; that lasted for over a year. Reverend Janice was terrific. She intertwined music, meditation and prayer into her morning services. She had a glowing smile and a personality to match. I went to many churches and synagogues throughout my years, searching for the right fit, but always disappointed. This church deviated from any religious institution I frequented in the past; there was no comparison. Reverend Janice embraced all religions and every parishioner felt welcome including Raquel and I.

Reverend Janice and I became friends. She helped me through a lot of emotional traumas during that year. She was my savior. I believe she is enlightened and if she isn't she soon will be. Janice brings so much joy to all.

A week after we were introduced, I asked Reverend Janice if the festival could be held at the Unity Church of Sussex County and she immediately loved the idea. The entire congregation jumped onboard. They organized the vendor booths. People from local businesses, public and private schools, non-profit and for profit organizations all gathered to help with the celebration. A grammy award nominee singer, Dalien from 13 Hands performed gratis. Aside from his musical career, Dalien is a professor, yoga instructor, sound therapist and trauma healing expert. In addition, he has self healed from several illnesses including Crohns and Colitis. You can peruse his website at www.13hands.com. Another singer performed for free. Kristin Hoffman produced and recorded "Song for the Ocean." I am convinced this song will soon be on the top 40 list. Kristin says "I wrote Song for the Ocean, so that, through singing, we can raise our awareness and get involved in creating positive environmental change." Listen to Kristin on you tube or her site www.songfortheocean.com. There were also local talent from the Biryukov Academy of Art and Music. Lena is the founder of this Sussex Country treasure for rising stars in the musical industry. Her students entertained the attendees with songs about peace and the environment. Lena organized an art contest as well that took place at the fair. Bright Beginnings teachers and students sold saplings a few months prior to the festival. Also, Maya, Kelly and Raquel sold the saplings in their schools; they were alumnus. The saplings were planted throughout the community and families learned how to care for their baby sapling and chart its growth. Under the guidance of Miss Turin, children preschool age to teens created a peace pole. On this pole, "Peace on Earth" was written in 12 languages including Braille. People throughout the community were invited to draw the symbols in their native language on the peace pole. Reverend Janice conducted a special peace ceremony at the labyrinth garden outside the church as the peace pole was unveiled. Native American drumming was played during this prayer ceremony. Moreover, we filled an entire school bus with medical supplies for the orphans through donations. Furthermore, planting and peace celebrations were organized in Haiti, Africa and United Kingdom on the same day. The day was fabulous! With intensity, any dream can be manifested.

Vanaja Ananda MA, MS

Rachel asked attendees of the fair to place their handprint dipped in paint on a butterfly banner. She was bringing it to Haiti to offer the orphans. The orphans outlined their handprints as well. The concept was beautiful. All human beings support each other around the world. Even though they have emptiness in their hands right now, there are people willing to fill them with treasures. Please visit Rachel on <u>www.howglobal.com</u>. Rachel is also an environmental children's author.

There was something even more spectacular that transpired on that day. Rachel flew two Reverends to New Jersey from Haiti. The spiritual leader I connected with was Pastor Augustine. He didn't speak English, but his soul was pure and his energy was at a high vibration. He operated one of the Haiti orphanages. Unfortunately, I never asked for his address. I pray in the near future, I find his orphanage and give healings to his students and give him a big hug!

Vanaja Ananda MA; MS

What's in a Name?

At Inner Awakening, Swamiji will give you a spiritual name. The commitment is to change it legally. At the time, I wasn't sure if I wanted a spiritual name. I pondered over the question for days. A part of me really wanted it, but I didn't know how people were going to react to it and I had a business to uphold. I wrote a letter to Swamiji telling him I would like a spiritual name as long as my family and people at the business embraced the name. He blessed my request and so I chose to have a new name. Swamiji meditated on me for three days to ascertain my spiritual path in life.

It was the last day of IA and I was shocked when I went up to receive my name. It was left on a table and looked like a diploma. It said Ma Ananda Vanaja, daughter of the forest. I was so disappointed. What kind of name is that? I thought he must be mistaken since my path should have been education or healing. I felt I made a big mistake. I agonized over it for a few weeks after I got home. I promised to change it, but I really didn't like it; I couldn't even pronounce it properly! I told a few people about it and nobody really liked it.

A few months later, Swamiji came to NY. When I went up to him, I told him I think he made a mistake with my name and I would prefer a new one. He totally ignored me like he had done on numerous occasions. I was annoyed. Shortly after that, I began to love my name. I learned how to pronounce it and thought it was exotic. When I started loving it and using it, other people began to like it also. Raquel, Kyle and Duane still don't love it, but now they tolerate it. Even Glenn, my brother, calls me Vanaja now.

I decided to have it legally changed with the divorce so a year later I was legally Vanaja Ananda and last year Swamiji said it meant Devi of the Forest. I interpreted that as being Snow White and therefore my prince was soon to arrive.

Why would anyone want to change his name? Our name is bleached with all our mental patterns whether they are negative or positive. Any incident recorded in our bio memory is associated with our name. When my parents screamed at me, they would use my full name, Pamela. Without even realizing the reason, throughout most of my life, I wanted people to call me Pam. Even Pam had emotional scars attached to it. In order to start a rebirth, it is important to have a new name because then you could add positive mental patterns or at least negative mental patterns that are at the surface so they are easy to remove. When I changed my name, many wonderful things occurred. In the past, I frequently went on nature walks and never looked at the surroundings; I just did it for the exercise and a good outing with Champ. However, once people started calling me Vanaja, I enjoyed the beauty of nature. Also, I felt like I had more courage and strength. I loved the little things in life such as a child eating ice cream, walking in the rain without an umbrella, organizing my room or watching the stars in the sky. I was content and joyful doing almost anything. Before, I always needed to be entertained by someone or a place. Now, I am happy anywhere, doing anything. I find the excitement in even mundane activities. Since I love to dance, I'll dance around the house or be innocent like a child. I want to try different adventures at least once since I only dreamed about it in my life as Pam. I want to explore and observe the creations on this planet. I want to talk to every being in their language so they know I care. I have to tell you I still don't like mosquitoes. I tolerate them, but haven't found joy when they attack my body.

Vanaja Ananda MA, MS

My Huge Failure

I wanted to become a doctor in psychology, but I majored in other subjects. Prerequisites were required and although I had two Masters Degrees, I didn't have enough psychology classes. I was admitted into the Doctoral Program at Teachers College at Columbia University and I loved my advisor. However, he didn't like any of my dissertation ideas. Even though I planned to expand upon his brilliant research, I also wanted to incorporate yoga, meditation and healing; he felt his expertise was elsewhere. I tried to persuade him, but he wouldn't budge. So, I didn't see any point going through the program just to get the degree although I knew the diploma from that esteemed school would be respected by society. I could share my passions easier with the world I kept telling myself, but my higher consciousness was disagreeing. The conflict brought me a lot of anxiety. Next, I finally was accepted into a Psychology program at the California Institute of Integral Studies. I was going to be a Doctor of East/West Psychology. I was all set to go there until I found out classes began in August and Raquel and Kyle's schools in New Jersey didn't start until after Labor Day. I wanted to be there for the first days of school because Raquel was a freshman and Kyle was in a new school as a junior. I decided to defer enrollment until the spring semester, but still was uneasy with the decision.

In September, my friend Sona gave me a gift; it was a psychic reading. I asked the psychic if I was going to school in New York or California. She said New York. I assumed it was Teacher's College and asked her. She told me it was not Teachers College, but it was a doctorate program. That's when I thought I found the perfect school for me. I decided to become a Chiropractor and this is the reason. For a long time I have wanted to see the disease inside the body and heal it. I know a lot of information about neuroscience, but very little about the remainder of the Central Nervous System—the spinal cord. I believed if I could locate the cause and disease in the anatomy, I would be able to heal children with neurological disorders. I rationalized, once these children's brains are working at full capacity, they will change the educational system on their own. I thought it was a brilliant plan until I drove up to the campus.

Jill and Neela took me on the 5 hour excursion to the school. She, of course, went an extra hour and we visited the Devi Temple. I was having uneasy feelings the entire trip; I thought it was the separation from my kids. When we got to the school, the wind was blowing fiercely, but I felt I had to unload everything so I felt like this dorm was home. Clothes and boxes were blowing everywhere. We were laughing hysterically as we collected garments and other necessities along the lawn. That should have been my first sign. The next morning, we went back to the temple. The energy was forceful even though the building was small. When we came back to the dorm, I couldn't speak. I had laryngitis for a week.

On my first day of class, I was emerged in a classroom of mainly 21 year olds, with the oldest at age 29 years old. I was 51 years old. I can easily get along with people at any age, but the thought of 3 years with the same student base was a little daunting. Even though I graduated only two years before from Teachers College, there were several people my age or older in the class. Every professor was programmed to say the same thing. They told us we were going to be stressed and don't worry because it goes quickly. They also told us to just focus on passing. There was a quiz in every class every single week, then midterms in every class, more quizzes and then finals. Basically, they were saying we had eight quizzes or tests every single week of the semester because we were mandated to take 23 credits. To make matters worse, all exams were multiple choice tests because their curriculum was developed to pass the boards. It went against everything I believed in and what I wanted to change in the educational system. I never heard of anything so bizarre and in, my opinion, inhumane. There was no other means of assessment.

I was living such a beautiful, peaceful life and all of a sudden I was in anxiety; this was only the first day. I liked some of the classes. I actually was fascinated with the lectures. However, one professor talked a mile a minute and it was about organic chemistry which I never had. I raised my hand and told the professor I was totally lost and so she asked a student in the class to help me. Nick was a Godsend. He spent time with me and explained every detail. Other people in the class also helped. I felt much better, but still I wasn't my typical self. I got up at 4:30AM to do my Bikram yoga in the room, then went to my first class that began at 8AM, studied through lunch, went to class till 6PM, studied through dinner and studied more until I went to sleep. Swamiji wasn't on because he was helping victims of a natural catastrophe in Chennai. I wondered how I was going to do this for 3 ½ years and keep my sanity. I was determined to stick it out at all costs. I wanted to give healings because the students were suffering as much as me, but nobody wanted one.

Vanaja Ananda MA; MS

My suitemate and her husband were beautiful people. We hung out one night for a couple of hours; I felt like I knew them forever. Ironically, they lived in New Jersey too. She was away on a family emergency when everything crashed in front of my eyes.

I woke up and followed my normal routine. It was sunny outside so I sang to class and was set for a wonderful day. I took my first quiz and failed it so that started my stress. Then, I sat through anatomy stupefied by the lecture on bones. Afterwards, we analyzed the bones and everybody in my group grasped the teachings except me. This is the piece de resistance. One of the girls in my group was taking it for the second time because she failed the first time. Immediately, I thought about my financial aid and loan; if you fail a class, the government doesn't pay. Moreover, I didn't know if my failings would affect my children's financial aid package. The minute class was over, I ran to my advisor and withdrew. Even though seven departments needed to sign my withdrawal form, including tutoring and counseling, not one department head offered to help; withdrawing was a simple process which was unnerving. In fact, the bookstore allowed me to return all my books and the skeleton for full price even though it was against their policy. I looked at this all as signs to get out of there. Raquel picked me up the next day. She drove 5 hours to get me and even though she was a fairly new driver, I knew she would be alright. I was so happy to see her. I was convinced I made the right decision and immediately wrote a letter to the Nithyananda group because I thought it was a valuable lesson about failure. Little did I know this was the beginning of a nightmare that lasted for weeks.

Here is the letter written January 10, 2012 . . .

Nithyanandam Everybody,

I am coming back to NJ. Since I haven't even been gone a week, I guess you haven't missed me that much lol. I withdrew from the Chiropractic program. It was extremely difficult and I wasn't having fun! Even unluckily didn't give me a sense of enjoyment. I thought I wanted to see the disease inside the body to help people self-heal. However, I realize I don't want to spend 3 ½ years of my life doing it. So, it must not be my passion after all which is a great lesson for me.

In addition, my biggest fear, other than the unknown, was fear of failure. I never allowed myself to fail at anything even if it meant giving up my happiness. In fact, I would excel. This time I actually failed because I chose not to continue with the program. Even though I failed, I am OK and I am willing to share this experience with anyone who wants to know. Now, I could go back to enjoying every moment of everyday . . . the essence of living! Once again, I am extremely grateful to Swamiji for teaching the importance of being aware of your feelings and delving into your emotions. Last night, he talked about fighting, flighting or freezing. There were points in the last week, I froze. At other times, I flew under the covers in flight into a deep sleep. Now, I am finally fighting for the bliss and joy we all deserve and is inherent in our nature.

I plan to get a job quickly even if it means working at the mall. If anybody knows of any jobs available or a good employment agency, please let me know.

See you all at satsung this weekend!

In love, peace, bliss, compassion and healing,

Vanaja

On January 11, 2012, I wrote the following, but only emailed it to a few people . . .

Nithyanandam Everybody,

The reason I am writing this email is twofold. First, I want to have all my thoughts down on paper. But, more important, I feel I have uncovered a deep negative mental pattern that I want to share with all of you—not only for myself, but I have the intuition it may be beneficial to some of you.

As you know I withdrew from Chiropractor College yesterday. I thought it was the best decision in the world; I convinced myself that healing was not my passion after all. I came up with every reason in the world to justify my behavior and I actually believed I was fighting for my happiness. I see now what Swamiji means when he says your minds are cunning and how one's ego takes over.

The other day, I felt Swamiji was talking directly to me—what a tremendous ego I still have! When he was talking about fight, flight and freeze, I figured it was a message to me. I knew he couldn't have meant I was freezing or running away, so I figured he meant I was fighting for my happiness. Isn't it interesting how our minds can literally justify anything to make us look good in the face of society?

Anyway, I realized I have been escaping from situations since early childhood. When I was 4 years old, I fooled around with my cousin who was 9 years older than me and actually enjoyed it. He sabotaged that enjoyment once he told me not to say a word to anyone including my grandmother who I adored. He added, she would no longer love me if she knew. I repressed the incident far into the deep recesses of my mind. I wasn't aware that the incident occurred until several years ago when I went through hypnosis. To make matters worse, my family moved to the suburbs away from my grandma who I worshipped at the same age. I associated the move with her lack of love for me.

The thought of my grandmother admonishing her love for me created several mental patterns in my subconscious. However, I am going to share the one that is relevant now. Sometime between the event and the move, I went into an escape mode because I was so conflicted. I believe the mental pattern I am referring to is this . . . "protect yourself because there is nobody there to protect you." As a result, whenever a tough situation occurred in my life, I would try to escape from it, instead of dealing with it head-on. In my mind, it was easier to admit defeat than experience the torture that ripped my heart apart.

I remember escaping from difficult situations all my life. I pretended I was sick so I didn't have to go to class and do a presentation. I would not even attempt to try something if I thought I would be a failure. As a result, I was never in any extra-curricular activities including sports, dance, or gymnastics during my childhood, adolescent and teen years. In addition, there were many times I wanted to close Bright Beginnings because I wanted to escape from controversy, financial matters and taking responsibility when times were difficult. Duane always pushed me through to persevere and I was extremely successful as a result. In my marriage, I told Duane I wanted a divorce almost every time we got into an argument. He would always try to keep the marriage together. Finally, he decided he wanted the divorce.

This time, I am escaping from a program because I am petrified of the outcome. All my grades have been exemplary in my graduate classes and I am used to excelling. Chiropractor school is extremely difficult. The professors talk a mile a minute and I wasn't able to grasp a lot of the concepts. I am not used to solely multiple choice quizzes. In fact, I haven't taken biology, chemistry, or physics since high school and I am 51 years old. I never took organic chemistry in my life and I am with a student body mainly consisting of 21 year olds. I felt totally lost even though there is a great support system. I physically went into panic mode and couldn't wait to get out of there. After class, I immediately went to the administration offices and asked to withdraw.

Now, that I am aware of this negative belief system, I am ready to take the leap and overcome it. I want to destroy, mutilate and expunge that mental pattern so it is permanently released from my inner being. Today, I humbly asked the institution to allow me to come back and they said yes! So, I am on my way once again to becoming a Chiropractor! Yippeee! I know it is going to be extremely difficult and I may cry or scream or panic again. But the difference this time is I am sticking it through until I graduate! I plan to be a fantastic holistic doctor!

You could all help in this process as well. Anytime you think of me, please send out positive vibrations. If your first thought is I miss her, she is too old for this, this is too hard for her, she will have no life, she should just get a job or anything else that goes against my passion to be a Chiropractor, please be aware and change it into a positive thought and send a blessing to me!

I do miss everybody especially my children, but they are off on their own adventures at college. I promise you every time one of you or all of you pops into my mind, I will send out a blessing to you! We are all one even though we feel like we are all separate individuals. The collective consciousness affects everyone. Let's all think positive thoughts for everybody and see the God in all. I love you all! I bless the NJ, NY, Philadelphia and DC centers/temples to be filled with tons of devotees! I am blessed to know all of you. Thanks so much for being a huge part of my life! We are all in this together so let's do it!!!!

In love, peace, compassion, bliss and healing,

Vanaja

Even though I was admitted back to school and they wanted me to come immediately, I asked if I could start on Tuesday, January 16th because Kyle and Raquel were returning back to school for their winter semester and Raquel needed a ride. I wanted to be there for her as she was there for me the day she drove 5 hours. Administration agreed. Since I was thrown off the portal, I asked her to notify the professors; I wanted to make sure they welcomed me back with open arms. She told me she was unable to contact the teachers. I agonized over this situation; should I go back or should I stay? I decided to check the portal again and miraculously my password allowed me to enter the portal. I emailed all my professors and explained exactly what happened. I am not posting that letter because it has all the names of the professors. It is not my intent to discredit the school at all. In my mind I decided if all the professors accepted me back, I would gladly be on the way back. On the other hand, if I received negative feedback I would stay at home. I received a positive reply; it was from only one professor. That was my answer.

Even though I had my answer, I still fought with myself over the decision. A week later an answer came to me once again through email. It was a video on you tube about failure. The film is a short 1 minute clip, but the message was compelling. It is worth watching over and over again. It is titled "Famous Failures." It put everything into perspective. If Lincoln, Grant, the Beatles and other great leaders of our country failed, then bring it on I told the cosmos. I responded to the person who sent me the video on January 17th, one week to the day later . . . .

> Last week I quit Chiropractor College after a week. I told myself I was fighting for my happiness. But, the truth is I was a failure. My biggest fear in life has always been the fear of failing. I would persevere to be the best at whatever I did at all costs. If I thought I was going to fail, I would escape. That is exactly what I did. A year ago I gave Swamiji a list of things I was interested in doing and he told me to get my Doctorate. He set everything up for me beautifully, but I wasn't aware of it until it was too late. He gave me a suitemate who was in her 5th trimester who wanted to help me. We had such a connection the moment we met as if we have known each other forever. There were students in the class willing to help me and we bonded as well. There were tutors available right at the college. However, I went into a state of panic and left. Even though they readmitted me now, I already missed 8 quizzes which I am not allowed to make up.

Vanaja Ananda MA; MS

When I was volunteering at the Ashram kitchen, I was able to go up to Swamiji twice. The first time I did pada puja and never thought to ask about college. In fact, I never asked about it the entire time because I wanted to be brave and figure it out for myself. The second time we were allowed to go up for darshan I asked him to help me release all mental patterns so I could be a perfect conduit for the divine to flow through.

We definitely have to be careful what we ask. I felt like I was in an abyss this weekend and I wasn't able to escape. I prayed, chanted, meditated, did yoga, live streamed with Braco 9 times and watched Swamiji's morning message. I released some major mental patterns this weekend. I am not sure if they are all gone, but I was aware of so much buried garbage from my past.

This video was a Godsend to me. I realized I failed even though society told me I didn't. Internally, I knew I did. Watching this film brought everything into perspective. It is OK to fail. I never tried so therefore I failed.

Swamiji and Braco put great jobs in front of me this year and I sabotaged them both before I was even hired. There is another job along the same realm. I pray this time I have released the fear so I could have the job I love and make the money I am worth. I am doing everything I possibly could do to release this mental pattern regarding self-esteem. Realizing that so many powerful individuals actually failed before they reached heights beyond their beliefs, confirmed to me anybody could achieve anything their inner being truly desires.

I realize what Swamiji means by we are all one. Swamiji, Broca, Jesus Christ, Buddha, Babaji, Sai Baba, Amma Karunamayi, Amma Gee and I could go on and on are all the same . . . just the cosmos in different form. We all have the cosmos inside of us as well. We just haven't figured out how to be released from the body and expand into the universe. However, our thoughts affect everyone and everything around us.

People told me I am too old, I shouldn't change careers, they miss me and wish I was back, it is too hard and so on and so forth. When all these thoughts go out to the universe, it sends a message since the universe doesn't know what is good or what is bad. With my doubts and everyone elses, it was easy to fail. I feel blessed that I failed, however, and was once again able to release deep seeded biomemory. So, I thank everybody.

It is a great lesson for everybody. Please be careful of your thoughts whether it is about the economy, a political candidate, your neighbor, global warming, etc. If we could all remember to have positive thoughts, we could manifest anything for ourselves, all of mankind and our beloved planet.

Thank you again for sending this video on failure. I sent it to all of my professors in hopes they will share it with the students. The entire student body is under terrible stress and duress. The faculty is extremely spiritual and wants the students to be successful. Maybe the students will realize at a young age (since most were 21) that it is OK to fail. In fact, great things could happen when we fail, it will give them some peace. That is my blessing for all the students, interns, faculty and administration at that school. I know fantastic Chiropractors are emerging from that school even though they are tortured through the process.

I thought everything was over and there would be peace. Boy was I wrong. I moved back to the house because I had nowhere to go. I asked Duane if I could stay there; since he didn't respond, I took that as a no. It was cold in the house, I was depressed, and there was hardly any food. I promised Duane I was going to be out of the house on January 1st and

I was reneging on our deal even though he adhered to every part of his commitment. At school, financial aid was paying for my room and board so I was set. I knew that, but I still chose to leave. Three friends offered their homes to me: Jacqueline, Michele and Heidi. I packed my bags and moved to Heidi's.

To back up a little bit, I want you to know I was extremely generous in my life, but found it difficult to receive. I emulated a friend and teacher, Turin. Turin would help people and animals in any situation. She had excellent ideas and enjoyed sharing them with anyone who was fortunate to be in her presence. The kindergarten children adored her and her colleagues felt the same. However, Turin would rarely allow people to do anything for her.

I know the divine wants us to give and accept graciously. So here was the test for me. I was apprehensive, but ready for my journey. I brought only two suitcases and a few books with me. It was President's Day and Raquel's dorm paraphernalia also had to fit in the small car. Heidi made me feel comfortable the minute I arrived. Many satsungs occurred in the basement of her home so I was familiar with the surroundings. She offered me my own bedroom. The first couple of days, I continued my daily routine of yoga, meditation and taking naps. On January 19, 2012, I began to write this book. Last year, I tried writing a book about the curriculum I developed, but I never made it past page 10. Apparently, the divine wanted me to write a self esteem book first. Every waking moment was spent and continues to be spent in the basement. I love it and call it my retreat. Nature girl has to wait a little while because this book was too important. The cosmos wanted it finished and I heard that message loud and clear. In between writing, I would do yoga, meditate and other techniques to clear the negative mental patterns.

The first three weeks at Heidi's were hellacious. It had nothing to do with Heidi; she was fabulous. In fact, she is a great cook and surprised me with terrific vegetarian meals and desserts often. Once I arrived at Heidi's, seven or more mental patterns reared their ugly heads simultaneously. Usually, one mental pattern or maybe two would appear at once. This time it was a smorgasbord of limiting beliefs and I thought I was going crazy. First, the incident with Shamadu and his girlfriend started it off with the replacement issue. Then, all these beliefs about school surfaced and my self-esteem plummeted. Fears about being worthy and being accepted by my peers were at the top of the list. I questioned my leadership abilities and whether I was still a good healer. Memories of being alone constantly gnawed at my brain. Since the students were young, I perceived they didn't want me to join them. Ironically, when I left, a few emailed and texted me and told me they missed me and to come back. We create our own illusions.

Initially, I was angry at friends from home because I blamed them for sabotaging my opportunity. Two of my friends told me I was too old to change careers and I should be concentrating on education because it was my expertise. I believe when people generate negative thoughts about a person, especially in unison, the cosmos fulfills their wish whether it benefits that person or not. At this time, I chose to blame them for my failure instead of looking within.

"Famous Failures" let me see the light. That video was the impetus to this book. Originally, this book's title was "Vanaja Writes a Book in a Week Thanks to Metatron." You will delight in that story shortly. I was in such a state of panic, I couldn't think clearly so Jacqui found the solution. She spent hours one night with me on skype and introduced me to EFT and several practitioners on you tube. We tapped that night and I felt much better. The next morning I was back to fear, but not panic. She told me to pick one of the EFT practitioners and tap all day if I needed. That is exactly what I did. I chose Brad Yates from the list of people because he was spiritual. Tapping was added to my repertoire of techniques and the results were uncanny.

Heidi and I started working on our mental patterns together. We were using the techniques I already knew and then ideas would pop into my head. She loved my ideas and never questioned them which I appreciate. We did puja to her parents photos and inanimate objects as well. I told her we had to remove pots and pans from the house because they harbored the negative energy from past relationships. She was ready to do this when all of a sudden I had a revelation. Since everything is divine, including the pots and pans, we need to show our love to them. We did puja to them for a week. Now, they are feeding us incredible delicacies.

After three weeks, I was back to my old self and I didn't require naps anymore. I was amazed. Sometimes, I felt I was dozing off during a meditation, but I always was awake and aware at the end. I may have been in samaddhi, no thought zone. Today, February 19th, I brought my purse down to the basement and Heidi's purse joined his friend. The purses were included in our puja ceremony. I believe it is the last thing we need to do before money is pouring on us from the heavens above.

Vanaja Ananda, MA, MS

Chop Your Way to Heaven

In November and December of 2011, I chose to volunteer at the Ashram for the Inner Awakening participants. The director of the volunteers asked me if I had a preference of locations and I chose the temple. The next day I went to the welcome center to retrieve my volunteer badge and was asked to help in the restaurant. I eagerly went. After all, if I was doing selfless service, I should go wherever I was needed. At the restaurant, we wrapped candies in cellophane. Since I love candy, this was a joy for me! It reminded me of the Lucy episode where the chocolates are coming so quickly down the conveyor belt. Lucy and Ethel had to eat some to keep up. All day long and half the next day, another person and I wrapped. When the task was complete, the head of the department didn't have anything for me to do. I went to the welcome center and asked to be transferred to the temple and she agreed.

The temple was a blessing. I was allowed to fold Shiva and Devi's clothes. I explained the significance of deities and the energy they transmit. The priest actually trusted me to care for the God's clothing. I was thrilled! I filled envelopes with vibhooti or sacred ash. I swept. I placed garlands on the deities. I got a hug from the banyan tree. Everything was magical. That night at the temple, I was there for aarti, a puja for the deities. After aarti, the priest conducted a ceremony to put the deities to sleep.

A lady who lived at the Ashram motioned for me to wait when the ceremony was over even though everybody left. She didn't speak English, but I understood what she was staying. We sat on the steps outside the temple; just her and me. We sat for about 15 minutes and I was getting ready to leave. To my amazement, Swamiji drove up in his car. I couldn't move; I was so surprised. Normally, you stand up when an Avatar comes into view. I just sat. We stared at each other for a few moments and then he offered his respects to the deities and drove away. The day was beyond perfect. I couldn't wait to go back to the temple the next day.

The morning started out well. I watched Swamiji's discourse, performed the kriyas and received my blessing from Swamiji; he blessed me with flexibility, grace and ease during yoga postures. Then, I immediately went to the temple. Shivananda, the priest, was doing another aarti. Wow! After the devotional ceremony, I began sealing the envelopes for the ash. A half hour later, I was asked to go to the welcome center. This time, they needed me in the kitchen. I was disappointed, but felt blessed to volunteer at the temple for a day and a half. I willingly went to the kitchen. Being in the kitchen was funny because cooking is not my passion. Here I was cutting and chopping 20 pounds of each vegetable and fruit. It definitely was a different experience for me, but I did the chore with love and joy.

All kitchen volunteers were asked to come to a meeting at 4PM. During the meeting they told us we needed to be at the kitchen at 5:30AM which meant we missed yoga and morning discourse. I told myself I could deal with this. The next morning, I arose at 4:30AM and arrived at the kitchen by 5:30AM. I began chopping, cutting, peeling and all the wonderful things they do in the kitchen. However, I was angry and resentful. I wanted to be at yoga; after all, Swamiji just blessed me to achieve yoga perfection. I missed morning discourse. I was miserable. As the day progressed, I was even more miserable. I thought about the temple and how much I loved it. I felt it was unfair that the director removed me from the temple and the banyan tree. By 2PM, I couldn't stand it and I went to the welcome center to tell her, I would prefer to be a guest instead of a volunteer. I told myself I was God and powerful even though I didn't believe it totally at the time. I felt I was going to poison the participants with my negative thoughts and anger. As a guest, I planned to help at the temple whenever I was allowed. It was all planned in my mind as I walked to the welcome center.

When I arrived, the Director was nowhere to be found. Her assistants saw my blotched face and knew I had been crying. They asked me to wait on the couch. I waited about an hour and a half and she was still not there. I decided to wait another 15 minutes and then go back to the kitchen because they had no idea where I was and they needed me that day. My friend walked in and I told her my course of action. She was walking out the door when the Director was coming in. The Director asked her to ask me how I was and I replied "not well." The next thing I knew the Director disappeared again. I couldn't believe it.

I told the assistant manager that this was my last day in the kitchen because I wasn't having fun. She said alright, but please be sure the head of the department knew. I went back to work happily knowing I would be at yoga, morning discourse and the temple the next day. Life was good again. However, the Kitchen Manager didn't appear that night so I was forced to tell him in the morning.

The next morning, I went to yoga and morning discourse then headed to the kitchen to speak to the Manager. The minute I walked in, the

Managers weren't there, but other volunteers came over to me. I began cutting and chopping because there was a lot of work and I wasn't going to sit while my friends were diligently working. I told the kitchen crew I would no longer be volunteering because I was blessed for yoga and didn't want to miss the morning discourse. At home, I drove two hours each way once per week to attend satsung; I simply couldn't give it up.

The next thing I knew, I had permission to do yoga and attend morning discourse.

From the moment I heard they cared about me so much to grant my wish, I put my heart and soul into my work. I worked till wee hours of the morning, I had so much fun! We would laugh constantly. The kitchen volunteers served the participants during darshan which was another blessing. Each day there were auspicious happenings and blessings.

I was so excited about the last day. The volunteers were serving 21 dishes from various states in India. The night before we were carrying in heavy bricks and pushing a car; life at the Ashram is so much fun, spontaneous and unpredictable. Anyway, we were setting the room up the entire morning for the luncheon at noon. We finished at 11:40AM and had to rush back to the dorm to put on our saris. My friend was going to pin mine; it was all arranged the day before. She had to get dressed as well so she asked another friend to do it and she agreed. We all went to the festivities and began serving the food on huge palm leaves on the floor. Apparently, my sari was revealing and I was told to go back and change. I ran back and put on a pants and shirt outfit and came back. Swamiji arrived 2 minutes later.

We had a great time and it was extremely busy so I had no time to think. When things calmed down, we were able to eat. I decided to eat by myself outside because all of a sudden I was angry. I was angry at my friend for not following through on her promise. I sat with the group at the end for dessert and then we were told we had a break and we could watch Swamiji's Pratyksha Pada Puja at 5PM because he was doing 3 pada puja's that day since it was the last day for everyone. I felt relieved and went to my favorite place.

As I was practically running to the temple, tears were rolling down my face. I was so angry, but now it was focused on me. I went to each deity and asked them to let me die and use my body for service to mankind because I felt time was of the essence and I didn't know how to have a totally pure body for the cosmos energy to flow through. Then, I went to my beloved banyan tree, hugged it for a long time and told it the same thing. I went to sit in my favorite crevice under the banyan tree and closed my eyes; I was distraught. Then, I became furious at Swamiji. All the anger I had inside of me toward him spewed out.

This is what happened. After I left the banyan tree I went to watch puja. It was a closed ceremony so we weren't allowed to watch. I went to the kitchen and began my normal routine. A mosquito was buzzing around me. Usually, I try to deal with the annoying varmints. However, I was enraged and inwardly told the mosquito if he landed on me, I would kill him. I felt I was talking to Swamiji; that is how furious I was. When the mosquito landed on me, I smashed him to smitherines! I felt so relieved after that. The rest of the night went beautifully and I woke up the next day in a fabulous mood! You may want to try hitting a pillow if you become this angry. Let's leave nature alone even if they are incredibly perturbing.

In March 2011, there was a huge scandal; Swamiji was accused of raping a girl and they apparently had video coverage to prove it. The media sensationalized the event and Swamiji was thrown into prison. He was tortured in prison. The guards would shine lights in his eyes, have him sleep on the floor and offer him no means to urinate or defecate. It never fazed or bothered him. The police couldn't break him down. They tried to find people to testify against him and none appeared. Swamiji started healing prison guards and prisoners and they didn't want him to leave. His devoted disciple, Swami Bhaktananda stayed in the prison with him.

Disciples and close devotees were leaving in droves. They believed the fabricated evidence. Swamiji was being crucified, similar to Jesus Christ. There are so many similarities between these two Gods. When I heard the story, I could care less. I knew the miracles and transformation that occurred within me and it was due to Swamiji. I knew it wasn't true and were shocked people succumbed to the gossip. The scandal was concocted to deface Swamiji because he was becoming popular around the world. After a month, the Indian government had to release him for lack of evidence. Even if a guru kisses a woman, the Indian government considers it illegal. I thought that is ludicrous; isn't that the luxury of being in a human body. I was convinced he was going to be released and come back even stronger than before. There were about 150 other people that stayed by him as well. He gave us all the best gift in the world; a **free** 48 day program titled "Living Enlightenment Program." Now, one year later, thousands tune into watch him every day for **free.**

Vanaja Ananda, MA, MS

At the Living Enlightenment Program (LEP), Swamiji told me I was going to be an enlightened Master. I thought of it as a status symbol at the time, not appreciating what it really was. I envisioned myself ruling the planet and people bowing down to me. I expected to be turned into a guru at the end of LEP and was crushed when it didn't happen. In fact, he became indignant when I asked him at darshan and yelled at me to take responsibility. I thought he lied to me, but my love for him never waned. How could God lie? That was in October 2010. His reprimand awakened something so strong within me; However, before I took responsibility. I followed Swamiji's advice, I wrote a letter to Swami Bhaktananda because I was angry and wanted answers. His response was to watch Peaceful Warrior so I rented the movie immediately.

Here is my critique of Peaceful Warrior. I sent it via email to Swami Bhaktananda on November 14, 2010.

Nithyanandam Sri Bhakta,

I watched Peaceful Warrior with Lena and Alice last night and today with Raquel. I am hoping to watch it with Kyle before I have to return it, but so far he doesn't want to watch it. It was amazing! So, I am trying to grasp many of the messages.

1. Life is a paradox—everything is a mystery—for me, I always want answers just like Dan did at the beginning of the movie, but I am trying to enjoy the now, present moment—today at yoga I was really in the moment most of the time and my postures are getting much better.

2. Laugh at yourself—I got a flat tire and Duane and Kyle told me to call AAA which I did, but Duane didn't sign me up (just Kyle and Duane) and he is insisting he did but refused to call. So, I called Kyle's friend and he helped. I thought it was hysterical. He tried to show me how to change it and maybe next time I could if I build arm strength. Raquel, Champ and I went on our nature hike after that and laughed about men—too funny.

3. Change occurs constantly—life is so full of spontaneity and you have to go with the flow. We had 2 of Kyle's friends for dinner tonight and you never know who is stopping by. I used to become distraught if I thought there wasn't enough food. But I figured if we run out, I'll make them a grilled cheese or something.

4. Enjoy the journey and not the destination—this was the most profound for me because you are so right all I wanted was to become an enlightened Master because I truly believed it was to bring love, compassion, bliss and healing to everyone and everything around me. While I want all those things, I also want to be done with the worry, fear, lust, greed, attention-need, jealousy, ego and discontentment I just want to live a care-free, blissful life. But, I also think part of me subconsciously wanted the identity of a Master. I never wanted to live enlightenment because I wanted to be chosen to be 1 of the enlightened beings. Now, I prefer having Swamiji in human form in my life and I am thrilled to be living enlightenment. I feel no pressure and am blissful. I could definitely bring people to Swamiji now and that is all that matters.

The destination is no longer important. And you know what is strange? I know if I was able to release Swamiji, I would meet the man of my dreams. But, believe it or not and this is even hard for me to fathom, Swamiji means more to me than anybody or anything in this world. At first, I thought it was a cunning game my mind was playing, but I am convinced this is true. Sometimes I wish I could release Swamiji, but I know I can't. I have decided to enjoy my journey and let the divine guide me.

So, maybe I will remain insignificant like the elephant story, but is that really so bad. I am no more special than anybody else. I was just lucky enough to be blessed with Swamiji and the divine and I intend to create that blessing for as many souls as I can. Another important lesson

I learned from the movie is to love the ones who are dishonorable because those are the ones who need it the most.

Thanks for always teaching me amazing lessons. Whatever I did to be blessed by you, I really don't know. But, I am truly grateful for you, Swamiji, all Masters inside and outside of their body, all existential energy and all the wonderful relationships in my life. It is like that song from The Sound of Music—somewhere in my youth or childhood I must have done something right.

Love always,

Vanaja

After that movie, I delved into the cause of every emotion and asked myself why I brought that circumstance into my life? What purpose does it serve and where did this pattern start? I meditated a lot and asked existential energy for answers. My higher consciousness, the God inside of me, revealed as much as I could handle. Finally, I understood enlightenment is not a name and fame game. Enlightenment is living in joy and bliss 24/7. Unconditional love is the key ingredient to enlightenment and understanding the power of love. I wanted to give something back to Swamiji for all he has done for me and that is why I volunteered at the end of 2011 at the Ashram.

I called volunteering in the kitchen "Chop Your Way to Heaven." I thought it should be another 21 day program since I felt like it was another Inner Awakening. Swamiji works on you constantly. Every day I would cry during kriya and get his blessing called seva darshan; he walks down an aisle and touches each person's head. Once you watch his morning discourse on en-tv, you will understand what I mean (www.nithyananda. org/en-tv and if you want to view his site go to www.nithyananda.org). After seva darshan, I was happy the rest of the day! If they ever turn "Chop Your Way to Heaven" into a 21 day volunteer program, the prerequisite should be that everybody has to send love and bliss to every fruit, vegetable or surprise food they are chopping, cutting, peeling or stringing! Yes, I now know that string beans actually have strings you need to pull off. It was an

Vanaja Ananda MA; MS

honor and a privilege to be working in the kitchen! Seva, or volunteering, is a quick way to reach higher consciousness, especially in the kitchen. In the kitchen, your mind automatically goes into a trance; chopping, cutting, and peeling don't require thinking. But, be careful because I did get a lot of cuts . . . definitely worth it!

PART 7

We Are Protected By The Cosmos

Archangels Are All Around Me

I was trying to remember the first time I began including Archangels in my prayers, but I don't really remember. I believe it was sometime in 2011 if that helps. Whenever an archangel was mentioned to me whether in a song, meditation, person, or in a book, I researched what they represented and thanked them for protecting me. Every single night, I thank Archangel Michael, Raphael, Gabriel, Uriel, Metatron, Sandolphon, Jophiel, Haniel and Raziel. I also thank the angels that appeared for me the last time I did Jacqueline's Tarot cards in December 2011. Now, I include fairies too!

My prayer goes like this . . .

I am grateful for all the blessings and abundance in my life. Thank you Swamiji, Lakshmi, Shiva, Devi, Ganesh, Kali, Durga, Saraswati, Pavarti, Patanjali, Krishna, Brahma, Vishnu, Shankara, Usui, banyan tree, Bhakta, Bikram, Buddha, Jesus Christ, Vanaja, Champ, Shamadu, Dheera, Reverend Janice, Pastor Augustine, Amma Karunamayi, Ammaji, Mother Meera, Braco, Sai Baba, Osho, Babaji, all the deities, Archangel Michael, Archangel Raphael, Archangel Gabriel, Archangel Uriel, Archangel Metatron,

Archangel Sandolphon, Archangel Jophiel, Archangel Haniel, Archangel Raziel, Angel Daniel, Angel Crystal, Angel Chantall, Angel Maya, Angel Isabella, Angel Aurora, all the fairies and Fairy Kayla, Lady Isis, the Arcturian healing team, Dr. Lorphan, Menokshee, King Solomon, Aschwini and the Aschwini twins, the sun and moon, all the planets, all celestial and terrestrial beings, dragons, all Ascended Masters inside and outside of their body, and all of existential energy for all the blessings and abundance in my life. Let me bring peace, love, grace, compassion, bliss and healing to the world. Amen. Also, if people are ill and need immediate prayers, they are included.

If you are interested in learning about each one of these divine beings with incredible powers, you can search google or read about them in books. I even started to include dragons because this is the year of the dragon. Dragons are real in other dimensions, but I was afraid of these fire breathing creatures. Now, they are included in my prayers. The dragon inside of us is the powerful, creative and passionate being waiting to be set free. Love the dragon inside of you because he loves you!

In this chapter, I will tell you about the Archangels I revere. Michael is my protector. He has given me courage and strength. In the morning, I ask him to place a blue ball on my throat chakra and balance all my chakras from head to toe. Raphael is the doctor and healer. I ask him to help me self heal and learn the skills to heal others. Gabriel is God's messenger. I ask him to let me be open to receiving all messages from the divine. Uriel is the angel of intelligence. I ask him to fill me with wisdom and ingenuity. Jophiel is the angel of beauty. I ask him to show me the beauty inside me and recognize the beauty of all that surrounds me. I was told Haniel is my special Archangel. He shows me how to be one with nature and be graceful in all my dealings. In addition, I ask him for eloquence when speaking in public. Raziel knows the secrets of the universe and I ask him to reveal those secrets to me. Metatron and Sandolphon were humans before they became Archangels. I am now going to share a reading with Metatron that took place two days before I left for college, December 30th, 2011. It was mind blowing!

Metatron's Reading

Jill had a channeled reading with Metatron and she shared its contents with me because it was recorded. All I could say is it blew me away; I am speechless for once in my life. Even though I had very little money left, I chose to spend part of it on this reading which cost $160 and worth every penny.

When I came back from India, I had about $200, and then I received my last child support check from Duane totaling $1500. I spent $1000 on Raquel and Kyle for Christmas; I told friends I wasn't able to buy anything this year for Christmas; I was just spending on my children. This left me $700. After the reading, I had $500 left. I knew my school and the kid's college were paid in loans and we each received $1,000 back. I planned to have work/study. I knew it would be tough financially, but since room and board were paid for, I was going to send whatever money I earned to the kids for clothes and miscellaneous items. All debts were paid because I sold my car to pay any bills I owed as well as the airplane ticket to India. I was sure the divine wanted me to have this reading.

Metatron is the Archangel who keeps the Akashic records, also called "The Book of Life." Everything is documented in this book about your past life, present and future; the book includes many past lives. If you ask questions, he will answer. Metatron asks permission to enter your DNA because this reading can only be done once in a lifetime. Once given permission, he asks for permission to enter your heart chakra. I will tell you key points in this reading. I was at a 5 point star with wings open and close to 7 points. I didn't even know what this meant, but I looked it up after. Humans are 5 stars with two arms, two legs and a head. I was moving into fairyland because the wings add two more points. This may sound strange and you are ready to call the paddy wagon, but it is true! I am 100% convinced. He said I need to help bring 20% of the population to higher consciousness. I believe right now it is at 17 or 18%; only 2% more. He confirmed what Swamiji said about being a Master. He also said I was going to write a book about self-esteem in a week, mainly for women and children. In addition, he said I was going to devise a mantra that people could use to improve their self-esteem. Furthermore, he explained every dimension and emphasized the entire planet was moving into the 4th dimension. I was told I was an Atlantean. The Atlanteans lived in a peaceful community. He also suggested I meditate on the dragon.

He told me to say a mantra along with the Pattern on the Trestleboard. This sounded esoteric to me, but fascinating at the same time. He mentioned King Solomon three times in the reading, so I asked him if I was related to King Solomon. Nothing is a coincidence he told me. I was shocked and told him throughout my life I would joke with friends and tell them I was a princess. I didn't ask him anything further about King Solomon.

The Pattern on the Trestleboard is from the Hebrew tradition. How ironic, right? Since that reading, I have followed his instructions. I tried to find out where the mantra came from. I couldn't find it anywhere, but I recite it 108 times every single day. Robone Oh Shalom and Robone Ohlan Shalom. It is powerful and reminds me once again that we all one! The Pattern on the Trestleboard is below.

The PATTERN *on the* TRESTLEBOARD
This Is Truth About The Self

0. All the Power that ever was or will be is here now.

1. I am a center of expression for the Primal Will-to-Good which eternally creates and sustains the Universe.

2. Through me its unfailing Wisdom takes form in thought and word.

3. Filled with Understanding of its perfect law, I am guided, moment by moment, along the path of liberation.

4. From the exhaustless riches of its Limitless Substance, I draw all things needful, both spiritual and material.

5. I recognize the manifestation of the Undeviating Justice in all the circumstances of my life.

6. In all things, great and small, I see the Beauty of the Divine Expression.

7. Living from that Will, supported by its unfailing Wisdom and Understanding, mine is the Victorious Life.

8.	I look forward with confidence to the perfect realization of the Eternal Splendor of the Limitless Light.
9.	In thought and word and deed, I rest my life, from day to day, upon the sure Foundation of Eternal Being.
10.	The Kingdom of Spirit is embodied in my flesh.

I asked silly things too about my twin flame; my bubble burst when he told me there was no such thing as a twin flame. He said I had one marriage contract; that was fulfilled and it is over. He said I have fifteen unconditional love relationships coming into my life and one man is coming very quickly. It will be my choice who I pick. I asked if I was supposed to go to Chiropractic College and the answer was yes. I asked if I was going to do well in school. He told me I would have a difficult period until March and then be successful. I said then I might as well start in April. He said not to wait because I would be in depression if I postponed. You know I didn't listen to that suggestion and he was absolutely right.

Those are the main components I remember. I thought I would have a tape to refer back to, but my recording had echoes so it was impossible to decipher. Who could figure? I believe he only wanted my subconscious to remember other details. Needless to say, it was the best reading I ever had and I had 5 within 8 months. I didn't even understand readings and Tarot cards; I thought it was hocus pocus. I was wrong, wrong and wrong some more! You can schedule an appointment for a Metatron reading at www.triolite.biz.

I embrace all religions, Gods and entities and I decided to come up with a new religion. I have added onto the HinJew, HinArcJewZen. This is what it stands for . . . Hin is for the Vedic tradition which I spoke about in detail. Arc is for the Archangels in the heaven that guide us to our true self. Jew is for the Pattern on the Trestleboard which is the truth about self. Zen is from the Buddha who believes in peace, happiness and tranquility. Om is the original vibration that first arose at the time of creation so it means one with the universe. Namaha is at the end of many mantras. When I looked up the definition it said "I submit and submerge myself or I become one with this. Maybe this is the mantra Metatron was referring to as a way to improve self esteem. **Om Hin Arc Jew Zen Namaha.** To simplify, we embrace the beliefs of all. We don't judge or criticize. We all support each other and as a result become one with the universe. If you wish, you could try this mantra. Say it at least 11 times for 21 days and let me know the results. We will experiment together!

There are two mantras I say every day as well: the Ganesh Mantra to remove obstacles and the Gayatri Mantra. Gayatri Mantra is explained below. I copied it from www.eagle.com. However, both mantras are on you tube.

Aum Bhur Bhuvah Swah, Tat Savitur Varenyam
Bhargo Devasya Dhimahi, Dhiyo Yo Nah Prachodayat
ॐ भूर् भुव: स् व: तत् सवितुर् वरेण् यं । भर् गो देवस् य धीमहि,
धीयो यो न: प् रचोदयात् ॥

A basic translation can be given as . . .

Oh God, the Protector, the basis of all life, Who is self-existent, Who is free from all pains and Whose contact frees the soul from all troubles, Who pervades the Universe and sustains all, the Creator and Energizer of the whole Universe, the Giver of happiness, Who is worthy of acceptance, the most excellent, Who is Pure and the Purifier of all, let us embrace that very God, so that He may direct our mental faculties in the right direction.

The Ganesh Mantra is **Om Gam Ganapathayi Namaha.** I say both of these 108 times. It is easy singing with the you tube clip.

Vanaja Ananda MA, MS

What's In a Number?

I had a numerology reading in September 2011. Your life path is calculated using your entire birth date. It is the sum of all the numbers including month, day and year and helps explain the nature of your existence. It contains your life mission. I was born November 29, 1960. I am an 11. Eleven plus eleven plus sixteen equals thirty eight or 11+2+9+1+9+6 = 38 and 3+8 = 11. Eleven, twenty-two and thirty-three are all Master numbers. The mission of someone with an eleven life path is to help humanity. However, if they are not grounded, it won't happen. People with a 22 life path have the same passion and they make it a reality. A person with a 33 life path is a Master Teacher.

Before you are born, you choose your parents. During the birth process, you go into a coma and forget your mission and samskaras, karma you bring with you into this life from past lives. You choose your name and birth date to help you remember your purpose for this lifetime. Every number has a special meaning. If you are interested in a name and number analysis, see Alison at www.visiblebynumbers.com. I was introduced to numerology at a Tarot reading with Vicky; it was the first reading by a psychic. After Vicky, I had four other readings, including Metatron and Alison. They were all conducted within an eight month period. Every single reading said I was a Master. It is a little difficult to digest that information after your visions of glory have disappeared. I am not saying this for notoriety. It is important you know this is the truth because major changes are occurring on our planet this year which affects our entire planet. On one hand, it is extremely positive and a miracle. On the other hand, many people may be suffering if they don't understand what is happening and techniques to overcome depression.

In a recent webinar on January 21, 2012, Swamiji explained what will be occurring in 2012 and for the next three years. You can watch this webinar on his site or you tube. Many experts have agreed with him. He told viewers around the world that the gravity of the earth is decreasing and therefore people will be experiencing fewer thoughts. As a result, many negative mental patterns will be released which is a blessing. People who have been meditating, doing yoga and finding inner peace will enjoy this experience and be in a state of bliss. However, the majority of the population who depend on the inner chatter in their mind to guide them will not know what to do. This feeling of helplessness will put them into a state of depression and possibly suicide.

Currently, our society depends on entertainment to keep us happy and we are going to be forced to live happily within ourselves without external stimuli to keep us occupied. All the techniques, websites, and methods in this book will help you get to a higher state of consciousness so the transition is stress-free. If you have a life path that is an 11, 22 or 33, the time has come for you to help humanity. The planet needs a lot of help. Use whatever methodologies you need including IA because it is the fastest way to transform. Next, if anybody in your family has these numbers, show them this book.

If you don't have those Master numbers, you still have the propensity to be whatever you want including a Master. You may realize the planet needs you and you want to help mankind on a mass level. But, it is important that you know if you simply just live enlightenment, you will be helping 100's of people just by your presence. The key is to heal yourself first and then you will be helping the planet as a result. When you operate at a higher consciousness, people are attracted to your energy. It is that easy.

Vanaja Ananda, MA, MS

Becoming One with the Divine

I have wanted to learn about tantra for over a year and the opportunity presented itself this summer. It was individual tantra so it was the perfect introduction for me. I read Osho's book about tantra and it was not based on human sexual lust; it was about becoming one with the divine. The class was great and I met wonderful people. I still keep in touch with some of them. In two weeks they were having a couple's retreat which I already knew about for three months. I was hoping I would meet someone so I could learn the art of tantra. The emphasis was placed on breathing techniques and the sexual act was not performed. Massage, sensuous dancing and couple yoga were the main topics. All workshops were conducted in clothing. It sounded perfect for me.

At the weekend retreat I met a man who was very nice, but I wasn't attracted to him physically. After the single retreat, he called and asked if I wanted to be his partner at the couple retreat. He said there would be no strings attached and I knew he was sincere. We shared breaths and hugged a lot. We danced and sang songs around the fire. He was a complete gentleman.

During the single retreat, many people went skinny dipping, but I had too many inhibitions about my body. Even though I was wearing a bikini, I chose not to go swimming at all. At the couple's retreat, they asked us to undress to go in the sauna and go swimming. They said it wasn't mandatory, but it was part of the tantra experience. All of a sudden, all inhibitions were thrown out the window and I was one of the first ones in the sauna. I enjoyed the sauna completely nude. They separated the groups. Women were in the sauna and men were in the pool.

It was time to go to the pool and once again I was the second one walking nude out to the pool. I was so proud of myself and I felt free. We went in the water and the women were asked to support the gentlemen while they lie on their backs and just relax; it was more of a trust exercise so that we don't drown our partner. There was only time for the men to enjoy this. At the end of the session, my partner and I chose to stay in the water. He was a very giving, spiritual person and he asked me if I wanted to float also. I willingly said yes. He put his arms under me to support me and I floated along the top of the water's surface with my eyes closed and the sun shining on my breasts and abdomen. The warmth from the sun sent tingles up and down my spine. I felt thoughtless for the very first time.

I felt like I was part of the water. It was incredible. I stayed like that for about 15 minutes, soaking up the rays. Then we got out and hugged in the nude. I realized I loved him as a soul to soul oneness. There was no sex or touching, just hugging. From that day, my inhibitions have disappeared. I was born nude and nudity is awesome. Society is overly concerned about body proportions, including me. I owe that wonderful man so much. Even though we never had sex, I felt a strong connection that brought me closer to the divine. He honored his word and helped me get through a major negative mental pattern.

Now, I am going to reveal something that I thought would be a buried secret forever. I never wanted anyone to know except Duane and a few close friends, but now I am sharing it with the world because I believe it will help people who have poor body images.

Here it goes. I was called Olive Oil as a teen and I despised that name. As a result, I began to hate my body. I would look in the mirror and be dissatisfied about all my proportions. I would continue to eat feeling there was no hope anyway. I was never obese; I had love handles and a belly. I continued this way until the early 30's, looking in the mirror and weighing myself daily and becoming angry at myself. If I only knew I needed to reprogram "I please everyone." I could have saved myself a lot of heartache. Who knew? Anyway, I started taking diet pills and pounds came off quickly; it was unbelievable to me. I continued taking these pills for over a year, ignoring the symptoms that appeared; I pretended they didn't exist. One day, the head tic I had for almost my entire life became exacerbated to the point where it was becoming debilitating. Moreover, my voice was beginning to slur as if I was drunk. And the final straw was I tried to pick up a cup and my fingers wouldn't wrap around it. I was convinced I had a major neurological disorder. However, I was addicted to these diet pills and wasn't able to stop. So, I decided to get a tummy tuck. Duane suggested I get larger breasts at the same time so I thought if he is giving me what I want; the least I could do is make him happy too.

I was actually excited about the operation, but I was so addicted to my thin frame I took the diet pill until the day before the operation. I didn't even want the doctor to see fat on my body. I know it is absurd. Because I took the diet pill, I now have a scar from my belly button down. During the operation there was not enough fat, so the doctor had to make abnormal incisions and take the fat from other areas.

Vanaja Ananda MA; MS

Even though I had perfect breasts, I never felt deserving of these coconuts and I hid them under clothes. I would get full coverage bras and bikini tops as well. My stomach was never flat like I wanted and I still had the bulge so I was never happy with the operation. This confirmed I wasn't even good enough to have the body I wanted. I actually had a good body, but I never felt it was good enough because my subconscious was telling me I didn't look beautiful. It is the self fulfilling prophecy. I have finally resolved that issue and love my body.

This theory was tested a few weeks ago. I needed to get my hair done; about 6 weeks had passed since the last cut and color. I didn't want to drive back to Sparta from the shore since gas is a fortune again. At this time, I had $300 left. I decided to try my friend's hairdresser. While she was cutting and coloring I was concerned because her energy vibration was off that day and I could feel it. I was praying this wasn't a lesson about vanity and I would need to cut my hair really short. The haircut and color turned out alright, but I didn't love it. It was still long so I was pleased. However, I wanted to know why I was so concerned so I delved into the situation and that's when all my "garbage" emotions about body image started to surface. I was aware, but I wasn't planning to write it in this manuscript.

I believe the divine had other ideas!

A few people said they liked my hair, but for some reason I wasn't thrilled. I was hoping for something unique. About two weeks ago, my friend and I were discussing my hair and a person came up and asked what we were talking about. I told her so she chimed in eagerly and offered her opinion. She told me I looked better with lighter hair because darker hair showed all my wrinkles. I had to laugh at that one because for the past year, almost everyone who knows me says I look 10 years younger. Also, it was close to my original birth color. In the past, I would perseverate and believe her words, but this time it was humorous. However, her words prompted me to reveal the truth about my body.

Like a tidal wave, it hit me; I was keeping the truth from Raquel who always thought I had a perfect body. She would compare her body to mine and I never had the courage to tell her the truth because she idolized me. The truth would have disengaged her from needless suffering. But, my pride and vanity was more important than my own daughter's anguish. I plan to tell her about this chapter over the weekend when I see her. I believe the truth prevails and will come out eventually. I have forgiven myself and I know she will forgive me as well.

The Patterns Keep Emerging

The first weekend I was home from college, I wouldn't move out of my bedroom. I didn't even go to satsung and I only missed weekly satsung twice since IA in 2009. The first time it conflicted with a Walk for Cancer and the second time I was lazy because it was raining. This was the third time I was missing satsung and I was too depressed to care.

I think I would have stayed in bed forever if I didn't move in with Heidi. The morning I was starting this book, I had a conversation with Heidi. I told her I was focusing on writing and may need to take naps during the day; I wanted to be sure she accepted this routine. Also, I explained I had $300 so I wasn't able to pay her right now, but as soon as I earned money I would reimburse her. Heidi was magnificent! She agreed wholeheartedly. She is an angel on earth and now I know the reason I was guided to live with her.

The webinar on 2012 was that weekend. I am not sure I would have gone because I was going through up and down stages; one day happy and the next day exhausted. Heidi drove and I went thank goodness. The webinar was fantastic as expected. Something even more auspicious happened that day. After the webinar, Hari Kaantaa, the New Jersey coordinator, was calling people over for healings. In the past, she never gave any healings. I usually was the one who offered the healings because I loved feeling the energy and helping people heal themselves.

This was too much for my ego! In the past, Hari Kaantaa and I would butt heads because we both loved Swamiji so we would try to outdo each other. Not always, but sometimes. I felt she needed to acquire better leadership skills and she felt I was insignificant even though she, Paul and I were the main volunteers for the first year or so. Now, we have many great volunteers.

Everybody was getting a healing from Hari Kaantaa and I was perturbed. I decided to go to Paul for a healing because I also didn't feel well from all the anxiety. Paul's healing was good. After all, it was Swamiji's energy. However, I kept watching Hari Kaantaa give healings and I was puzzled by the reactions of my friends. They never said a word to me because everyone was astonished, but they walked away with a huge grin on their face. I waited until the end and finally asked for my healing. This was huge for me!

I closed my eyes while she placed her hand on my head and my ego said it was like any other of Swamiji's healings. I opened my eyes to say thank you and I saw the most amazing image. Hari Kaantaa's hand was in front of me in a stop position and when I looked at her face, it was Swamiji's eyes and mouth. I was flabbergasted and it took my mind a few minutes to register what was happening. Hari Kaantaa was a perfect vehicle for Swamiji's energy to come through because her love for him was pure, unconditional love. At satsungs now, I leave the healing to Hari Kaantaa. In fact, I look forward to my turn with Swamiji and Hari Kaantaa. We have become good friends at last.

Yesterday, February 20th, was Shivaratri Day and it also has been 33 days from the genesis of this book; we know 33 is the Master Teaching number so I believe it has significance. Shivaratri is the day Shiva created, sustained and destroyed the earth. Until yesterday, I was afraid of Shiva because he was the destroyer. I invoked him in fear back in November because I knew he could destroy my mental patterns, but thought it might mean death. Our minds play funny tricks on us! Yesterday, I realized destroyer meant rejuvenator and he is the most loving and compassionate source of energy. There was a lot of energy in the room from satsung. When Swamiji came out, he looked like a mountain. That is the only way to explain this massive form of strength. While watching darshan, Heidi was compelled to get her crayons and paper. She drew three circles; gold was in the middle, light orange surrounding the gold and dark orange around the light orange. Purple bordered the entire design. You could feel the energy from that circle. I asked Hari Kaantaa to look at the picture to see if the symbol represented anything other than the sun. She couldn't decipher. I asked her to put her hand on my head and ask Swamiji if there was a message attached to that picture. The words that flew from her lips were "how are the kids?" I thought he was joking with me since he is a comedian because I was texting both children a few minutes before. I stopped texting.

MaryAnn put on the computer because Swamiji's discourse was translated from Tamil to English. Usually he speaks in English, but for this occasion it was all in Tamil. On my desktop is a picture of Champ. MaryAnn is an intuitive and said Champ is in the room right now which brought tears to my eyes. When everyone left and we finished cleaning up, we decided to do our meditation for the manipuraka chakra to release worry. During the entire 21 minute meditation, I was in tears and uncontrollable tears because a deep seeded engram or limiting belief was staring at me. The message was clear and devastating!

I saw a vision of Champ and he jumped into my arms; we hugged and kissed. Then the huge samskara emerged. My thoughts actually killed my baby. I asked Swamiji to allow Champ to come back as a human. My higher consciousness knew exactly why. I understood what my mission was on this planet. How was I supposed to accomplish this mission with Champ? I would think about that question constantly. I wasn't able to take Champ to any of the dorms when I went away to college. My higher consciousness knew I would never leave Champ behind because I idolized him. My persistent uneasiness and thoughts of him as a human made it a reality. As if that wasn't bad enough, I realized my thoughts also killed my dad, mom and April.

As much as I loved April at the beginning and still do, once she started misbehaving and lying straight to my face, I thought about her leaving. Kyle was born and April was a great sister. However, when we moved to New Jersey, she became a terror. I thought she was a terrible influence on Kyle. I was hoping she would leave because I didn't know how to handle her and my energy was drained by my parent's illnesses. I didn't realize how powerful my thoughts were.

Growing up I was so afraid of my dad, I wished he was dead on many occasions. I felt deprived of a male role model and blamed him often. I contacted the ombudsman to remove his feeding tube. I put him in a nursing home when I promised him years before I would never do such a thing. I was so relieved when the nurse called and said he left his body.

I was so angry at my mother because she was choosing to give up instead of fight for her life. She would forget to take her medicine. We would go places and she would just sit in a chair. She had no social life. I told her she would have to move out and find her own place. I thought I was doing her a favor, but the fear of being alone caused her to let the lymphoma devour her.

Negative thoughts are poisonous! It is the cosmic law to follow our thoughts when the subconscious and conscious are in alignment. I had so much internal anger for my parents and April and I also had external hostility. We need to be extremely careful. As for Champ, I needed him to leave so I could fulfill my mission. Once again my thoughts were aligned. I take full responsibility. Even though I cried for a half hour, I was fine after that. I released my guilt during that cry and forgave myself. My inner child was just trying to protect me so nobody is to blame. It is a great lesson though. Be aware of your thoughts and reprogram them now. You may not want to hear this, but we are responsible for everything in our lives whether it is good or bad. We all have negative thoughts sometimes, but the minute we are aware we can stop those thoughts just by saying the word STOP! You and I both know I didn't kill any of those people. I didn't stab or shoot them. However, I believed internally it was my fault and that I killed them. To me, it was real and so my subconscious believed it to be true as well. My inner child was tormented because she was convinced we were murderers. The guilt associated with that thought is tremendous. I was conflicted. I always knew I was a valuable citizen of society, yet my internal being disagreed.

We have a devil and angel inside ourselves. The devil is our subconscious and the angel is our conscious. To make matters worse, if your angel and devil were in cahoots, it could become catastrophic. For instance, your subconscious believes you are not good enough. Similarly, your conscious feels the same way. Then, this thought follows the self fulfilling prophecy and you will fail at many activities. If your subconscious believes you are not good enough and your conscious says you are going to win a contest. You may win the contest, but it will create illness within your body. The "win-win" situation is when the subconscious says you are good enough and your conscious agrees. You win the contest and you celebrate in joy! It is that easy!

I have learned to talk to myself. It is important to have a conversation with yourself. If the devil appears within you, talk to it and tell him you are in charge and he is not manipulating you. Tell him to stop the nonsense. When the angel appears, thank him for all the great blessings in your life and the lessons you are learning.

Searching For My Twin Flame

Once I heard about twin flames, I was positive I was meeting mine. After all, every psychic reading confirmed I was meeting my twin flame in March. A twin flame is your identical counterpart in the opposite sex. In other words, it's my mirror image in male form. I would have dreams since I was a little girl about my knight. We would be walking along the beach hand in hand. All I knew is he was taller than me with dark hair and a great body. I never saw his face.

As I got older, whenever I had sex, I would picture my headless twin flame passionately kissing me and more. Duane was always jealous of my mala because it had Swamiji's picture on it; he would tell me to wear his picture. There was no way! I would tell Duane Swamiji is God; it is like wearing a rosary. I guess Duane saw something in my eyes when I spoke about Swamiji and he knew I was in love with him before I did.

Swamiji and I have a lot of similarities. He loves healing and so do I. I could spend hours healing. He is opening up cancer hospitals and other types of hospitals to cure people from major diseases. He loves children and wants Indigo children to come to his gurukul so he could help them. He has love and compassion for all. Swamiji had a parakeet named Menokshee; the way he looks at that bird reminds me of me and Champ. He loves to sing and dance. He is hysterical. I was convinced he is my mirror image and since I will be a Master, it only made sense that he and I were together.

I would dream about Swamiji and me flying through the universe holding hands and hugging. I never understood why I could never get him to kiss me in my dreams because I know with intensity anything could happen. Even kissing could happen because it is the cosmic law. However, I realize there are things way beyond my logic as well. During a discourse, I remember Swamiji saying he was a sannyasi and the joy he experiences is way beyond anything we could imagine. He stated he gets excited when his lower back is rubbed and he is not interested in intercourse or having a relationship. I would dream about having sex by rubbing his back. Whenever I tried to dream about intercourse with him, nothing would happen. I realized he was giving me a message. Even though I wanted it, he didn't. That was clear. He chose to be born in the Arunachala Mountains for a reason. His love is to the entire cosmos and he doesn't want a relationship with one individual. I know there are other Masters who marry and have families. For instance, Braco fits that category even though he doesn't like to be labeled as anything other than Braco. So, that is something I have been trying to deal with because I still had attachment to Swamiji's physical form.

Yesterday, an epiphany occurred. The event with Hari Kaanaa awakened the revelation partly, but it was expanded wide open by another devotee Anupama. Anupama was explaining the story of Shiva, Brahma and Vishnu. Then, she turned the subject matter to Devi and Shiva. Anupama said Shiva is half Devi. Part of him is female energy and part is male energy. Swamiji taught us males have 51% male energy and 49% female energy and vice versa for females so that concept didn't surprise me at all. However, a click snapped after hearing that Shiva's human form was 50% Shiva and 50% Devi.

I realized I have been with my twin flame the entire time. My human form is composed of half Vanaja energy and the other half is Swamiji energy. That goes for every single person on this planet. If you are female. Swamiji is the male energy inside of you and if you are a male. Swamiji is the feminine form inside of you. If you wish, you could call this other 50% Jesus, Buddha, Babji, source, cosmos and so on; it is all the same energy in different forms. This divine energy lies dormant and needs to be awakened by a Master. They call it the kundalini awakening. Once it is awakened, it will bring you to higher consciousness quickly, but you also need to reprogram your thoughts. That is why I say God does 50% of the job and you have to take responsibility to do the other 50%. When these two energies reach 100%, you are outside your body and enlightened. To put it more succinctly, your God energy's sole purpose is to merge with the cosmos. The other half has fear, greed, jealousy, lust and worry so it is not aligned with its mirror image. Once those undermining emotions are eliminated from the ego, the male and female energies unite and merge into one. I feel like I am almost at alignment and I want you all to join me!

I didn't even realize this till yesterday on Shivaratri Day! Once the mirror images align, you are whole. There is no longer any need to look externally for a mate to make you whole because you are already whole. Everything else is just gravy at that point. You could have a relationship if you wish, but you don't need a person from the opposite or same sex to complete you. This is how we were born—totally whole. In other words, it is our birth right. As I am downloading these words onto paper, a lightning bolt just struck me. This is the absolute truth and it is so easy! I am willing to help anyone who is truly seeking peace, love and compassion instead of fear, greed and jealousy!

PART 8

Learn From Everyone And Everything

The Secret is Unveiled

What do Beethoven, Carnegie, Churchill, Edison, Einstein, Newton, Plato, Emerson, and King have in common? They are revered as some of the most influential leaders in history. They are also referred to in "The Secret," an acclaimed documentary a few years ago. The premise of the film is based on the "Law of Attraction." Our thoughts create our reality. What do Beckwith, Canfield, Proctor, Vitale, Walsh and sixteen other entrepreneurs, visionaries, authors, physicians and philosophers have in common? They are all the motivational speakers in this documentary who know the secret and want to share it with the world. The Secret is also one of the bestselling books of all time because people want an answer to the questions that always troubled their soul. Is there really a God or is the Bible a made up story? Is there really a connection between emotions and physical disease? Are our thoughts that powerful that we truly can obtain any desire we want? Yes, yes and yes are the answers!

I am expanding upon the brilliant workings of "The Secret" and I thank those 21 visionaries and especially Rhonda Byrne for sharing this enigma and making it public knowledge. I watched this film repetitively and while I knew it was true, I just wasn't able to achieve my dreams. Now, I know the reason. We need to change our thought patterns, but it won't magically transform. We have to completely reprogram them; to change a habit it takes 21 days.

I believe there is a stronger implication behind the number 21. However, you will have to research and let me know because this manuscript needs to be completed by February 29th and it is now February 22nd. I am also helping friends in between. All I know for certain is that it takes 21 days to reprogram any belief; it has to be 21 consecutive days.

Swamiji emphasized 21 is the magic number for a thought to be permanently embedded in our bio-memory. Based on this thinking, I organized a forum called Dreams Are Reality which became the title of this book. In short, Swamiji asked anybody who was watching en-tv that night to discuss our dreams, passions and visions at satsung. The following night, he elaborated upon this subject and added an essential ingredient. No judgment or criticism was allowed. If anybody had negative remarks, it needed to be discussed so there was positive energy flowing within the group. I was determined to participate in this assignment; however I wanted it to be meaningful. In the past, we would discuss ideas for about 10 minutes before satsung started; that would be the end of the discussion. Personally, I felt it was a waste of time and we weren't accomplishing our goal. A few weeks later, an idea came to me and so the tele-conferencing group session commenced.

On the first night, all participants agreed to pray for each other so we could achieve our dreams and make it a reality. There were 11 partakers and each person wrote one sentence that described their dream for this year. We always said a blessing before the prayer to thank Swamiji for all the blessings and abundance in our life. We ended with a prayer to bring peace, love, grace, compassion, joy and healing to the world. At our weekly sessions, downloaded meditations were used as a means to reprogram our current beliefs. Group prayer is powerful and it sends a message to the divine that we are united as one. The cosmos loves that message and will remove all obstacles to show you its appreciation. The following shows you what 11 people were committed to every single day for 21 days. It is funny, we started with 15 and we were down to 11. As Metatron noted, "there are no coincidences in the universe."

Vanaja Ananda MA, MS

Here is an example of a quick intro . . .

I am deeply grateful to you Swamiji and all of existential energy for all the blessings and abundance in my life. Thank you for making our dreams a reality!

You can put your own gratitude prayer and then put your name on the top of the list and read each of our visions.

1. **Dmitry** is deeper into the spiritual state.

2. **Lily** has an immediate source of income and is achieving her dream of a successful music career.

3. **Heidi** has discovered ways to have fun and joy in her life.

4. **Paul** made $300,000 this year, co-owns a $500,000 apartment building and is now in India with Swamiji achieving enlightenment.

5. **Helen** has adopted a healthy baby and the oil tank issue on the Hoboken house is resolved.

6. **Vanaja** is employed at a global education company that embraces and implements ABCPEACE curriculum in every one of their preschools.

7. **MaryAnn** is out of debt, is in India attending Inner Awakening, is completely surrendered to Swamiji, has a private practice and has started building the community she has seen in her visions.

8. **Michèle** is a yoga instructor specializing in teaching seniors, children and adults and markets a new exercise video.

9. **Josephine** is desire-less and enjoys life bliss and perfect health and has a website and web presence for spiritual counseling and healing with a focus on helping cancer patients.

10. **Radhika** has numerous investments, travels, sings while playing the piano, is a sattvic chef and enjoys perfect health.

11. **Jill** has a wonderful executive position on Wall Street, is a Siddha Medicine Doctor and is taking classes to become a Spiritual Director.

At the end please add "through my vision I bring peace, grace, love, compassion, bliss and healing to the world. Please do this daily for 21 days.

If you weren't able to make it last night, but are committed to the 21 day program and will be present at the next two forums, please add your name and sentence to the list and email it to everyone so you are included. You missed the first day of the 21 days, but we will figure out a way to do it so we all end on the same day. Also, Paul recorded the forum so we will be able to distribute it to everyone soon.

The message was clear as you could see. I even sent an email out the next day about the deadline to join the group. When people missed the deadline, they thought I would let them join anyway. In the past, I may have let them join to avoid confrontation. However, I knew this would only be beneficial if everybody was committed to the 21 day program so I asked them to join the next session. People became irate and asked to be removed from the list. Our egos are very cunning. Furthermore, I changed my sentence for about 2 days and I received comments about that as well. I was being bombarded with judgments and scrutiny, yet it bounced off of me.

Participants who missed the first 2 days agreed to say the prayers twice per day so they were caught up and we could end on the 21st day. At that time I had no idea the 21st day was also on February 29th. We began on the February 9th. I guess the cosmos wanted us to start on that day and now we know why. The date never crossed my mind. Now, the cosmos wants me to know all these numbers have significance.

I finally had the courage to reveal the truth in a letter to this group plus two more people who chose to wait for the next session without any complaints. Both Dionne and Marcia understood and didn't question the decision. I thank them both. The letter was sent on February 17, 2012 and is shown below.

Nithyanandam Everybody,

It is funny. Swamiji gave two sets of instructions for homework assignments during two discourses. First, he asked us to discuss our visions and passions in satsung. Second, he specifically mentioned we were to support each other and not criticize. While I wanted to do the homework assignment, I wanted to make it meaningful; not just discuss it for 10 minutes before the morning discourse. I really wanted people to achieve their dream.

So, after two weeks, the forum idea popped into my head.

The first session went great and then people were getting upset. I sent a letter detailing the forum and specifically announced the deadline people could join the forum for the 21 day period. I know that intensity and commitment are the ways to obtain our goals. If people missed too many days, they wouldn't have the commitment or intensity. I explained this to quite a few people and asked them to join the next one which was less than 21 days by that time. Two people agreed and I really appreciate that. However, about 6 people took it as an affront and exclusion.

Next, I revamped my statement and I was excited. People felt I didn't have the right to be a billionaire. Swamiji says the cosmos wants us to be wealthy and if we are poor, we are committing a crime, yet a few people have already decided I am not worthy of this abundance from the cosmos.

Next, I spent hours the day before our forum, as I did last week as well, writing the meditation so people could achieve their goals. It took hours because I looked at the goals of each person and meditated for a few minutes on every individual and your higher consciousness downloaded it into me. When people were leaving messages, they weren't joining us last night, I did everything in my power to try to convince them to join because there was a message for them. I couldn't tell them what the message was because during the meditation, each person needed to allow their higher consciousness to reveal it to them. The cosmos requires permission. I wasn't sure who was going to be on last night; it was all a surprise.

I am going to tell you the truth because it will be revealed soon in my book anyway. Before I begin, I want you to know my real mission is to help mankind in the quickest and most effective way possible. I actually wrote the script which was downloaded from the cosmos the day before our meeting. Heidi knows because I emailed it to her to print. However, I woke up thinking everybody may think my ego is involved when they heard mine, so I changed my entire section. I could show you both if you wish.

Here is the truth. You can interpret it any way you want, but I know I am extremely honest and even hiding something from yourself or others is dishonest. I am sharing this with our group only and the two people who are joining the next session. It is interesting, but my Dreams Are Reality letters circulated outside our immediate group somehow.

Last year, when I went to LEP, Swamiji told me I was going to be an enlightened Master. During the entire program, my ego was inflated as I thought about royalty and having everything in the world along with helping others. At the end of LEP, I expected to be enlightened. During darshan, I told him today is the day. Could you believe my audacity? He became indignant, crossed his arms and yelled at me to take responsibility. I was shocked, but asked him for a hug anyway and he obliged.

I was furious and thought he lied. I even wrote a letter to Swami Bhaktarananda. Something about his reply allowed me to start taking responsibility for all the injustices and traumas in my life. I realized I could help so many people now because I encountered all those experiences. I went through lots of quick surgeries as Swamiji calls them. I delved into the embedded emotion and found ways to reprogram beliefs that created illness inside my body.

I was scared about being a Master: I envisioned physically dying and an alien taking over my body and many other scenarios as well. The thought literally petrified me, yet I knew by making my body a perfect conduit for the cosmos, that body could help mass quantities of people. So, my higher consciousness made me meditate, pray, yoga, visit temples, and so on. I did anything spiritual and tried to release mental patterns. That was my new career. Also, I drove hours to help people who needed healings.

This year, I wanted to volunteer at the Ashram to give selfless service to Swamiji for everything he did for me. That didn't work though because he still worked on engrams that were still there. During darshan, he told me I knew the truth and said things similar to before. I know he and the cosmos have done their part and it is up to me to do the rest. I told him I wanted every mental pattern removed from my inner being and he blessed me. I know I have money issues, attachment to Swamiji and maybe more so I am still in my body.

It is important to get the truth out and all the disdain over the past few days has encouraged me to reveal it to

Vanaja Ananda MA; MS

you. I am powerful and so are all of you. I want you to realize you are just as powerful and can obtain anything you want from the universe. I could help you because I have been through so much and I believe others could realize the truth instantly once negative mental patterns are erased. Master is just a title I realize. To me, it is no longer a big deal. I felt the cosmos energy go through me the other day. I want to allow that energy to flow through me because it is an amazing, beautiful experience. I know there is so much more out there too. I want to help beings in other dimensions and other planets so I know I will achieve that someday soon too.

Right now, I want to help you achieve your dream. I also want to do the 21 day meditation in Washington, DC because Swamiji said that will help save the world. Wherever I am needed, I plan to be. I know my book is going to help so many people because it is about mental patterns in my life and how I have overcome them, techniques to help people overcome it, the importance of attending IA, Ascended Masters and angels who helped me along the way and friends, animals, inanimate objects who also left signs for me along the way. But the best part of the book is that even though I have no money right now, they are going to witness all my dreams and passions manifesting into reality as it all unfolds in front of them. It will be so much fun! Then, they will realize, if a person who had traumas like them (or maybe even worse) can achieve these things, they can too!

Swamiji says in 2012 and the next three years, people around the world are going to be extremely depressed and even suicidal. It kills me to hear that these people are going to be in so much pain. We are all one and I am already feeling their agony. It is time for at least this group to wake up and help as many people as we can.

Vanaja Ananda MA; MS

You are all Swamiji's close devotees. Your higher consciousness knows what I am saying is real. Please allow your consciousness to accept it so you could become self-realized quickly and follow your mission and passions. Together, we could help humanity; the more people we get to understand this, the more people will be saved from the tortures of our mind.

Next week, we will be meeting our inner child. I hope you will all be there; it may be emotionally difficult, but you can conquer that fear if you choose. Please let me know who will truly be on our forum next week. I believe it will be another meditation, but even I don't know that for sure. Also, please continue praying for each of the participants of Dreams Are Reality. Only do it though if you could do it with purity of heart and no negativity because it won't be fair to all involved.

So, now you know the truth and I feel so relieved that I could be me and not have to walk on pins and needles. I will leave you with one last thought. Your higher consciousness knows you are ready or else you wouldn't be part of this group. As you know, I only read the contents of the individuals who were present last night. Everybody told me Josephine wasn't coming on because she was packing to leave for vacation and we waited to start until 7:15PM because I thought for sure she would be on. When she didn't come on and I know she is always punctual, I was convinced you guys were right. However, during the meditation I felt her in the room and so I read her section as well. When we came back from our astral travel to Bidadi, Josephine was present. I will end on that note.

Love,

Vanaja

You are going to laugh at this one because I laugh everytime I think about it. I was revealing a secret I had kept hidden since October 2010 and not one person made a comment. Instead, they all interpreted the letter exactly the same. They felt I was upset that people didn't want to join the forum. Our perceptions are illusions that are so far from reality. I realized that was a lesson from the cosmos on courage; the divine wanted to see if I had the moxie to perform. I surprised even myself.

Heidi helped me a lot with courage. I have been helping her with various limiting beliefs. In addition to the techniques I mentioned throughout the book, we added a 21 day manipuraka meditation which clears blockages in the navel center. It releases worries so you are able to release the pattern. Anything I asked Heidi to do, she did without question. I guess her higher consciousness recognized I was here to help her. Heidi watched me do some strange things like puja to pictures and pots and pans and yet she never judged.

Recently, we began doing puja to our purses. It is essential to respect everything and treat each object as a deity from the cosmos. I organize my money so that every bill is facing the same direction. When I spend the money, I thank the cosmos for giving it to me so I am able to purchase commodities. I even kiss it. I also do the Lakshmi ashtothram because Lakshmi is the Goddess of Abundance. Abundance is showered in many ways: prosperity, health, relationships, success and joy.

Heidi and a few other people believed what I was saying. Paul, Michele, and Jill proved their allegiance. I needed help today and all four of these blessed souls are ready to help. I need a letter to get to Louise Hay so Hay House will publish this book quickly and efficiently. Louise Hay is the globally renowned spiritual author of many books including Heal Your Body which I refer to like a Bible along with Living Enlightenment by Swamiji. The cosmos wants Louise Hay to publish Dreams Are Reality and I know the minute she reads the content of the letter, she will agree. Her administration won't give her the letter. I documented the day and time it was sent to her office and Balboa Press, the subsidiary company to Hay House. At this moment, I don't know the exact reason. This is more like the game "Clue" or an Agatha Christie novel without a murder. The suspense is killing even me!

I woke up today knowing I had to write this letter and get it distributed. However, the cosmos always plays games and since I love games, I am playing right along. The cosmos has decided society has to merge together

Vanaja Ananda MA; MS

to get this book published so you will understand that you have power beyond belief once you tap into it. As I mentioned before, group prayer is the key. The world is going through significant changes and we all need to ban together so people are saved from themselves.

There are no demons out there. We create our own heaven and hell right here on earth. The existence in the cosmos is complete and utter fulfillment. Look for yourself. Birds flying in the sky never worry about crashing into a tree. A tree grows when it is watered from the heavens above. You will never see two trees arguing about the water each one receives. The cosmos is constantly in a state of chaos. Animals in the forest do not plan their day; they just go with the flow and allow the cosmos to guide them. If they are hungry, they search for food. If they are tired, they sleep. If they want to rest, they just sit. That is all. They don't say I have to get up, brush my teeth, eat breakfast, go to the office, and blah blah blah. We need spontaneity. We don't need to know what is next because it is so much more fun and exciting not to know.

I am not saying don't work. It is important to create, create and create some more. I am saying allow yourself to enjoy life through fun and play. Laugh a lot, smile often and dance your feet off! Release your inhibitions and just be. The cosmos is there to protect.

I will never forget this story from Swamiji. It will put things into perspective for you.

The story . . .

In a village, trappers would catch birds without having to shoot them. They would adjust the branch so it was wobbly. When the bird came to perch, he would become disoriented and turn upside down. The bird would go into panic mode and just hang there; the trapper would put a cage over the helpless bird. All the bird needed to do was flap his wings, fly off and escape. However, he was paralyzed with fear. Swamiji says we are like that bird. All we have to do is release our grasp and fly. If we fall, he says he will be there with a net to catch us. You will not get hurt.

I have heard and read this story on many occasions; it is my favorite story in Living Enlightenment. With this book, I ask a question and then close my eyes and open the book to whatever page appears; the answer is right in front of me. I read a few pages or more and go to sleep. I gave all my Living Enlightenment books away to people who really needed it more than me so now I just remember the information contained inside that phenomenal book. To me, there is no book that compares—even the Bible. The Bible was always difficult for me to read and understand. Living Enlightenment is written at a level where anyone can understand the message.

As far as the letter goes, I was ready to put it on the Facebook "I am Enlightened" group page. I cut and pasted and pressed send. However, the document was too large. I didn't know how to attach a letter on facebook, so I decided to ask some friends to help me. As I mentioned before, my friends were willing to help but because I still lack patience, their reply wasn't quick enough for me.

I knew the letter was going to create controversy and disbelief so I needed someone with credibility who could persuade the Nithyananda follower group. That person was Dheera. Dheera means courage although when I first sent it, the name was the furthest thing from my mind. I thought Dheera would love it and release it to the public eagerly. His response surprised me and without thinking I told him he needed to read between the lines and realize it was the truth. I told him to show the world what his name really meant. I guess the cosmos liked that because he asked me to send him the manuscript for perusal. As I am writing this, I am awaiting his response.

Here is the letter that was downloaded from the cosmos this morning . . .

PLEASE READ EVERY SENTENCE CAREFULLY BECAUSE IT WAS DOWNLOADED FROM THE COSMOS . . . GIVE YOURSELF PERMISSION TO LEAVE YOUR JUDGMENTS ASIDE

I am a Master. Swamiji told me at LEP and he confirmed it this year when I was volunteering at the Ashram. When I first heard this back in 2010, visions of grandeur was my number 1 concern, even though helping humanity was not very far behind. On the last day of LEP, I expected to be enlightened and a Master. When I told that to Swamiji (I kids had the same situation. I sold my car to pay off debt room and board with about $1000 left over for me. My homeless with $300 left. Financial Aid was paying for Heidi graciously offered me her home because I was

my one week failure at Chiropractic School.

fruition. A cascade of emotions simultaneously arose after you ask Swamiji for something with intensity, it comes to do it as gently and quickly as possible. As you are aware, if vehicle for the cosmos to flow through. I also asked him to remove every negative mental pattern so I was a perfect slight doubts penetrating in my mind. I asked him to I knew the truth and I believed I did, but there were still Your Way to Heaven." During the program Swamiji said Awakening participants; it was amazing. I call it "Chop volunteered in the kitchen for 21 days and served the Inner The bottom line is I didn't die and I volunteered at IA. I

is the truth.

Swamiji because he has transformed me totally and that cosmos (like an alien). I was willing to give up my life for and someone was going to take over my body from the destroyer means rejuvenator, so I thought he may kill me selfless service for Swamiji. At the time, I didn't realize and remove any negative mental patterns so I could do Bidadi. I invoked Shiva and asked him to enter my body this past year, so a week before I went to volunteer in and clear it out. I was convinced I would be enlightened everything in my life. I would delve to the exact causation something clicked and I started to take responsibility for Bhaktananda expressing my dissatisfaction. With his reply, Bhaktananda. In fact, I wrote a letter to Swami After that, I became angry at Swamiji and Swami

course he gave me one.

I was hurt, but I asked if I could still have a hug and of didn't even have the courtesy to ask), he became indignant, crossed his arms and yelled at me to take responsibility.

Vanaja Ananda MA, MS

and go to India so I didn't have a car on campus; gas wasn't an issue. I was planning to do work/study and send that money to the kids, so everything was set for the next 3 ½ years. However, I withdrew from Chiropractic College and was homeless because I told Duane that I would be out of the house on January 1st and here I was coming back on the 9th; I didn't want to renege on my part of the agreement especially since Duane adhered to his end of the bargain.

When I arrived at Heidi's, I felt like a complete failure. However, I knew I was supposed to write a book. This information came from a channeled reading with Archangel Metatron. Originally, I was told the book could be done in a week. I am convinced it will be done on or before February 29th. Today, is the 35th day of writing.

Yesterday, I finally understood the truth. Everything is revealed in the book with techniques to achieve whatever you want quickly. It took me 2 ½ years, but you could achieve anything and I mean anything much easier. The truth is so simple. Swamiji is in every one of us; he is the other half. He is the opposite gender in everyone. He is our mirror image. However, negative mental patterns keep us at a lower energy vibration so we are not aligned with our mirror image. Once we are able to reprogram beliefs that occurred from early childhood and thousands of past lives, we will be in alignment. Then, our thoughts will allow us to obtain any dream or desire. Right now, our conscious wants one thing, but our subconscious is sabotaging it. The subconscious believes it is protecting you. If you could create agreement between your subconscious and conscious, you are aligned with your Swamiji half. Then, you can get whatever you want.

It is the Law of Attraction explained in the Secret, the Living Matrix and What the Bleep. It is real and easy and I help you every step of the way through my book. The most important thing is to get to Inner Awakening because only an Avatar could awaken your kundalini which is the Swamiji in you. Any Avatar could do it, but there is significance behind the 21 days. It takes 21 days for a habit to be changed in your bio memory. This is proven! If you have gone to IA, you already have this power. If you haven't gone to IA yet, get there as quickly as you can. During the 21 days Swamiji removes negative mental patterns from its roots and then you need to do the rest by reprogramming the thought pattern in this life time. Swamiji actually removes all your past life samskaras; it is truly amazing and an incredible blessing.

I need help now! The name of this book is Dreams Are Reality. Swamiji gave homework a few weeks ago and a forum materialized from the assignment. We turned it into a 21 day program so our passion and mission will be a reality. The name of the forum is Dreams Are Reality and it became the impetus for the title. The first day I named it Vanaja writes a book in a week thanks to Metatron. Last year, I started a book on the education system and it never made it past 10 pages. The cosmos has downloaded this book and it is the total truth because I am almost a pure conduit.

Swamiji always said he doesn't want you to know he is God; he wants you to know you are God. It is true you and me and everybody else on this planet have power beyond belief. I am going to show you what you are capable of right now. There is God in every one of us and every entity. We are all created from energy source and you could call that source whatever you want. The truth is we have tremendous power and the capacity to get anything we want. Collective consciousness is the fastest way to achieve this.

Swamiji told us during the 2012 Webinar that the gravity of the earth is decreasing and as a result people will start having fewer thoughts. It is happening already. He said the people that meditate, do yoga and know how to achieve inner peace will love this transition. However, a massive percentage of our population, including our politicians, will go into a state of depression and make destructive decisions. That is why we are conducting a 21 day peace meditation outside the Capital Building in Washington DC; so the leaders of our country make decisions out of love and compassion instead of greed and fear.

It is time to achieve your dreams. The more people that reach higher consciousness, the more people will be helped. Swamiji says if one person lives enlightenment, hundreds of people also achieve that state just by being around that energy. Imagine how many people we could help together and save our beautiful planet. I am not just speaking about mankind. I am talking about mountains, rocks, oceans, and so on and so forth. Every being on this earth, living or non-living has energy and therefore is God and is a part of ourselves. We are destroying ourselves when we harm anything!

Dreams Are Reality is the truth. It is a compilation of my life and the mental patterns that developed in my subconscious and how these were revealed to me when I took responsibility. There are techniques and strategies to help any person reprogram these beliefs. It intermingles brain research as well. In addition to Swamiji other Avatars are mentioned as well as Archangels, the Arcturian Healing team, angels and many other divine entities. Even in the heavens, there is a hierarchy and each divine being has a particular job. I believe Archangel Haniel is writing this letter right now and Archangel Raziel revealed the truth to me. It combines the Vedic tradition, Hebrew heritage, Christian beliefs and Buddhist philosophy to show people religion, creed, sexual orientation or anything else is irrelevant because we are all one. I want to show scientists that this is real so I am offering my body for experiments at Ivy League Universities. Teachers College at Columbia will have the first choice because I am an alumni; the beautiful souls there offered me the chance of a lifetime even though my GRE scores were horrible. I am forever grateful. The ending is the best though because everybody will watch Vanaja's life unfold as the cosmos showers me with abundance right before your eyes. Then there will certainly be no doubt.

It is imperative Louise Hay publish this and she gets the manuscript on or before February 29th. The bureaucracy at her offices won't give her a letter I wrote. I know she will understand it because it sounds a little bizarre even to me, but that is what the cosmos wants. We are each like a small atom compared to the universe. However, we are in the human body so must do the work the cosmos wants us to do. That is all there is to it. We need to figure out a way through collective consciousness to get this manuscript to Louise Hay because many people will be suffering needlessly and this book will help.

I know you are thinking I could just ask Swamiji or Swami Bhaktananda and it will be accomplished. This is all true, but the divine wants you to realize what you are capable of by yourself and as a mass community. This is difficult for me to write. I am asking Swamiji and Bhakta to trust the souls you created and allow them to do this mission on their own. So, I am asking you not to interfere with this huge mission. I hope I didn't offend you with these words since you both mean the world to me. I also have a caveat in my intensity to see our Dreams Become Reality. I am not allowed to help with this part because I have to finish this book. I leave it all in your hands. You have the power; just choose to believe in yourself and all those around you. Moreover, if you need help, go to Brad Yates on you tube and start tapping. He will help you release mental patterns quickly. The divine is counting on all of you to save our planet.

Vanaja Ananda MA; MS

Here are a few ideas. Go to Hay House and stay until they allow you to give a letter to Louise Hay. Call Hay House every minute so you tie up their phones and they can't do business. I am sure you will have creative ideas. Please designate one or only a few leaders and figure out a way for this manuscript to arrive in Louise Hay's hands on February 29th. Heidi has the letter because I emailed it to her the same day I sent it to Louise Hay. The cosmos wants Jill to be the liaison. Jill, please give the Louise letter to the leaders of this campaign.

Everybody circulate this letter everywhere. In the past, the media was a great channel for me (no pun intended). When I went to sleep last night, I never thought I would be writing this letter today. My entire life is on the line here. I don't care if I get persecuted; the mission is to help the planet. Swamiji, like Jesus, was crucified and they were innocent. By the way, I am 100% convinced Swamiji is innocent and if you have any doubts, it is your illusion playing tricks! One human, even if it is an Avatar, can't help the earth. The scandal proved that. However, the mass population united will save this planet! It is all up to you!

In case you are still having doubts, today is February 22, 2012. Twenty-two is a Master number. There are also a lot of 2's, but I am not sure what that means. Shivaratri was on the 20th, 33 days after I started the book; 33 is a Master number. The 29th equals 11 which is a Master number. Also, my entire birthday 11/29/60 adds up to 11. In addition, it is Ash Wednesday today. Check with numerologists and they will tell you the significance. Do you think I like the entire world to know my age lol?

Love,

Vanaja

I just decided I will wait this entire day and night for Dheera's response. If I don't hear from him, the letter will go out across facebook tomorrow and to esteemed spiritual authors like the visionaries of The Secret, Dr. Wayne Dyer, and Eckart Tolle to name a few. Time is of the essence right now.

A Preteen Taught Me the Meaning of Courage

I met Alice when she was three years old. Her mother, Lena, came to Bright Beginnings. Lena, Max, Alice and Lev are my friends for many years. Alice had focusing and academic issues. I always knew there was brilliance behind that frightened exterior. Alice has a charismatic personality. In elementary school, she was labeled as learning disabled. I really don't like labels, but that could be a book in itself.

Lena brought her to me for Neurofeedback and other therapies. I owned another business called Educational Healing. Educational Healing was a healing arts practice that utilized Neurofeedback and other modalities to help clients achieve vastly improved alertness, attention, relaxation and inner peace. I implemented effective holistic treatment plans for children, adolescents, teens and adults with learning impairments specifically ADHD, Pervasive Developmental Disorder, Dyslexia, depression and anxiety.

Sometimes, I felt I was torturing Alice because she had a short attention span. I tried to make it fun, but some of the modalities required work and delving into deep emotions that were painful. Alice, like a trooper, came every week. Recently, she attended En Genius, the Inner Awakening program for kids.

The perseverance and determination Alice demonstrated gave me the courage to pursue my dreams even against adversity. A lot of people slowly disappeared from my life over the past two years. The name change scared them as well as the changes they saw in me. Most of them couldn't understand how I could abandon Bright Beginnings. In reality, I saved Bright Beginnings so the families, teachers and curriculum would continue under strong leadership; Sonel was the perfect person to maintain the school's philosophy, mission and integrity. One day, they all may realize that. I will welcome them back into my life at any time. That statement holds true for anybody I have lost contact with throughout the years as well.

891

Vanaja Ananda, MA, MS

Science and Spirituality Merge

Clinical evidence has always been important to me. I chose to go to Teachers College at Columbia University because of its stellar reputation. The school didn't prove me wrong; the esteemed professors are brilliant. Moreover, the advisors at Teachers College looked outside the box and admitted me into the program even though my GRE scores were atrocious. It probably helped that I prayed everyday for a year to get into this school as well. Once again, you are witness to the power of thoughts and intensity.

I was convinced my advisor would accept my dissertation proposal. However, my subconscious had other ideas. No matter how much I tried to persuade my advisor, he wouldn't budge. I was expanding upon his study so it didn't make any sense to me until recently. I had a limiting thought pattern engraved in my memory. Negative mental patterns are brutal for the psyche. It is also an illusion. Reality is the present and it is new every minute. Spontaneity is the key. Being in control will leave you exhausted and following your intuition enables you to be blissful, enthusiastic and creative.

Sharon Begley, author of "Train Your Mind, Change Your Brain," discusses the neuroplasticity of the brain. Neuroplasticity refers to the ability of the brain to grow new neurons. Begley explains that neuronal growth continues through adulthood. This research was discussed at the Mind and Life Institute in 1990 where the Dalai Lama met with scientists. By understanding how the mind works, "Train Your Mind, Change Your Brain" is a breakthrough in emotional, cognitive and behavioral problems. Buddhist Monks participated in a study at several universities. The compelling evidence confirmed the monk's brains were unique and these beings have more neurons than the average human. What do you think the reason is for this phenomenon? You are right! It is because they meditate and have learned the secrets of inner peace.

Begley's book is phenomenal yet it never received the accolades it deserved. I believe the title has a lot to do with that. People automatically switch into the fight or flight mentality when they don't feel adequate. In this case, most people haven't studied neuroscience and therefore have little knowledge about the intricacies of the brain. They fear when they pick up Begley's book, it is going to confirm what they believe about themselves. The truth is this book is fascinating and you don't need to know the neuroscience jargon. You don't need to be a brain surgeon. All you need to know is that neurons communicate with each other in an enriched environment and read it with an open mind ready to absorb whatever you can. You will understand the connection between science and spirituality when you read this book. I recommend it highly.

As I wrote that last paragraph, I thought of the movie Young Frankenstein. Gene Wilder was told to go to the laboratory and get a brain for Frankenstein. There was an entire room full of brains and he chose the brain with the label Abbie Normal. Of course, Frankenstein received the abnormal brain and the movie was hysterical. My personality definitely didn't change as a result of this transformation. I still laugh at my own jokes.

No human on this earth has a brain that can't be reprogrammed; all it takes is desire, intensity and determination. Wherever there is a will, there is a way. You will see miracles raining down from other dimensions. Leave your umbrella at home and lavish in these blessings. Always remember to thank the divine in you, soul sisters and brothers and those in other dimensions for all the blessings and abundance in your life.

The Protector

Throughout my entire life, I have always protected children. It may be because I felt abandoned at such a young, impressionable age. I was and still am a huge advocate for children and their families. I would even be willing to lose customers if the way to solve the problem was contrary to my mission, philosophy and curriculum. I knew, beyond a doubt, that ABCPEACE benefited children in every developmental area. This claim was based on the reputation of the school and the success of the students within. Also, I would do anything for Kyle and Raquel to protect them from the malice of society. In fact, I sat along with Kyle in detention for two hours because he was unjustly accused of plagiarism.

I was always loyal as well. I would protect the staff at Bright Beginnings because I felt we were a family. I would also protect anybody I felt needed protection. While I have a lot of compassion, I also become emotionally charged sometimes. This happened two nights ago. It is now February 24th and even though I know I have no time to waste. I wasn't able to write anything yesterday except a letter to someone which is shown below and a meditation for the Dreams Are Reality forum which took place last night. I didn't understand the reason for my block until I meditated late last night.

Dear . . . . ,

I sent you a letter yesterday and I was shocked by your reaction. Instead of reading the contents of the letter carefully, you chose to focus on the last line. While I am not going to expound upon the merits of numerology, your comeback was both hurtful and judgmental. After reading that harsh response, I began to wonder how the rest of society would respond. I decided to procrastinate and wait a day to hear your reply after you read my incomplete manuscript. However, there was no feedback from you.

I know what I say is the truth. People who know me well are cognizant of the integrity behind my words. I also know one person can be persecuted, but the mass united can make a difference. This was proven when

Barack Obama was elected; this only occurred because the majority of the American population banned together.

Throughout history great leaders have been oppressed because their beliefs were contrary to societal norms. Even Gods were punished because concepts were beyond our logic. Jesus Christ was crucified on the cross and a year ago Swamiji was crucified by society as well. The only way massive changes will occur on this planet is when everyone joins hands in uniformity with passion and intensity to help mankind. That is the law of the universe. Otherwise, dissention and contention will result leading us to wars and separation.

We are all divine. Separate, we are just matter in the universe taking up space. However, when we assemble together, miracles could happen. Moses parted the sea to save the people. Does that sound logical? Absolutely not! I have no doubt it is real though. If Moses went by himself, he would have probably drowned, but because he merged his energy with those all around him, he brought his people to safety; they did it together, not detached.

Everyone who knows me understands the undying love, commitment and attachment I have for Swamiji. He is extremely powerful. I also know all the Gods, Archangels and angels are extremely powerful. Swamiji is a form in a human body. Jesus and Buddha are forms of matter not in the body, yet they all have the same ability. Every animal, ocean, mountain and so on and so forth is made of energy. We are all one whether we choose to believe it or not and not one person or divine being in the heavens is any better than anyone else. That is just the way it is.

I know the truth and it is revealed in the book Dreams Are Reality that I am sure you started reading. I have a lot of knowledge about the brain and how negative thoughts create disease in the body. I know the techniques to help people deal with anxiety and the depression they will soon be experiencing due to the changes in the earth's gravitation. Through my experiences, I am able to teach others.

You said I didn't explain what I wanted people to do in the previous letter so I am clarifying that right now. Dreams Are Reality needs to be published by Hay House Publishing. The owner of this corporation is Louise Hay. She is a globally renowned spiritual author. I need everybody to work together and assimilate into one energetic force to make this happen. I need this letter and the letter I wrote yesterday on facebook, twitter, and blogs. I need it sent to the media and other leaders such as Tony Robbins or Dr. Wayne Dyer. These two letters need to be circulating around the world. There are so many brilliant minds out there so I am sure more ideas will be generated as well. All I know is this manuscript, which will be finished today except for editing, needs to be in Louise Hay's hands on February 29, 2012.

Even if you have doubts, I don't. There are four people who received this letter after you and they believed me because they know me as a person. Also, my angel Raquel has always believed in me even in the face of adversity. These four people who will remain nameless to protect their identity, are willing to help me get the message out to the public. I hope you will join as well because the planet needs you right now.

Even though I have transformed, I am the same person. My name change helped me to realize my path and that is all. Pam and Vanaja are the same. The difference is I no longer have the stress, fear and anxiety. It is a miracle. My birth name is Solomon. I chose that name for a reason.

Am I scared? The answer is unequivocally yes. I know the truth is esoteric and society is ready to pounce. I realize I could become ostracized from all of society; that feeling is inhumane. I should know since I have experienced it from many people over the last two years. Also, I know Eckarte Tolle, the author of "The Power of Now" was institutionalized in an insane asylum before he became a renowned author. I am aware Van Gogh cut off his ear because his thoughts were beyond his logic and he thought he was going crazy.

I am intelligent, sane and passionate about my mission in life. My mission is to bring love, peace, grace, joy and healing to the world. In order to help humanity, I am willing to take the chance of being excommunicated from the public. Also, my trust and belief in the divine is invincible. I have surrendered completely to the entire cosmos. I will end with a passage from Dreams Are Reality. This excerpt was written yesterday.

The Secret is Unveiled

What do Beethoven, Carnegie, Churchill, Edison, Einstein, Newton, Plato, Emerson, and King have in common? They are revered as some of the most influential leaders in history. They are also referred to in "The Secret," an acclaimed documentary a few years ago. The premise of the film is based on the "Law of Attraction." Our thoughts create our reality. What do Beckwith, Canfield, Proctor, Vitale, Walsh and sixteen other entrepreneurs, visionaries, authors, physicians and philosophers have in common? They are all the motivational speakers in this documentary who know the secret and want to share it with the world. The Secret is also one of the bestselling books of all time because people want an answer to the questions that always troubled their soul. Is there really a God or is the Bible a made up story? Is there really a connection between emotions and physical disease? Are our thoughts that powerful that we truly can obtain any desire we want? Yes, yes and yes are the answers!

Vanaja Ananda MA; MS

I am expanding upon the brilliant workings of "The Secret" and I thank those 21 visionaries and especially Rhonda Byrne for sharing this enigma and making it public knowledge. I watched this film repetitively and while I knew it was true, I just wasn't able to achieve my dreams. Now, I know the reason. We need to change our thought patterns, but it won't magically transform. We have to completely reprogram them; to change a habit it takes 21 days.

In love, grace, peace, bliss and healing,

Vanaja

I showed Raquel this letter and the previous letter. She has always supported me and I wanted to make sure she still did because I wanted to prepare her for what may occur. Her reply makes me crack up. She said "What am I supposed to believe? That u are being transformed by the divine? I mean I get what ur saying, I told u I don't like swami and ur giving everyone credit. If its wat u believe then go for it." That is all I needed to read and I knew that my angel was always with me no matter what.

We Are All Unique, Yet All The Same

Two nights ago a pattern was exposed and I tried to embalm it way beneath the earth's surface. Even though I knew the technique to remove my funk all day, I never used EFT which would have taken about 30 minutes. Instead I chose to sulk all day and all night. Clarity came when I meditated at midnight.

On this particular evening, I went to a meditation group. As I explained prior, I am enrolled in a Siddha Medicine Doctor 3 year program. The meditation was based on the teachings of the Malaysian Masters and Yogis. Before the meditation, there was a discussion among the group. The discussion evolved into a heated discussion between me and another woman. She proclaimed this Malaysian Master was superior to any other Master. Of course, I had to chime in and protect Swamiji. We had a slight altercation; it was nothing momentous. However, I was able to analyze where the pattern stemmed from. All of a sudden the realization hit me like a ten ton brick.

I always believed that Swamiji was the Supreme Being. To me, he was the elite of all the Masters in the heavens. To rationalize my strong connection with Braco, I would tell myself he was an angel, but not a God. Even though I witnessed Braco healing people through live streaming, similar to Swamiji, I wouldn't allow my mind to believe any entity was stronger or more powerful than Swamiji.

Oh my God, the truth is coming, but this is so hard. I just screamed and cried at the top of my lungs. I feel like a traitor right now. Just give me a moment. Here it is. The truth is every being on this planet or other dimensions have dreams, passions and visions. Each being is unique and specializes in certain areas. That is why "United We Stand, Divided We Fall." A teacher could not mentor her students without the knowledge of authors who wrote the books. There would be an endemic in a town if the sanitation department chose to go on strike and rats decided to scavenge through the refuse; it could potentially turn into an epidemic. There would be no bridges to cross from one state into another without the expertise of engineers. The mailman drives through snow, sleet, and hail to deliver your mail and packages. Did you ever wonder what would happen if people decided they didn't like that occupation?

Every being who follows his passion, brings joy and bliss to the world. Happiness automatically radiates from the person who gets up in the morning looking forward to the day ahead. The person who takes the time to smell the flowers on the front porch or looks at the formation of the clouds in the sky transmits wonder and curiosity to those around. The person who gets caught in the rain without an umbrella, but doesn't care shows spontaneity is a key ingredient to living.

I still haven't said what I set out to tell in this chapter. We are all divine. Every single one of us is God. There is no difference between the divine in other dimensions or the divine on earth in the third dimension. It all has to do with our thoughts. Whatever we think is what comes back to us. So, Swamiji is not any better than the Malaysian Master. Sai Baba is no different than Babaji. Jesus is no better than Buddha. Archangel Michael is no better than Angel Crystal. All of these entities are no better than me and you. We are all the same and the faster we realize that point of contention, the better.

There are a number of infinite possibilities in our lives and ways to obtain any desire; it is simply our choice which route we want to take. Do we want to travel from the east coast to the west coast by car, bus, train, airplane or teleport? I choose teleporting. It is up to you to decide which way you want to travel. The secret is all inside this book.

There is a gentleman by the name of Burt Goldman. I have frequented his site on many occasions. This man is over 80 years old. Starting at the age of 80, Burt has published a book, learned photography and his works are displayed in the International Photography Hall of Fame, learned painting and designed an art website, released a CD even though he never sang, and set up a multi-million dollar internet business. Do you think he knows the secret? Since 30 years old he has been seeking the truth. On his journey he met many spiritual Masters including Yogananda. Google Burt Goldman and Quantum Jumping because it is real. Believe that your dreams can become reality; Burt needed to wait until he was 80. You could do it right now!

Am I Worthy?

Throughout my life, I haven't felt comfortable accepting praise and recognition. I am not sure where this pattern originated. It is easy for me to release this pattern easily now without knowing the root cause. I have always had the ability to transform, but my fear of the unknown kept me in bondage. It was socially acceptable to keep my opinions to myself and that is what I learned to do.

As a result, I never accepted credit for anything I did. At Bright Beginnings, I would always say the success of Bright Beginnings is due to the teachers. The teachers obviously are essential for the business to triumph, however I was the leader of this school. I was the person who trained these teachers.

I wrote a charter school 180 page proposal in three months. There were 5 other founders, but to be honest they wrote small sections of the proposal. The New Jersey Department of Education liked the contents of the program and we made it all the way to the final interview. Even though I wrote this huge document, I told everybody all of the founders developed the curriculum for True Potential. I thought we were denied for other reasons, but today I understand why we weren't chosen. The curriculum is outstanding so that is definitely not the reason. It is because I was the only one who knew anything about the workings of the charter school. At the meeting, all questions were directed to me, so it was apparent there was no collaborative effort. It was done by one person and the state knew one person could not run the entire school; it is just not possible! As painful as it is to admit, the state administration made a good decision.

Last night, we gathered through tele-conferencing for our forum. At the brainstorming session we were discussing Dreams Are Reality and ways to place this manuscript in the hands of Louise Hay. During my explanation of the book, I told people this book was not written by me. In fact, I planned to put Dreams Are Reality, by Vanaja Ananda and all the beautiful souls of our society who collaborated together to make this dream a reality. Once again I wasn't taking credit for my work and didn't even realize it until after kriya. Am I joking? Of course I wrote the entire book and it happened in less than two months. Nobody contributed to the script. However, I know the divine's positive energy was always surrounding me in the form of the divinity in other dimensions as well as humans, animals, nature and inanimate objects. Whenever I felt defeated,

I heard the voice telling me to persevere against all odds. So, in a sense you all did write this book.

I uncovered a big mental pattern. It may take me a little bit of time to get used to the notoriety because I never strived to achieve fame. Also, money was never my big motivator either. I always believed money would be available when I needed it and that was that. It would create anxiety inside me; don't get me wrong. However, the divine within always knew the universe provides.

I have $200 left. A check was addressed to me for $1,300 and was mailed to the house. Duane opened it. Apparently, Kyle's financial aid refund was addressed to me. I thought it was strange since last semester, the check was in Kyle's name. I knew the answer. My thoughts involved finding a way for Kyle to realize he could be anything he wanted to be. He is a finance major and he is trying to convince himself he likes the business world; he and I both know, and anybody who knows him realizes, his passion is film and acting. His self-esteem is so low he doesn't believe he has the power to make that dream a reality even with me as his mother.

My intense thoughts to help him brought the check to me. I knew I didn't need the check because soon I will be a billionaire; my predictions are for a month or less. Then it hit me. Kyle said he wanted to transfer to NYU Tisch School, but he knew he wouldn't get in. I offered him a deal. There were two components. First, he needed to apply at NYU that day. Second, he needed to tap with Brad Yates on you tube. In return, I would give him the entire check for $1,300. I thought he would jump at the chance to receive this amount of money. However, he said he had to think about it. He called me about two hours later and said he was on the NYU site and the Tisch School requires a portfolio. Kyle has been told by several teachers that he has natural acting ability, but he never performed so doesn't have a portfolio I agreed, but was satisfied he took the time to research the possibilities. I decided to change the agreement. I told him if he Tapped to Excellence for 21 days, I would give him the check. I said all he had to do is give me his word and I would believe him. I am thrilled to say he has been tapping for about a week now. As you know, Kyle has to change his thoughts on his own and he is on the way to his own success!

Fame and money really are irrelevant to me. I have been doing puja to my purse and I have chanted the Lakshmi astothram every single day for over two years. I know I am going to be blasted with money and abundance in every way. I plan to enjoy the money! I am excited in fact. I plan to have a personal shopper and a house on the ocean. I plan to have a maid, chauffeur, chef and anything I want to get and there is no guilt involved. I will be enjoying the riches of the universe. But more important, I will use that money to send true seekers who have the intensity and determination to succeed at all costs, but don't have the financial means, to the Inner Awakening program because that 21 day program removes all mental patterns in thousands of past lives. Through my book, you will be able to remove the mental patterns for this life time. Also, I plan to help orphans around the world and change the educational paradigm. I also plan to travel wherever I am needed to help people heal. Amma Karunamayi says it perfect "I love you my babies." She says these words over and over again at her programs. She is not referring to infants or toddlers. Her love is showered on beings of any age and she calls even senior citizens her babies. I decided I am going to follow and help people of any age, race, color, creed, sexual orientation, or alien. There are so many happenings way beyond my logic. I am looking forward to the adventures that await me. I have the intense desire to astral travel so Jetsons move over please!

PART 9

Love Always Wins

My Biggest Concern

The writings within Dreams Are Reality are extremely powerful. If followed, people will realize their innate ability quickly. If greed and fear are intermixed with power, the outcomes are catastrophic. The 21 Day Peace Meditation in DC provides an avenue to generate positive energy to the leaders of America so their decisions are based on clarity, not fear. In fear, the choice would be war. In clarity, peace and compassion are paramount.

I need to be sure this book doesn't create a new Hitler in any form. I have the power to do this so this is what I choose to do. I am telling all of divinity in any dimension, including anything that hasn't been disclosed which is beyond my logic right now, the following. This book will help anybody. I want it to help people who live in poverty as well as the elite. Our subconscious really doesn't care about social status. I want to help the prisoner who wants to reform. I want to help orphans who feel all alone. I want to help soldiers because even though they are fighting for the rights of a country, war is still not acceptable.

I am asking the people who benefit from this book to please help others and Pay It Forward. Through your own healing, you are automatically helping 100's around you. Together, we could help millions of people around the world. Whatever is your passion, use that intensity for the benefit of our planet. Even helping in a soup kitchen, allows that homeless person to experience the energy that belongs to all. Offering this book to a homeless person, could potentially help that person to live the life he has always dreamed. I am here to help and there are enlightened beings around the world helping right now as well. Reach out to them. They will all help you. You couldn't be enlightened if you weren't pure of heart. It is imperative that you know whoever you encounter whose mission is for love, peace, compassion, bliss or healing is a blessing; learn as much as you can from that person.

Moreover, anybody using this book as a means of destruction, conquering land or war over other countries will not benefit from its contents. I am not referring to the past because that is over. Everybody makes mistakes; you read about all of mine and I am sure there are more to come. Always learn from your mistakes. Whatever you put out to the universe comes back to you. If you put out hate, hate will come back. If you put out greed, you will meet greedy people in all your rendezvous. If you put out jealousy, someone will probably stab you in the back; figuratively I mean. If you put out love, love will come back to you. The universe is filled with love and peace and all are rooting for you to achieve success. Let's join our universe and become one together. We are just fragments when we live our lives through fear, greed, jealousy, worry or other limiting beliefs. However, when we are connected, we are a beautiful transparent mirror.

Vanaja Ananda MA, MS

Because You Loved Me

The song "Because You Loved Me" by Celine Dion is dedicated to Swamiji for all the love, faith and trust he had in me that allowed me to reach the ultimate, but not the final!

You were my strength when I was weak
You were my voice when I couldn't speak
You were my eyes when I couldn't see
You saw the best there was in me . . . .

I intended to include the entire lyrics to this song. However, I was told I was legally permitted to put four lines. Please read the lyrics to the entire song "Because You Loved Me". There is even a video on you tube with Swamiji's pictures and the song lyrics on each photo. Every word in this song conveys my feelings and gratitude for this divine being.

Yesterday, the publisher asked me if I have permission to include the words from "Because You Loved Me" and my answer was no. Today, I had an epiphany (June 2, 2012)! I wrote a song at the Living Enlightenment Program (LEP) on October 9, 2010 and I decided to include these lyrics in this book. The song is called "I Wanna Be Enlightened Now." Since we kept a daily journal at the Ashram, it was easy for me to locate the song and the exact date I wrote it. There was a group of 6 people at the LEP program who agreed to perform the song at entertainment night for Swamiji. We rehearsed for a few days and were so excited. It was fun to sing and comical as well. Unfortunately, due to time constraints, our group was unable to perform. I realize many people may not understand these lyrics because they are about the Hindu Gods, but I know you will enjoy the message. The tune is from the rap song "I Wanna To Be A Billionaire" by Travis McCoy.

I wanna be enlightened now
So very bad
Bring peace and love to the planet
I want to be in the cosmos with
All blissful beings
Smiling next to Shiva and Devi!

Oh every time I close my eyes
I see Swamiji's face shining bright
The ultimate experience every night
Oh I
I swear the world better prepare
When we're all like Swamiji

Yeah! I would be just like Ganesha
Clearing out the obstacles
Everyday engrams
Trampling the new ones

I'd probably pull a Shiva and Devi
And help a bunch of orphans
Who never had peace
Lift away a few tears
Like here baby hug this
And last but not least
Chant the dancing Shiva past twist
It's been a long time that I've been blissful
So you could call me destroyer minus the ego
Get it . . . hee . . . hee

I'd probably visit where the earthquakes hit
And make sure I bring abundance like Lakshmi did
Yeah can't forget Goddess Lakshmi
Everywhere I go I hear the Nithyanda music

Oh every time I close my eyes
(Watcha see, Watcha see)
I see Swamiji's face shining bright
(Uh huh, Uh huh)
The ultimate experience every night
Oh I
I swear the world better prepare
When we're all like Swamiji
(Oh ooh, Oh oooh)

For when we're like Swamiji
(Oh ooh, Oh ooh)

I'll be eating butter like Krishna
Being very mischievous
Dunking all his donuts
Then I'll compliment him
On his love and compassion
Toss a couple million in the air
Just for the heck of it
But keep a few billion completely separate
And yeah I'll help the poor and sick with no racket
They don't meditate but let me take a crack at it
I'll probably heal whoever I see
And just laugh a lot
So everybody I love will have a lot of luck

And not a single tummy around me
Would know what hungry was
Eating and sleeping soundly
Goddess Devi has a similar scheme
Look at your mala
Pull out your sutras
And pray to the Divine Mother and sing

I wanna be enlightened now
So very bad
Bring peace and love to the planet
I want to be in the cosmos with
All blissful beings
Smiling next to Shiva and Devi

For every time I close my eyes
(Watcha see, Watcha see)
I see Swamiji's face smiling bright
(Uh huh, Uh huh)
The ultimate experience every night

Oh I
I swear the world better prepare
When we're all like Swamiji
(Oh ooh, Oh ooh)
When we're like Swamiji
(Oh ooh, Oh ooh)
I want to be enlightened now so very bad

Vanaja Ananda MA, MS

The Truth Always Prevails

I have been procrastinating, not wanting to write this last chapter even though I know it is essential. Today is February 26, 2012. There is now a video on you tube thanks to Paul and the website is ready and yet only seven people viewed the site. I have helped hundreds and maybe even thousands of people over the years and yet nobody truly believes me. At one point I thought five people believed me, but I am not sure anymore.

I just left to take Raquel to the store and I told her the secret about plastic surgery. I am telling you what I told her because I know it will help a lot of people in the same situation. First, I explained I hid something from her for years; concealing the truth is the same as lying. I explained how I was always called Olive Oil because I was flat like a board. My stomach was flat too. I abhorred that name so subconsciously I programmed a mental pattern to change my proportions. I was never heavy, but I had a pot belly in college and up into my 30's. I started taking diet pills and became addicted. I had no body fat, but I still had a pot belly no matter what I did. The chemicals in the drugs started altering my brain. I became jittery at times and started slurring my words. I really panicked when I wasn't able to bend my fingers to hold a cup. Even though those symptoms occurred, I was so addicted, I was unable to stop.

I had the idea to get plastic surgery on my stomach and Duane wanted me to get the breasts done. In addition, I thought my nose was too big so I decided to do that too. Up until the day of the surgery, I was taking diet pills because I wanted the doctor to think I was skinny. During surgery, there was no fat on my body so the surgeon was forced to make incisions that shouldn't have been necessary. I have a line below my belly button that is a reminder every day of my life. I also can't stand fake breasts.

Even after the surgery, I had a pot belly. The reason was buried in my subconscious. My inner child was protecting me from the ridicule of teasing. I know my friends meant me no harm in my teenage years, but my subconscious had other beliefs. I never felt pretty even after surgery, but guys would definitely look. My low self-esteem couldn't handle it so I would cover it up with clothing.

Then I decided my nose was too big so I decided to have rhinoplasty. My nose looked exactly the same after surgery. I think if it looked different,

I would have gotten foot surgery too because I hated my feet. I loathed my body! All the plastic surgeries in the world didn't change that. I massacred my body because I hated it so much! Taking a knife to your body is horrible. We are all a child of God; we are all beautiful inside and out. Now, I have a flat stomach because I was able to reprogram that negative mental pattern.

I thought Raquel would be angry, but she said she was happy I didn't tell her because she probably would have wanted plastic surgery as well. She is thrilled she has a great body and she sculpted her body through yoga, good eating habits and going to the gym. She is proud of herself. I know the mental pattern still exists in her and if she allows me to help her, she will release it forever. She has to be willing to delve into the emotion and it is painful though.

I tortured myself for a week about telling Raquel and she made it so easy. However, today she didn't support me. She, like most of the population, thought I was going crazy. I felt like I was all alone and people weren't going to join together in prayer. Even though I don't have any evidence right now to confirm they will help humanity, somehow my trust and belief in mankind has been restored. Archanaa, my soul sister, believes me and she has shared the link with family and friends. Heidi spent all day trying to figure out facebook so she could convince me of her loyalty. Paul just sent me a message that gave me clarity. He was the one who gave me the clue to send the Schiffer Publishing email. Jacqueline said she has been trying to go on facebook, but yet she never texted me so I am not sure I totally believe that is a valid excuse. Josephine was in California on vacation so didn't even see the emails till about 6:30PM. It is now 7:15PM.

I jumped to conclusions that weren't valid probably because I witnessed what happened to an innocent soul last March. As you could see, I still have mental patterns to unravel. I was crying all day feeling alone and abandoned. I felt crucified and it is torture! My letters may have sounded irrational, but I am totally sane. I just want to help humanity in the quickest way possible. Patience was never my virtue and that was clearly shown today. Below is the letter I wrote and posted on facebook.

WHAT HAS THIS PLANET COME TO?

I already have a contact at Balboa Press and 3 people received my email on Friday night. Balboa Press is the subsidiary to Hay House. On Monday, when they come into the office, they will see my you tube clip. The book will be in Louise Hay's hands on February 29th. In addition, Schiffer Publishing was interested in my book. Whether you believe I am crazy or not, the media will love this and the book will be published to help people.

Do you really think I don't know what I am doing? I am shocked about how fear paralyzes people and the threats from society scare people beyond belief. I have been ostracized for 2 ½ years by people who swore their love and devotion to me and today I was able to release that mental pattern so there is no more fear.

I brought this into my life for a reason. I wanted to feel what Swamiji went through when he was vilified by disciples who professed their undying love for him and accused him the minute a scandal broke out. He was vindicated, but he lost his faith in humanity. Yet, everyday for FREE he broadcasts live around the world.

I went through the same thing today when only 7 people went on the Dreams Are Reality site. Out of 1,000's of friends, only 7 chose to visit. I would go hours each way to give healings to people I didn't even know and I ask you to go to a site and share the link and nobody is willing to do it. Let me tell you it is the most excruciating pain and I pray nobody has to go through it. It is literally inhumane. What has our planet come to?

The only way to help the planet is to ban together. The power of prayer is the only way to stop manmade catastrophes. The divine wants the people of the world to pray for a planet filled with peace, love and compassion. That is all! It is not about a book. Give me a break! It is about uniting as one entity because we are all God.

Would I ever sell Bright Beginnings to any corporation? No! Did you know there was a person who wanted to buy it for more money, but I didn't think he would follow the mission and philosophy so I chose not to go that route. I never spoke with him because I promised Sonel and I never break a promise.

I need 100 people on the site today because there is important information I have to share. It is about happenings in 2012. People need to be prepared so they are not fearful because it is all good once we come together as one.

It is your choice! Please have the courage and share the link.

I think the hardest part for me is that my own children didn't believe me or my ex husband who lived with me for 24 years. My own brother didn't believe me! So, how was I really going to get 100 people on that site when the closest people to me let fear take over? I know Champ and Fluffy would have been there for me. If I didn't put up the email from Schiffer Publication, I don't think any of the above people would have come to my rescue either. I am not sure so I will not judge. Her email is below and it was dated February 23rd.

Hello Vanaja and thanks for writing!

I would like to see a couple chapters, a chapter outline, and contents page. Also include 2 or 3 images that you intend to use for your book. I'd like to know how many

Vanaja Ananda MA; MS

words you anticipate, too. It sounds interesting and I'd like to pitch it at my next pitch meeting with the publisher (in about a month's time—I'm not really sure when). Thanks!

Dinah

Dinah Roseberry
Schiffer Publishing
4880 Lower Valley Road
Atglen, PA 19310
610-593-1777 phone
610-593-2002 fax
www.schifferbooks.com
www.schifferghosts.com
dinah@schifferbooks.com

I am a little numb right now. I stopped writing last night and watched Swamiji. I was emotionally drained and missed most of the discourse; I was dozing during the teachings. Miraculously, I was wide awake for the kriya. After the satsung, I said my prayer for the Dreams Are Reality forum people and went to bed. I prayed all night to be able to be able to forgive people; I cried off and on throughout the entire night so I am exhausted today. It is February 27th. During yoga this morning, I cried uncontrollably; I am going to start calling it crying yoga. Then I did puja.

I decided to do puja by myself because I still was not able to forgive anyone, so I really didn't want Heidi doing my sacred prayer to the Divine this morning. I did my mantras and at the end Heidi came down and told me she was mad and I didn't wait for her. I told her how I felt. Her response surprised me because she said more people are supporting you than you think. Of course now everybody will be supportive because I just gave them evidence. Prior to that, they were willing to cut off my head at the guillotine. I wanted to hold a grudge, but yet I couldn't. I did puja all over again . . . the entire ritual.

I know I brought this pain into my life for a reason. However, the torture is unbearable. Excruciating is not even a word to describe this torment. I thought of Swamiji and knew he didn't experience any of this emotional pain because he was enlightened when this occurred. Then, I thought of Jesus. He was still a human when he was tied to the cross, but

I know he didn't experience any physical pain because the minute a knife was coming toward him, he was released from his body by the universe. However, the emotional suffering he had to endure was unrelenting. I felt that same pain whether it was being nailed to the cross or being ostracized for years by people who claim they love you; it is the same. So, what am I supposed to say? Forgive them Father for they do not know what they have done. Bull crap! Every single one of you knew exactly what you were doing. You were afraid to support me because you didn't know how your friends or family would react! TAKE RESPONSIBILITY! You had a choice and you went with your fear.

You did the same thing to Jesus in other lifetimes. You go to church and talk about how spiritual you all are. Is it spiritual to torture someone for years because she believes something that is contrary to your beliefs? Look in the mirror. We bring every situation into our lives for a purpose to learn a karmic lesson. Who knows who you were in a previous life? Maybe you were a rapist and in this life you are the victim. We play different roles each time in hopes of achieving self realization so we don't have to come back to this planet ever again.

I was thinking about what has happened over 1000's of years to make people so brutal. I concluded it is just fear and our subconscious causes us to be monsters without even realizing it. How could I truly blame anyone? I have cleared out all my limiting beliefs except one huge one and maybe a couple of small ones in this lifetime. Thanks to Swamiji, all my past life negative mental patterns have been removed. Most of you, however, have so many mental patterns consuming your very existence. Jesus is right when he says "they do not know what they have done." I guess therefore I have forgiven. It just may take me a few days to release the betrayal pattern. I know the technique, but I am not sure I want to let it go yet. I'll have to contemplate.

Anything that has been written in this book stays. I will not be editing this book except for typos or grammatical errors. I have been agonizing for a few days about writing something. Even though that person has conspired against me, I am unable to crucify him like he willingly did to me. My passion is to help mankind and if I intentionally hurt even one person, that goes entirely against my mission. Even though I told him I keep my word and I was going to write it, my heart just won't let me do it. He will have to live knowing he could have made the last few days much easier for me. But with the techniques in this book, he will be able

Why do we allow jealousy and greed to come first? Why are we so oblivious to the true nature of our being? Why do we think wars are fine as long as our country wins? War is not fine people! Innocent women, children, animals, and men are getting hurt whether it is in our country or not! We are killing a part of ourselves every single time another being dies. Why are we polluting our waters? Why do we leave lights on all day and night without thinking of the ramifications? Why do we leave garbage at the side of the road thinking someone else will pick it up? I really don't have the answers to these questions. All I know is it is disheartening! We are destroying our planet and we have no one to blame except ourselves. We could choose to join together and become one or be defeated.

I am now going to give you the main reason for this book. The earth as we know it will be different. We will be going into the fourth dimension and experiencing things we never thought were possible. Enlightened entities have been protecting our planet from other dimensions for thousands of years. Now, they are ready to come meet us. Our planet needs help fast! It has reached a state of urgency! Our political, health, educational and financial systems are all corrupt; they need to be totally revamped. People living in the third dimension don't have the ability to save the earth. The planet is in such a state of disarray that only advanced teachings way beyond our logic will emancipate us. They are coming soon and you may be scared and immediately propelled into fight or flight mode. These beings, although they may look different than you or I, have the same soul and their souls are totally pure with thoughts of love, peace and compassion. They are here to help. They will be removing the corruption and offering new jobs to all of humanity so the unemployed will be financially secure. Unfortunately, they will not make their grand appearance until they know they are welcome. Cosmic Law will not allow them to interfere even though they have started a little bit already.

When we elected Barack Obama, we showed the divine we are ready to be a planet of love, peace and compassion. Some people thought Obama was a terrorist and tried to defame him. However, the majority of the American population was fed up because our souls were seeking peace. Obama has incredible public speaking skills, intelligence and charisma which combine into a great leader package. Obama is so different than any President we have ever had and yet we had the courage to vote for him. The high energy vibration from the majority of our citizens not only brought Obama into office, but told the universe earth is finally ready for transformation.

In the book "21 Days To Braco," Angelica mentions the Obama election brought Braco to America. Before that he only offered his eye gazing to European citizens. Now, with live streaming Braco has healed thousands of people around the world. There are many enlightened beings on this planet in human form like Braco and Swamiji. Now, enlightened beings will be arriving in different forms and we must be able to accept this. Let's all pray together with all our neighbors no matter what color, gender, religion. Let's pray for each other because we are all one. Let's not focus on the external appearance and concentrate on the inner souls. Let's show these beings we not only welcome their help, but are willing to collaborate with them to bring peace, love and compassion to this planet and all the inhabitants on it. Let's protect our bodies of water. Let's protect our animals since many are becoming extinct. Let's protect our natural wonders. Let's create a beautiful society of peace and happiness. Only humans could do this. Do we really have the right to allow nature to suffer because of our fear? Let's take the plunge. I am here to help you and teach you the ways out of emotional turmoil. Please allow me to help you.

Vanaja Ananda MA; MS

The Last Gigantic Negative Mental Pattern

I have fallen in love with Swamiji. I did everything in my power to erase that thought, but yet it still vibrates. Or didn't I? I realized I don't want to release this pattern. Swamiji and the Divine in every form have tried every possible way to help me release this desire, however it is even more important to me than enlightenment.

I knew in December 2011, I could have been enlightened because Swamiji told me I knew the truth and once you know the truth you are enlightened. However, I immediately installed a prerequisite. I wanted to be a totally pure channel for the divine to flow through so I asked for every single negative mental pattern to be released from my subconscious. I believe I knew that I would never release this pattern just like I knew I would never give Champ away.

I knew without a doubt that when I was enlightened I could have any person on this planet as a lifelong partner. Yet, I didn't want that. I always wanted someone to love me for myself and not because I am wealthy and successful. I always craved unconditional love. I wanted to meet that person before I transformed and now that is impossible. I have two days now and I will be metamorphosing into a butterfly. I know miracles could occur easily and do. How would someone be able to convince me they have always loved me? They didn't even know me before my transformation. There were only two beings that offered me total unconditional love: Champ and Swamiji.

I thought about Champ coming back to earth as a walk in, but that wouldn't be fair to him. I want him to experience the human body from birth. However, I want him to be born enlightened! I don't want him to suffer at all! That is my wish for my little angel Champ!

As for Swamiji, I love him so much! I know he doesn't want romantic love and that is truly what I want. I offered him the choice and I know. I told you in my visions, he didn't kiss me back. I lied and that is the only lie I have told in this book. I wanted to protect him at all costs. He did kiss me, but anything else I tried he didn't respond except when I rubbed his back. That is the truth! When our lips met, it was the most amazing experience for me. Whether it was real or in my fantasy doesn't matter because my brain doesn't know the difference. I would rather keep that fantasy instead of meeting another guy. I know once I am enlightened, that intense passionate feeling for Swamiji will no longer be there and I am unwilling to give up my fantasy.

I guess I will have to live with the torture of being rejected to protect society. I am strong. I can do it! I could still help mankind on this planet. I just won't be able to help beings on other planets except when I am sleeping. I am truly sorry to the universe. I guess I am not the Master you expected after all. I am just a human who has been traumatized and needs a few days to cope; then I'll be my happy self again. There are no smiles or laughter right now and I know the world needs my bliss. Don't worry! I will supply it in a few days.

Vanaja Ananda, MA; MS

One Last Thought

I have one more thing to say to all of mankind. The next time you see a bum on the street, give him some change or offer him your coat so he doesn't freeze. The next time you abuse another human being whether through words, thoughts or physical force, stop and put yourself in the other person's shoes. The next time you are the victim of abuse, stop blaming the other person and look inside yourself. We are mirrors of each other. As much as we believe we are all separate we are not! We are all one.

See the God in everybody and everything around you. Feel the beautiful energy vibration. Enjoy every minute on earth. Nobody is punishing you. You are punishing yourself. Love yourself! Forgive yourself! Remind yourself you are God in every way, shape and form! Laugh, smile and have fun! Be spontaneous and creative! Life is not boring; it is our perception. Start enjoying the little things in life and you will be blessed tenfold.

PART 10

I Am Awake

I Am Taking Responsibility

I just took a break to eat lunch. Before I went to eat, I received a text from Raquel. It said she got an A in English. Yesterday, after I gave her the boots I was wearing that she loved so much, she was offered the solo at her college musical production. I was too distraught last night to comment except I said great and congratulations. Today, when she told me about her grade, I said awesome now do you believe me? She told me she always believed me and the minute I dropped her off yesterday, she posted the link on her facebook.

I am no better than any of you. I was ready to condemn the one person who has always supported me against all odds just because I thought she let me down. I may have more limiting beliefs than I think. Human nature is based on fear! Once I heard Raquel stood by me, nothing else mattered. If she believes me then I have to show her that humanity and helping others comes before anything else. I posted a passage from the book on Archangels. Here it is in case you forget.

Vanaja Ananda MA; MS

Archangels Are All Around Me

I was trying to remember the first time I began including Archangels in my prayers, but I don't really remember. I believe it was sometime in 2011 if that helps. Whenever an archangel was mentioned to me whether in a song, meditation, person, or in a book, I researched what they represented and thanked them for protecting me. Every single night, I thank Archangel Michael, Raphael, Gabriel, Uriel, Metatron, Sandolphon, Jophiel, Haniel and Raziel.

In this chapter, I will tell you about the Archangels I revere. Michael is my protector. He has given me courage and strength. In the morning, I ask him to place a blue ball on my throat chakra and balance all my chakras from head to toe. Raphael is the doctor and healer. I ask him to help me self heal and learn the skills to heal others. Gabriel is God's messenger. I ask him to let me be open to receiving all messages from the divine. Uriel is the angel of intelligence. I ask him to fill me with wisdom and ingenuity. Jophiel is the angel of beauty. I ask him to show me the beauty inside me and recognize the beauty of all that surrounds me. I was told Haniel is my special Archangel. He shows me how to be one with nature and be graceful in all my dealings. In addition, I ask him for eloquence when speaking in public. Raziel knows the secrets of the universe and I ask him to reveal those secrets to me. Metatron and Sandolphon were humans before they became Archangels.

I will be posting Hinduism next. But, right now, I feel compelled to tell you about Charley Thweatt. Charlie was performing at the Unity Church. I had no idea what to expect, but when I heard his music, I felt like I was in heaven and all the answers from the heavens were contained in his music. I bought his CD and listened to it every single day for a year. All the songs are fantastic; the song "Love Finds Its Way" touches my heart the most. Here are the words to that magnificent song. I bless him with tons of abundance in every form; he saved my life on many occasions!

UPCOMING STAR CHARLIE THWEATT
From The Popular CD "Wave After Wave"
Love Finds Its Way Within
Listen to the Preview on Dreams Are Reality You Tube
Link On This Page
Visit <u>www.musicangel.com</u>

Love . . . finds its way within
Like a long lost friend
Finds its way from all around me
Love . . . finds its way within
Like a long lost friend
Finds its way from all around me
As I reach into
Into all I am . . . I am
I step into the truth of who I am . . . I am
I am . . . I am

Peace . . . finds its way within
Like a long lost friend
Finds its way from all around me
Peace . . . finds its way within
Like a long lost friend
Finds its way from all around me
As I reach into
Into all I am . . . I am
I step into the truth of who I am . . . I am
I am . . . I am

Joy . . . finds its way within
Like a long lost friend
Finds its way from all around me
Joy . . . finds its way within
Like a long lost friend
Finds its way from all around me
As I reach into

Into all I am . . . I am
I step into the truth of who I am . . . I am
I am . . . I am

Grace . . . finds its way within
Like a long lost friend
Finds its way from all around me
Grace . . . finds its way within
Like a long lost friend
Finds its way from all around me
As I reach into
Into all I am . . . I am
I step into the truth of who I am . . . I am
I am . . . I am

Life . . . finds its way within
Like a long lost friend
Finds its way from all around me
Life . . . finds its way within
Like a long lost friend
Finds its way from all around me
As I reach into
Into all I am . . . I am
I step into the truth of who I am . . . I am
I am . . . I am

After I wrote this, I realize there is one more person who means the world to me and I pray he will support me! Kyle, you are also my angel. Please hear my prayers! Hinduism is now posted on you tube as well as the lyrics by Charlie Thweatt. Charlie . . . thank you for helping me achieve oneness with the divine.

Am I Crazy or Brilliant!

Swamiji told us a story which explains February 28th, the day the planet was saved!

> A man woke up feeling great, ready to go to work. He went into the kitchen and his wife said are you feeling alright? He replied I feel great. Then he went to get his car and he met the neighbor on his driveway. The neighbor told him he looked pale. He told the neighbor he felt good. As he past the receptionist at his office, she told him he was looking sick. His boss met him in the hall and said take the day off because you look horrible. When the man walked in his house, his wife took his temperature. He had a fever of 103.

The reason I am telling you this story is because that is what I brought into my life. I didn't realize it at the time, but it was the only way to create some noise. I sent 10 emails out; one right after the other. Since people already thought I was insane, I thought I would honor their wishes. The idea was to create unity and that is all. Although I didn't realize it yesterday, I needed to feel what it was like to know you were right, yet doubting yourself because society was telling you something completely different. Yesterday, even I was beginning to doubt my sanity.

Today, I woke up and tapped to Brad Yates unstoppable and boy was I! The messages always amuse me after I write them. I am Kali, I wrote. It is too funny! What is that really supposed to mean? It just meant I was strong and taking initiative . . . geez! Then, I wrote I am leaving my body which to me meant enlightenment. To everybody else it meant suicide. I also said if that doesn't happen, I am going away. I meant to my friend Shamadu's house because he called me last night and told me he was in Florida. I told him everything and he said he totally believed me! He really is my best friend.

Michele called before visitors arrived and she didn't even read the emails yet because something was wrong with her computer. However, after speaking to her, I immediately asked Heidi to get her Tarot cards. We did Tarot two nights ago. I asked for the best way to get the book in Louise Hays hands on the 29th. It said there was an emperor who was older than me; a teacher and a father figure who will make this mission successful.

There was also an upside down woman which meant bad communicator and egotistic. Of course, I figured it couldn't be me, but of course it was. I was convinced Dheera was sabotaging everything, but in reality it was me who was sabotaging everything. Five minutes before MaryAnn and Paul arrived, I asked the Tarot Cards if Dheera was sabotaging the mission. The card dropped out of my hands and it was the empress. It meant I was the one responsible!

Paul and MaryAnn came rushing over wanting me to commit myself. I talked to them for awhile. It was hysterical, but I kept a straight face once I realized what my higher consciousness was telling me . . . the Swamiji in me. I will tell you in a minute. I want you to see the emails I sent out to the Nithyananda family . . . you will be lying on the floor laughing. Are you ready? Just so you know, I was serious at the time.

Clues In Swamiji's Discourse

- **There is no organization to back us up—meaning Swamiji or any enlightened being can't help us right now**
- **There will be a net, but don't look down because you won't see it—meaning Swamiji is always protecting, but you have to trust because there will be no signs from him**
- **Have the courage—meaning release your fear and listen to signs from others**

Messages In Past Discourses From Swamiji

- **I have been preparing you for 2 years to face 2012**
- **2012 is the year feminine energy takes over**
- **Only female energy could bring the planet to a place of love, peace and compassion**
- **There will be no natural catastrophes, only man made**
- **Fear will cause people to make destructive decisions**
- **We are celebrating Devi for 10 days starting 2 days ago**

There Is A Female Willing To Help

Please listen to everything she has to say today. Only a human can lead the planet to love and peace. It is the cosmic law. Here is what I have said in my prayers everyday for over 2 years. I add to the prayer whenever a new enlightened being comes in my path. I am extremely connected to the entire universe and I am a pure channel for their messages.

My prayer goes like this . . .

I am grateful for all the blessings and abundance in my life. Thank you Swamiji, Lakshmi, Shiva, Devi, Ganesh, Kali, Durga, Saraswati, Pavarti, Patanjali, Krishna, Brahma, Vishnu, Shankara, Usui, banyan tree, Bhakta, Bikram, Buddha, Jesus Christ, Vanaja, Champ, Shamadu, Dheera, Reverend Janice, Pastor Augustine, Amma Karunamayi, Ammaji, Mother Meera, Braco, Sai Baba, Osho, Babaji, all the deities, Archangel Michael, Archangel Raphael, Archangel Gabriel, Archangel Uriel, Archangel Metatron, Archangel Sandolphon, Archangel Jophiel, Archangel Haniel, Archangel Raziel, Angel Daniel, Angel Crystal, Angel Chantall, Angel Maya, Angel Isabella, Angel Aurora, all the fairies and Fairy Kayla, Lady Isis, the Arcturian healing team, Dr. Lorphan, Menokshee, King Solomon, Aschwini and the Aschwini twins, the sun and moon, all the planets, all celestial and terrestrial beings, dragons, all Ascended Masters inside and outside of their body, and all of existential energy for all the blessings and abundance in my life. Let me bring peace, love, grace, compassion, bliss and healing to the world. Amen. Also, if people are ill and need immediate prayers, they are included.

Vanaja Ananda MA; MS

I AM LEAVING MY BODY TOMORROW

- Swamiji told me I knew the truth in December 2011.
- I immediately asked to be released from every negative mental pattern to be a pure channel for the divine to flow through
- 29 is the number I chose to join the cosmos and it is tomorrow
- I have released every negative mental pattern except I which I may choose not to release . . . my undying love for Swamiji is something I may not be willing to release because I don't want to even though every being in the universe wants me to
- The secret of the universe is alignment between your subconscious and conscious so you could merge with your mirror self and meet the divine . . . I love Swamiji more than enlightenment
- If I don't leave my body tomorrow, I am going away anyway so today will be the end of my emails

SWAMIJI HAS GIVEN YOU ALL MIRACLES

It is time to return the favor. You heard his plea last night for people to come together as one!

SWAMIJI, THE UNIVERSE AND PLANET NEED YOUR HELP

There are 2 Missions To Prove to the Divine You Really Want A Planet of Love And Compassion Instead of War and Destruction

- The book has to be in Louise Hay's hands tomorrow—it has ways to help people quickly
- People need to see and hear important messages on the facebook site . . . I am delivering the messages

little by little in preparation—all will be revealed today!

READ THIS LETTER AGAIN

It has clues on ways to help!

LETTERS ARE CURRENTLY AT THE FOLLOWING PLACES . . .

Except nothing is happening because the cosmos won't allow me to do it on my own. Only when they see everyone joining in unity, will they be convinced.

- Visionaries of the movie "The Secret"—Michael Beckwith, Lee Brower, Jack Canfield, Bob Proctor, David Schirmer, Marcy Shirmer, Joe Vitale, Denis Waitley, Neale Donald Walsch
- 3 Letters are at Balboa Press, subsidiary to Hay Publishing
- Letters are with . . . Eckart Tolle, Dr. Wayne Dyer, Dr. Bruce Lipton, Tony Robbins, Joseph Chilton Pearce, Heart Math, Howard Gardner, The Living Matrix movie
- Letter to Shame On You Fox News
- Blog on Oprah Winfrey site
- Letter to Mike Milliken of Knowledge Universe

IT IS UP TO YOU TO FOLLOW UP

Create blogs, twitter sites, call the people, call Hay House . . . whatever you need to do to get that book in her hands and people on that site . . . that is your mission today!

DHEERA I TRIED TO SAVE YOU

Even though you conspired against me because in my love to save the planet, I was not able to even allow one soul to be tormented. However the Kali in me has emerged. As you can see, Bidadi knows about this and has done nothing to stop it . . . my reply was helping mankind . . .

On Sat, Feb 25, 2012 at 6:20 PM, Achala Ma <en.structuring@nithyananda.org> wrote:

Nithyanandam!

Ma Vanaja, structuring at the ashram needs to know what you have to say in this matter.
Please respond.

Thanks
In Nithyananda

DHEERA ARE YOU REALLY COURAGEOUS?

Or is that just your name? I need Dheera to contact all centers and temples around the world.

On or the day after the 29th Swamiji will be talking about this . . . don't disappoint him.

- Swamiji has already been persecuted once as a human . . .
- If I leave my body, I am not sure I will choose to come back if people are unable to join forces and save the earth—humanity has crucified me enough and yet I still love you all unconditionally . . . even Dheera
- If I am stuck in my body, I am leaving the area

- The book will be published, but history will repeat itself once again

YOU WILL ALL BE FINE

- Swamiji told us people who know how to achieve inner peace, will be happy with the changes
- However, the majority will suffer
- If you truly care about others, prove it!
- Help mankind!

QUICK METHOD TO RELEASE FEAR

Go to Brad Yates on You Tube and Tap to Releasing Fear and Worry . . . do it over and over if you have to until the fear is released . . . he is amazing!

I STILL BELIEVE MANKIND CAN DO THIS

I AM SWAMIJI IN ANOTHER FORM . . . I AM ATMAN . . . I AM GOD . . . I AM SELF-REALIZED . . . I HAVE INCREDIBLE POWERS . . .

SEE IF BHAKTA ALLOWS THIS ONE TO STAY!
GOOD LUCK WITH YOUR MISSION

This definitely does sound like the ravings of a lunatic. However, when MaryAnn, Heidi and Paul talked to me, I was totally sane and they were in a quandary. I asked them to ask Dheera to send a message to all the centers because I felt that was all the cosmos wanted; they wanted people to join as one and go to the site for the message. I explained to them if they could do that, I won't write another email. I told them it wasn't about the book and that is what I truly believed at that point. I asked all the people in the Dreams Are Reality forum to convince Dheera to send the message out across the world. Paul didn't want to do it unless Swamiji told him specifically to do it. I felt defeated and knew there was nothing else I could do.

Vanaja Ananda MA; MS

I started to write the final chapter of this book and then it hit me. Everybody joined together to help me get over the biggest mental pattern of my entire life. I always wanted unconditional love and felt so betrayed throughout my life. So, I brought this episode into my life to see if anybody really offered unconditional love. Of course, this was all created at a subconscious level so I really believed I was saving the world. Me with my ego . . . unbelievable! People from everywhere came to my rescue.

Duane called before anybody, but he never received the email. He is not spiritual remember. I told him everything I was going to put on the site and he said he knows I believe what I say so he is trying to support me. Also, he told me he was keeping me on his health insurance. In addition, he may know a publisher for me. He was amazing after all. How could I ever have doubted him? Kyle called out of the blue as well. We had a beautiful conversation and he knew nothing about the emails. He was still doing Brad Yates tapping and I heard a joy in his voice that has been missing for years. I am so proud of him. Lena sent the email to Raquel so of course she was concerned, but the minute I told her I was fine, she believed me. We had an awesome conversation about a new potential boyfriend. She is also tapping to Brad Yates. Brad Yates is a miracle worker! Lena sent about five texts because she was so concerned. Michele kept telling me about all the chocolate she was manifesting for Train. She needs to meet that band already. I can't keep hearing about them! Michele has written a perfect song for them. Wait until you hear it! I just want to thank Michele for keeping me laughing through the last couple of days. Shamadu automatically knew I was fine. I really think he is enlightened and just doesn't know. Dheera, India, Hari Kantaa and Igor were all calling. Poor Heidi! They wanted her to call 911, but Heidi told them I am coherent and typical Vanaja. If they came, I told her to tell them to bring donuts! I don't think she will ever let me or anybody else move in again; not after this adventure! I bless her with tons of abundance in every way; she is truly a pure soul. Marcy texted and asked me to send her my resume to forward to companies. It just showed me I have so many friends who love me no matter what I do and that means the world to me! I am so blessed!

I thought the universe wasn't with me. I really believed it was a human mission. The truth is the universe is always with us; we just have to trust and believe. In Swamiji's discourse last night, he told us to walk on the tight rope and there will always be a net for us. However, if we look down, he will make sure we don't see it so we will always have doubts. Today, I walked on that tight rope without looking down. I actually surrendered to the divine! I feel fantastic! I am ready to be blessed with the abundance of the universe! Watch out world! Vanaja is traveling around the world!

There is one last thing I want to tell you . . . at least I think it is one last thing. Paul told me he texted me a week ago to tell me he would send the letter Federal Express to Louise Hay. He said he sent it to me 3 times because I never responded. Do you know I never saw that text. See how cunning our subconscious could be. It protects us at all costs, even though it is doing the complete opposite. Once we are aware, the world opens up right in front of our eyes and the joy is indescribable!

Vanaja Ananda MA, MS

The Book Goes On and On

There is a new title for this book. I am calling it "The Book That Goes On and On and On," just like the energizer bunny! It is February 29th. I thought my mission was accomplished yesterday, however it will be consummated after my last postings today. I feel like I am on the TV show Mission Impossible. Your mission Vanaja, if you decide to accept it, is to bring peace, love, grace, compassion, bliss and healing to the world. Then the music comes on, the match is lit and the paper disappears. Of course, the person accepts the mission and is off to the races! I think if I knew what I would be going through for the last month and a half, I would definitely do it again if it meant helping our planet.

I was told by Vicky, the first Tarot reader, that I would meet the guy of my dreams in February or March of this year. He was going to be sensual, romantic and passionate among all of the other things I had on my vision board. He was going to be like a guru. I believe Jacqueline has met this man and once she releases the fear, she will realize it herself. I guess in all my prayers for her to find the man of her dreams, I subconsciously sent him over because I knew even a guru couldn't match up to my fantasy. Jacqueline called last night and she sounds so happy; in fact they are talking about a honeymoon. I wonder if she even realized she said that. I bless them with a beautiful, loving and mutually satisfying relationship that brings many auspicious surprises in their lives!

In all the emails and texts I sent out, I never sent them to my friends at college. I don't know the answer. I just want Nick, Barbara, Glory, Alex, Amara and John to know that I think of you guys often and I always pray you learn the techniques to be free from your stress. I love you all!

I promised my friend Ash I would do a healing as soon as I got a job. I believe that promise will be fulfilled very soon. I received a text from Hari Kaantaa yesterday. To refresh your memory, Hari Kaantaa is the person who manifests Swamiji's eyes and mouth through her healing. It still blows me away. This was the message "whatever job comes up, you should take that to support your expenses and do whatever you like on side and also look for a job that you like." She interpreted the clue as Swamiji doesn't want you to depend on someone for your needs. The message I derived is to expect a call from Michael Milliken because your curriculum is going worldwide! We all perceive things differently . . . let's see who is right!

Yesterday, I thought when so many people came in support of a friend, it showed the cosmos we are ready to be a planet of love. However, I believe today people are going to release some fear so they could all become one. My dream is to live in a world where peace, love and compassion are paramount. It is a world where people truly see the inner beauty of everyone and everything around them. External appearances are like a costume; what is inside really matters the most. Look at the divine inside of everyone and be aware they are a mirror image of you. If there is something you don't like about them, it most likely exists within yourself as well. Today, February 29, 2012 is dedicated to all the beings on this planet who truly seek peace, love and compassion in their heart. God bless all of you!

As soon as I put up my last three postings, I am off to visit my baby boy! Even though he is 21, he will always be my baby. On February 18th I told him about his birth experience and asked for forgiveness. He said "come on, I don't even remember . . . who cares . . . of course I forgive you and love you." The other day he said I was crazy and he didn't even know about those emails. Join the club! He still said he loved me though! He is so funny!

Please don't ever bow down to me unless you are my prince with my magic slipper! By the way, my shoe size is 10. Only offer me smiles and hugs! Remember, I am no better than anyone else on this planet. Hey! If a Brooklyn girl could do it, anybody could reach their dreams and make it a reality. The sky is the limit. A wise man once told me it is the ultimate, but never the final! Who could that be?

The vision just came to me and I know it is real! Swamiji has chosen me as his bride! Not only that, we are having a baby boy. He will be born on December 12, 2012, but not out of my svelte body, thank goodness! Only kidding, but not really! A beautiful soul has agreed to go through the birthing process. May you and your husband achieve enlightenment! That baby is my Champie in human form! I also decided since I could be immortal, I am choosing the age 35. First, because it is one year older than Nithyananda and I love younger men; they are so much more fun! Second, it is the age before I mutilated my body. Third, I already look 35 and I love it! My knight in shining armor has really come to whisk me away to far off places. I am still in shock! Now do you believe Dreams Are Reality? Fairytales really do come true!

Clues All Around Me

There are so many clues in this book to remind me about my mission. The mission is for people to realize the power of their thoughts and to understand what is happening in 2012. As much as I would love to believe it was over, March 1st was the crucial day.

I woke up in the morning feeling agitated; I thought what if everybody is right and Swamiji and I aren't going to be together. I already wrote it so I can't delete it. If anybody saw what I wrote, they really would think I am crazy. Imagine me telling Kyle and Raquel that I am getting married to Swamiji and we are having a baby. By the way, I am not going to be pregnant; someone is doing that for me. And . . . the best thing of all is your baby brother is Champ. The men in white would be at my door lickety split!

I began my daily yoga routine and even though I had doubts, I was determined to get the message to the public. I remembered the poems I received in the email a few days ago on patience and space. I decided I was going to take my time because precision and calculation were crucial. I remembered last night I told Heidi I love psychological thrillers because I am fascinated by the brilliance of the serial killer. Their method of success was taking their time and planning.

After our normal morning routine including puja, aarti, and a half hour meditation, I began tapping to Brad Yates unstoppable. After that, I put a list of clues together in the past couple of days. I needed to get the message from the divine to as many people as possible. At the same time, I had to prepare them for what was coming. One comment I made to Heidi last night continuously bothered me. I told her Jesus was human when he was crucified and she reminded me he wasn't. Of course, I knew he was enlightened at 12, so why did I say that? I wasn't sure. However, Shamadu sent me a text about **prophets.** I asked him to elaborate, but instead he sent me a link which is posted here.

Jeremiah-1:4-10

Being called by God to be a prophet is awe-inspiring, humbling, more than a little frightening, and often dangerous:

- Moses: "Who am I? . . . What shall I say? . . . They will never believe me . . . . I am slow of speech."
- Isaiah: "Woe is me! I am lost!"
- Jeremiah: "Ah, Lord God: behold, I cannot speak, for I am a child."
- Ezekiel: After the vision in which God calls him, "For seven days I stayed with them, dumbfounded."
- Hosea: God said to him, "Go. Take a prostitute for a wife, and get children of her prostitution; for like a prostitute, this land is unfaithful to the LORD."
- Jonah: He kept quiet, but immediately bought a ticket for Tarshish (roughly equivalent to Timbuktu.)
- Daniel: Thrown into a den of lions.
- John the Baptist: Imprisoned and beheaded.

In similar circumstances, all we can do is say, with Isaiah, "Here am I. Send me." God's assurance is that he will go with us, protect us, and tell us what to say. Also, he sent another message which clinched it!

In Mark 6:4-5 Jesus affirmed that a prophet is without honor in his home town, and in view of that reality, He could not perform any miracles in Nazareth except for healing a few sick people. The people of Nazareth were apparently plagued by unbelief and paid little attention to the claims of Jesus.

At first glance, one might get the impression that Jesus' miraculous power was utterly dependent upon peoples' faith in order for it to work. That is not the meaning of this verse, however. It is not that Jesus was unable or incapacitated in performing a miracle in Nazareth. (Remember—Jesus is the sovereign Creator of the entire universe according to John 1:3, Hebrews 1:2, and Colossians 1:16). Rather, Jesus "could not" do miracles there in the sense that He WOULD NOT do so in view of the pervasive unbelief in that city.

Miracles serve a far greater purpose, from the divine perspective, than just providing a raw display of power. Indeed, Jesus' miraculous deeds are often called "signs" in the New Testament because they serve to signify His identity as the Messiah. Since the people of Nazareth had already made up their minds against Jesus, and had provided more than ample evidence of their lack of faith in Him, Jesus chose not to engage in miraculous acts there except for a few healings of sick people. He refused to bestow miraculous deeds on a city that had rejected the miraculous Messiah. Unbelief excluded the people of Nazareth from the dynamic disclosure of God's grace that others had experienced.

Because of Nazareth's rejection of the person and message of Jesus Christ, He went on to other cities that did respond to and receive Him. We have no evidence that Jesus ever again returned to Nazareth.

Right before me was the message that the universe is always with me, even when I think I am alone. I started writing all my clues to concoct my plan. It was a little thrilling and exhilarating. Clues are interspersed within all things around us. Read all the clues and see where the messages came from.

CLUES

- I reminded myself . . . from past chapters, I made the analogy this book is like the game of clue!
- I listened to Charlie Thweatt in the morning and one of his songs reminded me no one's alone . . . we are all divine
- The Empress card is about Mother Earth, helping and healing . . . that was me since I am Vanaja Ananda . . . blissful Goddess of the Forest
- The Emperor card is Dheera who is a teacher and very courageous . . . his one text to me a few days ago was "I am saved." . . . interpretation . . . I am enlightened

- Shamadu broke up with his girlfriend and the last thing she said was that you and Vanaja should go on a retreat. Heidi said Paul wanted to buy me an airplane ticket to India . . . it meant we were heading to India
- Michele said John thinks you are over the edge. She is sick last night, but says she felt a lot better during our conversation. She asks to see book at least 3 times within past 2 days . . . interpretation John and Duane want insanity evidence
- On February 28th, Swamiji's discourse was about hormones being responsible for our actions . . . I expected to be absolved that night . . . he was telling me the mission wasn't over
- Paul's story about demons had MaryAnn thinking I was taken over by demons . . . demons are just our thoughts in our subconscious
- Swamiji spoke about people who have courage and work even without an organization are liberated . . . I must lead by myself because there is no organization backing me up
- Vanaja jokes about paddy wagon and men in white over the weekend . . . people are thinking I am crazy
- Lena said no matter what you do, I don't care. I love you so much . . . she is over her anger
- Vanaja writes a text to Raquel and uses the word miracle . . . a miracle is about to come
- When I went to the bank to cash Kyle's check, my password wouldn't work which was strange since it has been my password for years . . . reminded me facebook password didn't work to link to twitter . . . need to use twitter later
- Disconnected from gmail . . . universe knew I was irritating people . . . however I Am Enlightened facebook worked for messages
- People went on a new site and were no longer on I Am Enlightened . . . Archanaa already invited me as a friend on the new site . . . easy switch over

Vanaja Ananda MA; MS

- Alexandra sent me a message on facebook . . . when you whisper people listen, but when you shout with Capitals people ignore . . . tone down my messages

- I stayed on spiritual singles because I only met two people through that site. One helped me with The Rhythm of Peace Festival and I am friends with the other. I always check who views my profile because you never know. A man called honest soul looked nice, but I was going to delete him. However, I couldn't delete him so I looked at the profile. Carl Jung was in his profile! His profile sounded perfect as well and it was a message from Swamiji that we will be together.

- I Googled Carl Jung and read about "The Red Book." It was 100 year old book that was published in 2009 by heirs. The reason for its secrecy was disclosed in the article . . . in a quote from Carl . . . "to the superficial observer, it will appear like madness." . . . this told me my findings were similar to a brilliant psychologist who delved into the subconscious mind

- MaryAnn called and told me she got a trident tattoo . . . the trident symbolized knowledge, desire and implementation . . . the drum referred to allowing the holy scripture to guide us . . . the cobra's head meant the ego has been Mastered . . . I knew this from my Siddha Yogi class

- Heidi asked what color comes to my mind when I think of peace . . . immediately I said blue . . . she asked what shade . . . I said like the ocean . . . I put Kristin Hoffman Song for the Ocean on the site

- Michele asked what charity I would give money to on the site . . . I said something with orphans . . . she said Train guitar player was an orphan she thinks

- Train lead guitar player has a Dragon and Tiger tattoo . . . Year of Dragon means power, creativity, excitement, intensity and unpredictability . . . Year of Tiger means radical change and growth

- Swamiji said always live in uncertainty

- Shamadu asked me what letters I was on Meyer Briggs . . . I took test . . . ENFP . . . Champion
- Heidi had a message from India . . . it said tell her to become financially independent . . . meaning book was success
- Pop up of Eckhart Tolle . . . reminded me he sat on a park bench for 2 years before writing "The Power of Now"
- Vanaja says I make political and media noise and a bill was fast tracked through the legislation . . . message to be released about NESARA . . . need media involvement
- Poem about patience and space . . . do it slowly and methodically . . . send messages out incrementally

Once I wrote out this list, I decided what information I was going to post on the site and the exact times they were going to be released.

10AM	Song For The Ocean with message about saving our environment
12PM	Carl Jung "The Red Book"—author explanation
12:30PM	Carl Jung—article from New York Times
1PM	Jesus and Nazareth
2PM	Drunvalo Melchezidek & Mayan Calendar video
3:15PM	Swamiji's 2012 Happenings
5PM	Awakening the Planetary Mind—Why All the End of the World Fears? Could it be that Something GOOD is Coming?
6PM	TONIGHT AT 11:11PM . . . WORLDWIDE NEWS BREAKING STORY . . . THE END OF THE WORLD AS WE KNOW IT . . . 1st LETTER IS BELOW . . . READ THE SECOND LETTER FROM THE ASHTAR COMMAND

<table>
<tr><td></td><td>http://www.facebook.com/
MakeYourDreamsReality#!/
MakeYourDreamsReality</td></tr>
<tr><td>6:39PM</td><td>Link to Brad Yates to Release Fear and Worry</td></tr>
<tr><td>11:11PM</td><td>The Messages Were Released . . . Shown Below</td></tr>
</table>

This forwarded Channeling is a very clear & powerful Channeling, which Greg Gile's own contacts in the Galactic Federation of Light have Confirmed of it's very clear and direct focus on what is to very soon occur; of first the mass public arrests, which will then be followed by all those other many long awaited events; NESARA & Disclosure, etc.

Also the second forwarded e-mail, of the—as of a few days ago—over 39 "resignations/quitting/removing" of these first of many corrupt financial and political figures to be forced to step down/leave their positions of power, is the beginning of the initial process of their public arrests.

Perhaps the most "telling" of who is actually forcing these corrupt individuals to face their inevitable punishments, was what the corrupt Australian foreign minister (#39 on this list, which is growing longer & longer) stated, that he blames his resignation/leaving/quitting on *"faceless men"!* I think it is pretty OBVIOUS who he is actually referring to.

Message from the Ashtar Command

As channeled through Greg Giles

February 22, 2012
http://www.ascensionearth2012.blogspot.com/2012/02/message-from-ashtar-command-22212.html

Care is called for at this time as we proceed with the many plans to free your world from your oppressors. The speed at which these events proceed is not important at this time, although we do strive to maintain forward momentum as we push ahead with the many scheduled phases of this, as well as other aspects of the overall plan.

We see we remain on schedule, and we also foresee no delays to this operation. Remain ever patient as you will experience the fruition of this plan, as we will not permit any obstacles to stand in our way.

Many of you are waiting to see action, and it is action you shall see. By now many of you know what is asked of you, but these tasks do bear repeating. Please look after your fellow human family members as many may experience fear and confusion upon seeing so many political and financial figures taken into custody simultaneously and also in rapid succession. The arrests will climb high into your political arenas, and it is here where we foresee the bulk of those who fear suffering a greater emotional toll.

No one and no office within your world governments are off-limits, and legal indictments have already been prepared against some of your most powerful political figures. They will be taken into custody just as anyone who commits a crime against another has in your legal systems, and they will enjoy no luxuries due to their alleged stature or wealth.

They will be removed from their offices and positions within your governments and financial systems and will be arraigned in a court of law at which time the charges against them will be made known to them and to the public as well. You are the victims in these cases, and therefore you will be kept abreast each and every step of the way throughout these prosecutions.

We ask you to assist to spread the news of these pending arrests as to strengthen the impact of what they will mean to the people of your world. It is not overestimating these connected events when declaring humanity will finally be free from the tyrannical rule of those who have oppressed you for so very long.

We see this day as your true Independence Day, and we see this day replacing in stature many of your current holidays which may have little to do with important matters of your world. This day will be remembered and celebrated by all throughout your world no matter one's nationality or religious background, making this a truly global holiday celebration.

Many of you are impatient at this time awaiting action, and we say to you action is what you will see. You will not be let down in this regard, as nothing can or will delay these proceedings any longer. We see a date when you can begin to witness these events for yourself, and on this day this is what you will see. Get ready, as this day is not far off.

"What then?" many of you are asking. Upon these arrests we, along with our allies, will begin the next phase of the overall operation which is to make our presence known to all of your planet who will not turn a blind eye to us.

We have a very meticulous plan that we see successfully reaching its desired outcome, and upon our readings that a suitable number of you understand who we are and why we are here, we will immediately proceed with the next phase of the operation which is the landings of many of our ships and personnel that will interface with you, the people of Earth.

These introductions are necessary as many projects must get underway and it is you that will be undertaking them, with our assistance. These projects must be completed according to a restrictive time schedule, so as you can see we must begin these series of events as soon as is possible.

Remain vigilant, for these arrests will be the catalyst for the many events to quickly follow. There will not be long delays between each successive project, as once the Cabal is obliterated there will never be a reason for us to slow our progress in any way. You will witness a meticulously laid plan unfolding with precision each day throughout the rest of this year leading up to your ascension, and it is your ascension that necessitates the undertaking of many of these projects.

Many of you will be taking a hands-on approach to many of these projects, and we look forward to working with you in the near days ahead. There is much to do and as we said little time to do it, so prepare yourselves for your new careers with us, the Ashtar Command. We have been journeying throughout this universe on missions of peace and liberation for many eons, and through our travels and work we have enlisted many beings from throughout the cosmos who share our passion to assist worlds in their times of need.

Not all of our crewmembers and officers are of the humanlike species, and many of you will soon be meeting many different beings from many different star systems. Some of these beings will appear quite different to you and even sometimes what you have least imagined. We say to you that all the members of the Ashtar Command are ascended beings, which is only accomplished through love and spiritual understanding.

There is never a reason for you to be fearful or concerned with your safety when interacting with any of these beings, and you will find that many different beings interact not only professionally, but socially as well, and many close friends have been made throughout our command.

Vanaja Ananda, MA, MS

We look forward to enlisting humans from your planet to join us as new recruits ready to begin your new careers that many of you may find quite satisfying in so many different areas. We also look forward to welcoming back some of our crewmembers who have incarnated into the physical to carry out their duties as our agents in the field.

Your positions and stations await your return, and your careers will pick up just where they left off no matter how long it is that you have been gone.

The Ashtar Command plans to see humanity's ascension through, and remain here with you for a time afterwards ensuring the safety and well-being of the newly ascended human. Upon the decision that our work here is done we will move on as there are many other worlds that can benefit from our assistance.

We will never be far from you, and possess the means to travel back to these universal coordinates in quick time. Many of you who will become members of our team will continue to call this planet your home and you will have the opportunity to travel back here for visits and rest and relaxation.

You will also have the ability to visit many other planets throughout this universe with your fellow crewmembers, and we feel you may enjoy these trips very much as well. There exists such a blessing a variety throughout this universe and there is something for everyone no matter what your particular tastes may be. There are sandy beaches and snowy mountains and everything in between. There are scarcely populated locales as well as bustling communities if this better suits your liking. Your adventure will only be beginning once we make contact with you as a new life and a new career awaits you.

This moment is just up ahead as events are moments away from unfolding in blissful excitement. Your buildup of anticipation has been long, and this also suits a very important purpose. All has been for a reason, and we see many of you understand this clearly. Your experience every step of the way has been carefully designed and implemented, and this is just as true for these last years and months as it ever was. As a matter of fact, your recent history has been more meticulously orchestrated than any other time in your history. Nothing has been left to chance, and nothing about your experience has been overlooked.

Some of you may feel certain aspects of your recent experience has been nothing more than a waiting game, but we assure you that it is we who have been waiting on you. As we have often made very clear, it is your world and it is up to you. We are assisting, this is all we have been permitted to do and we cannot overstep our bounds. We await you to reach certain levels of understanding and consciousness, and we also await certain actions to be undertaken by you. Upon the reaching of these milestones, we can then assist you to reach another.

At this present time we are focused on the arrests of the men and women of the criminal Cabal and we await the actions of our human Earth allies in the field. Again, you're not waiting on us or our signal that it is time to proceed.

This signal has been given by all parties involved, terrestrial, as well as extraterrestrial, and we see the successful implementation of this carefully laid plan at any moment. We hope you enjoy this moment, you assuredly earned it, and as we have said, this event is merely the beginning as the fireworks will continue unrelenting for many months to come.

Vanaja Ananda MA; MS

Your world will experience wonderful advancements throughout this period in your history and your world today will barely resemble your new Galactic society we will begin to create together. This would surely be a wonderful and exciting time to be here, and this is why many of you chose to be here today.

You felt it was worth all what you knew you would have to endure to reach this point, and yet you made the decision without hesitation. This is what awaits you dear ones.

It is quite appropriate for you to display a childlike expectation of excitement, as this will all be new to you and you have not experienced anything new such as this since you were a child. Feel free to enjoy this moment and celebrate it, for it has taken you many long years to get here and you have earned every part of it.

Enjoy this moment, for it is your moment, as each and every one of you has contributed to your journey in one way or another. Your achievement has truly been a team effort, and all deserve to take part in your celebration.

We are your Family of Light from the stars.

My Favorite Martian is coming! Boy! I used to watch a lot of television! We are so blessed to be on this planet in 2012. I still can't believe I was the one who let everyone know about the transformation soon to occur to all of humanity! As of this morning, there were 39 people who liked the site. I really haven't looked all day. I sent messages to ABC-TV, NBC-TV, CBS-TV, CNN, Fox News and more. I also linked to twitter, but for some reason I was suspended; they thought I was a scammer because I was sending messages too fast . . . patience my dear. One day I will totally understand the word patient. I don't think any of the broadcast stations cared. Maybe when it actually happens, it will be worldwide news. Who could figure?

The End

PART 11

The Suspense Is Killing Me!

The Tarot Cards

Last night after watching Swamiji's discourse I was extremely disheartened. He discredited everything I said. I didn't blame him because I knew it was something I had to figure out. I asked Archangel Raziel to give me the hidden message. I woke up knowing what I needed to do. Once again, it was time for clues which I will reference in a moment.

Right now, I am totally exhausted because I had to do everything by myself; not one person helped me including Shamadu. I know the mission is a success because after I finished with my postings today, I asked the Tarot cards if I was finally done. Six cards fell out of Heidi's deck and I had my answer.

- Five of Swords—people were gossiping maliciously . . . I was already aware of this and I know when people are talking about one individual, that energy connects with the universe . . . the cosmos doesn't know if it is good or bad . . . so I guess gossip helped me in this case . . . this card also said I had a fear of defeat which definitely crossed my mind . . . I was in panic actually but then released it easily

- Ten of Wands—carrying a huge load . . . I was taking full responsibility . . . not one person was supporting me . . . only the divine . . . and they couldn't do the human work
- Nine of Cups—get what you want internally and externally
- Knight of Wands—traveling is coming quickly
- The Tower—healing, restorative and renovation . . . it also said released from bondage . . . old mental patterns are released . . . shocking enlightenment
- Page of Wands—being in the limelight . . . great news

As you can see, everything turns out fantastic. However, it is appalling to believe that people find it easier to brand someone as insane rather than understanding her desire is to help the planet. Why are people's first reactions to gossip? Why do people want to condemn and not see the truth right in front of them? Why do people want to live in an illusion? I truly hope you now understand the importance of love. First, you must love yourself and then you could love others. Otherwise, you are creating more negative mental patterns for your loved ones. If I wasn't a pure channel for divine energy, I don't know what may have happened to me. Maybe I would be sitting on a bench like Eckhart Tolle for 2 years. Or maybe I would be starring in "The One Who Flew Over The Cuckoos Nest."

While I always love to joke, this is very serious.

What if I didn't have Swamiji and all the other divine beings? What would have happened in 2012 to our society? The thought scares me, so I choose not to focus on it. Please release your fear and greed so you could luxuriate in the wonders of our planet.

I believe this was a great lesson for all of humanity. It is time to move into the 4th dimension and we are all going to blossom into loving and compassionate beings. Our innocence will be back and we could do and be whatever we want. It is such a beautiful time and I am thrilled you are all going to be successful in every way. You all deserve it because even though you didn't believe at first, you released your fear and helped our planet. You are all powerful especially when joined together. Thank you for saving our fabulous planet!

Here is a list of today's clues for all you spies out there.

Vanaja Ananda MA; MS

- Kinder Care was the first thing on the internet today so I thought it meant I would soon be working for Knowledge Universe. When I was ready to send the two last postings on facebook, I tried to find Mike Milken. I had to google him and I was shocked. Milken was known as the "Junk Bond King" because of Wall Street Greed. He was indicted years ago, but only served for 2 years.

- Last night, Swamiji said he didn't want marriage or kids. At first I thought I was still in fantasy, but I knew all my chakras were balanced except throat chakra . . . this chakra deals with expressing oneself and I certainly have no trouble with that now. Also, Swamiji already gave a couple a baby and the husband said he didn't want more kids. So, Swamiji said give him to me . . . this was a past discourse. I knew there was unfinished work.

- Michele said read Doreen Virtue and Karen Atkins bios because they believe in angels. When I read them, I had the idea to facebook all the authors, media and more instead of twitter.

- My friend Dave came for a healing a couple of weeks ago. After the healing, we listened to a radio program about Project Pegasus. I never listened to the entire program so I woke up feeling I had to listen because it was about Clinton, both Bushes and Obama time traveling in the US defense community . . . the notice that went out 2 days ago was about our political system.

- When I checked emails on google today . . . remember I was suspended from sending . . . there was a message from Dave and I knew this message needed to go to the public today. It was about arresting Worldwide leaders, but that could only be accomplished when everyone sent the message to friends and families.

- Swamiji discredited Freud and Jung last night . . . he never defames specific people so it was surprising . . . also he knew Jung separated from Freud so they weren't linked together . . . he also knew "The Red Book" was billed as the most influential unpublished book in the history of psychology . . . I knew it was a message to me that I had more to do. I felt like Jack in the TV show "24."

- Text from Shamadu last night and he always talks in semantics so it is a puzzle in itself . . . "Passion of Christ carrying sword to be crucified"—he was doing it to help humanity . . . "how much divine LORD God loves us"—God is with me . . . "Have you experienced terror-ific sadness of this movie"—I was living it unfortunately . . . "did u die ur hair blond"— telling me I am transforming . . . "ur brain must still be tired from all the intellectual and emotional drama leading up to last night"—reminding me its an illusion . . . "painful to watch, but necessary to grasp Jesus's mission and sacrificial love of mankind"

- Last night, March 3rd (India time), Swamiji released his new book, Jeevan Mukti . . . Jeevan Mukti means enlightenment

- Paul texts thinking I am off facebook and email . . . I told him I had a hotmail account and I was on facebook . . . after this I felt the need to send messages to other sources on facebook

- Dheera sent email at 6AM . . . "how r u . . . I am blissful and great . . . how is book project coming along" . . . reminded me to send my book to Louise Hay . . . texted Paul to send letter and passages . . . he said he would do it

- Padmaja email . . . "congrats Vanaja . . . best wishes to you . . . supporting all ur efforts in silence . . . adding energy to your asks . . . I ask the divine consciousness to support you to fulfill ur desires and goals . . . be it . . . om!" . . . she was already telling me I was successful

- Josephine email . . . "I want to thank u for Dreams of Reality sessions . . . . I truly appreciated the structure of each session and of course the meditations . . .

regarding the dynamics . . . some of which were great and some of which were not so great . . . it was all grist for my processing mill . . . I learned some deep lessons" . . . I had to be organized and structured . . . use meditation if needed . . . I have strength . . . don't rush because you made mistakes . . . process before you react . . . delve into the subconscious

- Josephine email also said . . . "today reading NYT, you came to mind . . . Lady Gaga has started a new foundation . . . Born Not To Be Bullied . . . she may be the person to talk to regarding curriculum" . . . don't listen to others . . . think back to NYT article on Jung . . . send message to Lady Gaga on facebook
- Email about retreat with Masters . . . thank God
- Autism Finds Inner Voice . . . article linked to my facebook page . . . focus on my inner voice and stop external chatter
- Jacqueline sent an email . . . "Written by a Cop for Safety . . . Tae Kwon Do tip . . . elbow strongest point on body" . . . on Shiva Ratri day I felt burning near my elbow which turned into a rash
- Biryukov email . . . "It's A Small World concert" . . . keep going
- Sophia email from Archanaa . . . "will sail ahead" . . . one of Charley Thweatt's songs about sailing to the divine
- Fred email . . . "I was curious about emails from yesterday and thought that I needed to reach out to u and see how u were doing . . . I hope that all is well for I was concerned for u . . . love u dearly" . . . I pictured Swamiji reaching out to lift me up as in Celine Dion's song
- Shamadu text . . . 'when I checked facebook nothing came up . . . maybe I jumped the starting galacti gun" . . . I put the post up too soon . . . tread carefully

Vanaja Ananda MA, MS

- MaryAnn a few days ago said . . . "why are we the only ones helping," . . . gave me idea to send posts to other groups on facebook

- There were two messages after I finished Tarot Reading and Meditated . . . advertisement said . . . "what if Eckhart Tolle was available right now to support spiritual awakening" . . . I did it!

- I went to close out of hotmail when an email appeared from months ago . . . on it was the song "Dance Me To The End of Love" by Leonard Cohen

I chose the following people to send the last two facebook posts:
Doreen Virtue, Dr. Wayne Dyer, Oprah Winfrey, Jacqui Johnson, Joan Borysenko, Tom Cruise, Angelina Jolie, Brad Pitt, Lady Gaga, Keanu Reeves, Rachael Ray, Louise Hay, Heal Your Life, Hay House Radio, Hay House Writer's Workshop, Dr. Michael Beckwith, Bob Proctor, The Mayan Secret, Eckart Tolle, Tony Robbins, The Living Matrix, Drunvalo Melchizedek, Paris Hilton India, Shakira Loca, Shakira, Metallica, Pitbull, Akon, Celine Dion, CNN Company, CNN International, Drudge Report, Fox News, ABC News, Gay Hendricks, Evolvefest, Galiana Retreat, Kristin Hoffman, the 2 Nithyananda sites and Project Pegasus.
Below are the two posts . . .

Coast-to-Coast AM with George Noory, 11/11/09
Andrew D. Basiago: Project Pegasus . . . Find Out How
Clinton, Bush and Obama Time Traveled . . .
http://www.projectmars.net/

After You Listen To . . .

Coast-to-Coast AM with George Noory, 11/11/09
Andrew D. Basiago: Project Pegasus . . . On This Site
Find Out About Worldwide Political Arrests At . . .
http://www.facebook.com/#!/MakeYourDreamsReality

On the Dreams of Reality site was the beautiful message from the divine . . .

How to do Your Part to Spread the News of the Imminent Arrests of the Criminal Cabal!

Easy Copy & Paste Method! Fun for the Whole Family!
By Greg Giles
March 1, 2012

http://ascensionearth2012.blogspot.com/2012/03/how-to-do-your-part-to-spread-news-of.html

The Galactic Federation of Light has assured us that once a suitable number of our human family understands that the imminent arrests of many members of the criminal Cabal means that humanity will finally be free from the tyrannical rule of our oppressors and from the shackles of poverty and debt, we will bear witness to these events. The Galactic Commands have asked us to do our part and share this information far and wide, and the following announcement has been created to assist us in this task. Please feel free to copy and paste these following words on Facebook and throughout every online social network and in no time we will together accomplish our goal. (*Helpful hint* If you include a photo with this announcement on Facebook, it will not be sent to the 'Facebook Notes' page due to it containing too many words. This is advised as your post will receive more views on Facebook's main page.)

Additional Facebook tip: "Just as a reminder, if you wish to share this far and wide . . . set the Facebook privacy settings to Public for the post you create. On the upper right of the post there is a drop-down menu where you can select that.—Casey"

We Interrupt Your Regularly Scheduled Lives

For A Life Changing Newsflash!

Vanaja Ananda MA, MS

All your life you have waited for the good news, and that day has finally come. Very soon you will witness large-scale mass arrests all over the world of many men and women who you have come to know as the world's political and financial leaders. These arrests will reach high into the U.S. Government and include many members of the financial and banking worlds. Many of these names you will immediately recognize, though some you may not immediately recognize, but all have actively taken part in serious crimes against the people, leaving our nations bankrupt while they looted our hard earned money.

These arrests are groundbreaking, and these arrests are Earth changing. Humanity will finally be free from the tyrannical control of these power-brokers commonly known as the Cabal. These arrests should come as no surprise to many of us as we all know deep down that there is something very wrong with this world, a place where so many go to bed hungry at night while a few others possess not millions or billions, but trillions of dollars, pilfered from the labors of the people.

There has always been enough wealth on this planet to go around, yet these few men and women have been dividing up for themselves virtually all of the wealth of our world, leaving only crumbs for the rest of us to compete over. Upon these arrests, this will now change.

Many new projects will immediately be implemented under the new leadership of men and women of the highest integrity who are committed to restoring our world to the utopia it once was, governed by a constitutional and true democratic process.

There are many men and women dedicated to this cause throughout the US Government, agencies at the Pentagon, militaries, the financial sector, as well as the private business sector who have committed so much of their lives to this effort, and they are so eager to present to humanity our new system of abundance that they have been working so diligently on in secret for years. As part of these proceedings, vast sums of wealth that have been stolen from the people will be redistributed through programs that will benefit greatly every man, woman and child on the planet. No one will be overlooked, and no one will be forgotten.

But there is more.

Upon the arrests of these many members of the criminal Cabal, the second phase of this operation will commence. Today our world is being visited by many spiritually enlightened beings who wish to openly reunite with their ancient family. These spiritually advanced men and women are assisting in the disarmament of the criminal Cabal which has controlled much of the world's military and possessed highly advanced weapons systems.

These advanced ancestors of the human race appear just as we do, although there are other beings that we shall meet as well that do not look like we do. All are ascended spiritual beings who are only here to assist us make the changes we all know deep down inside need to be made. These beings are the original planners of this world, and are the same advanced civilizations that built many of the great archaeological mysteries such as the pyramids in Egypt. They are not strangers to us at all, as we are their ancestors, all of us.

A very important social experiment has been conducted here over many years and each of us has been a part of it. We have been left here, seemingly all alone, to work things out for ourselves. This experiment is now over and it has been a tremendous success. We are now about to reunite with our brothers and sisters from the stars and be welcomed into the greater Galactic Community.

As they are many worlds that go by many names, it is easier to refer to them at this time by the name of their peaceful alliance: The Galactic Federation of Light, although other spiritually advanced organizations are here as well including the Ashtar Command.

Upon these arrests and our reunion with our Star Family, all the problems of our world will be quickly and smoothly brought into the alignment of our new Golden Age society through the leadership of souls of pure hearted intent.

Through a worldwide community effort, all wars, hunger, poverty, illness, and pollution will soon be a thing of the past, as will our lives of daily servitude. Advanced technologies will replace our need to labor our lives away, and everyone will be free to pursue every creative dream they have ever had.

All this will begin with the imminent arrests of the many members of the criminal Cabal, and these arrests will take place as soon as a suitable number of our planet's citizens are aware of what these proceedings will mean for our society.

This is why you are reading these words today, as many members of your human family are doing all they can to share this news with you and do their part to usher in our civilizations new Golden age of peace, freedom, and prosperity for every man, woman and child throughout our world.

Please participate in this great cause by sharing this message on Facebook and other online social networks. This is your chance to really make a difference and be a leader of your fellow man. If we all do our part to spread this news, we will all begin to witness these high profile arrests all around the world, and this will be your sign that everything you just read is true.

Justice is finally being done! Since I never believe in punishment, only consequences, I have had an idea for years. We should put all the corrupt individuals on a deserted island with no means of escaping. They could use their skills to create a civilization on that island. They could choose whether they want to fight and continue being corrupt or if they would prefer to learn how to love and work together. Once a person on the island truly achieves a pure heart, then he or she could be released to explore the rest of the world. Once back in society, they should no longer be judged and be welcomed back with open arms.

We had satsung last night and Swamiji spoke about name and fame. The date is March 4, 2012. He said it was good to have those desires and he even enjoyed being on the top 100 Most Spiritually Influential People list. Then, he said don't expect people to give you praise; just love for the sake of loving. He didn't do a kriya last night either. After satsung, a conversation ensued about demons and the people speaking unequivocally believed demons possessed them or others. I needed to leave the room because I knew they wouldn't believe me if I told them the only demon was buried inside themselves. I went to sleep and asked the divine the lesson I was supposed to learn. Even though I knew I won, it felt anti-climatic.

I woke up with the answer. First, I want to apologize to all the beautiful souls in the world. At times in this book I was reprimanding and blaming you when I should have taken responsibility. I would have deleted those passages, but as you know I can't. I guess it is a good lesson to see I am only human and my first inclination was to blame as well.

I know there was no malicious gossiping occurring. Instead, everyone in the world gathered together in prayer for Vanaja. I could feel the energy. People truly loved me and wanted me to be OK. I was the one who had conflicting thoughts. How could this be real, I thought? What if I am wrong? Why aren't people coming on the site if I am a hero and have power? These questions percolated often the last few days. The answer was in front of me the entire time. I know the power of thoughts. All your thoughts told the universe to concentrate on Vanaja. However, Vanaja was afraid to release the fear of the unknown and she was petrified of name and fame. I even sent the News stations my home address even though I am living at Heidi's because I pictured news cameras at my door. All I need to do is align that thought pattern and there will be a lot of people on that site. That is what I plan to do.

The book I always carried around in my purse was "Heal Your Body." "Heal Your Body" is a compilation of diseases, the probable cause and the new thought pattern. Sound familiar? That is why I only wanted Louise Hay to publish this book and I know when she reads the letter and the beginning passages, she will agree. Heidi had the book "You Can Heal Your Life." I asked the divine to tell me what I am supposed to know about this book. I closed my eyes and opened it up and there before me was the answer. I am writing the paragraph exactly as Louise wrote it.

"So many people want to be rich, and yet they won't accept a compliment. I have known many budding actors and actresses who want to be the stars and yet they cringe when they are paid a compliment. Compliments are gifts of prosperity." I want to thank Louise Hay for this insightful passage. I saw this a week ago, but a click didn't go off until today.

Last night, Anne massaged my shoulders and neck during satsung and she kept saying I was knotted. I went to Louise Hay's book to ascertain the probable cause. Shoulders represent creating a burden out of life by our attitude. I immediately thought of the Tarot card that said I am carrying all the weight on my shoulders; no pun intended. According to Louise, the positive affirmation which I plan to start reciting today is "I choose to allow all my experiences to be joyous and loving." Neck problems referred to stubbornness and inflexibility. That is me in a nutshell. Once I am convinced about something, I stick to it like glue and the only thing that pries it apart is verifiable evidence. I will be reprogramming that as well starting today. "It is with flexibility and ease that I see all sides of an issue. There are endless ways of doing things and seeing things. I am safe."

The message has been there the entire time. I was convinced everyone had to go on that site and that was the only way people would understand the power they possess. Nobody could convince me otherwise even though many tried. The truth is you all showed your power when you all joined in unison in prayer. Thank you so much for having faith and trust in me. I realized people from Bright Beginnings were praying for me. That was indicated by my emails from both Betsy and Fred. I knew the teachers were praying for me. I could feel Kelli and Turin's energy and I also saw pictures of Sandy, Debbie, Denise and Tara. I knew Duane, who wasn't sure if there was a God, was praying for me. I knew Glenn, Karen and Josh were praying. I knew people from the Nithyananda family around the world were praying for me. I also knew Jill was praying for me even though she couldn't call or email because her heart was breaking for her love for me. Archanaa sent me an email yesterday suggesting I do pratysha pada puja and she would pay for it . . . thanks soul sister. I could feel everybody's energy and it was overwhelming. God bless you all! Please don't be offended if I didn't mention your name in this book. You are in my heart and that is all that matters.

I have one more thing to tell you. Here I go with the one more time . . . too funny! Anyway, I realized I am not in love with Swamiji. The love I have for him is so way beyond lust and the love is transmitted to every soul on this planet. Also, I don't want a baby. I already have the two best children a mother could ever hope for. On my vision board, I wrote I want to be married by Swamiji and my lifelong partner has to love Swamiji as much as I do. Even though Hugh Jackman is all over my board, I chose him because he is sizzling hot! I knew I couldn't have him because I would never break up a marriage so it was easy to stay in my fantasy world. However, the person I have always dreamed about is single and although we have never met I feel a strong connection. I adored him from the first time I saw the movie "Speed." Also, I don't think it is a coincidence he was the lead role in the "Matrix." I forgot all about him the past two years because I always thought I wasn't good enough.

A couple of weeks ago Michele mentioned she saw Keanu Reeves in her dream. I immediately thought that message was for me. I told her how I adored him for years. I googled him and read he played in a band, rode motorcycles and more. He sounded like so much fun. Michele told me he might be gay. I forgot about him until yesterday. I posted on his site yesterday and when I saw his profile picture, I couldn't take my eyes off of it. I told myself I loved Swamiji and to stop the nonsense. However, I realized last night that my knight is someone else.

I will know if Keanu is my true prince if he tells me 2 words when I meet him and the words are not I do. Otherwise, it may be someone else. Also, I want to tell Keanu if he is gay, it is fine. It always bothered me that gays and lesbians were treated differently. At one point I thought I was gay because porno movies excited me and it didn't matter what sex. However, when I went to a sex club and actually experienced a woman, it really didn't turn me on. After that, I would lower my eyes and look at women's

Vanaja Ananda MA, MS

neck area; I always wondered why because I knew I definitely wasn't a lesbian. Women would become uncomfortable and covered themselves up. The reason hit me today. I wanted to put myself in a gay person's shoes. It is not fun and it is not fair. People should be able to choose whatever sexual orientation they want as long as their inner being is full of love and compassion. The universe doesn't care about gender so why should we. I hope this paragraph liberates all those beautiful souls who only chose a different way of living. Their love could only benefit the planet and not harm them. Also, I want them to get married and have children if they so desire. I also believe transvestites and cross dressers should be treated with love and respect. We are all unique in our own way and that is what truly makes life fun and interesting!

I want a mutually satisfying relationship emotionally, physically, cognitively, sexually and spiritually. I know I could be with many men, but I have always been a person who prefers one man in my life. I hope that man is Keanu. I wonder if he is a Scorpio because you know what they say about Scorpios.

As for Champ, I want him to be a human because he deserves it. But, to me, my Champ was a Pomeranian. I miss the feel of his fur and his tongue licking my face. I miss him jumping on my lap and humping my arm; yes he was a typical male lol. I miss his beautiful brown eyes staring into mine and him greeting me at the door. Tears come to my eyes just thinking about him.

I decided I love my age! It is only a number so who really cares. I look 35 and act about 25. The other day Paul told me I acted like a 10 year old. Is it my fault he didn't want to play? I plan to be around a long time so I feel more like an infant being reborn on this beautiful planet! Watch Leonard Cohen's video "Dance Me To The End of Love." It personifies true love.

Ever since I saw South Pacific, I have wanted to go to Bora Bora . . . or is there a Bali Hai? Now, I heard they have huts in the middle of the ocean! How cool is that? I believe I will be with the "Happy Talk People" very soon. Here are the beginning lyrics from the song. Happy, happy, happy, happy talk . . . . talk about things you'd like to do . . . you gotta have a dream . . . if you don't have a dream . . . how you gonna have a dream come true?

I want to thank Swamiji and all of the divine for always being there for me. You are right! When I fell down, you picked me up and placed me right back up. Many times you carried me because I was simply too tired!

My last wish is for Swamiji's wish to come true. He wants to celebrate December 12, 2012 by having 10,000 people at the Ashram. Everybody start packing . . . December is only 9 months away!

I just had to tell you . . . it is March 6th and Raquel and Ralphie both put the letter on their facebook page! You are both awesome!

Vanaja Ananda MA; MS

I Am Trapped

Today I woke up in sheer agony; that is the only way to describe it. It is March 9th. Yesterday, I was banned from attending satsungs and that is like nailing me to the cross. Satsung is my favorite time because it is when Swamiji sees me through the cameras. I thought the nightmare couldn't possibly be worse, but that is no longer true.

I wanted to end this book on a happy note; that is why there are so many endings. I feel like I am writing a screen play. Producer . . . which ending would you like? The truth is I am trapped. I put myself in this situation, but nonetheless the pain is horrific. Why I choose to suffer when I know the strategies to release or at least subdue the agony always puts me in a quandary? I guess I wanted to write my feelings down on paper so I could remember these dark times. Possibly, this experience is to help you as well, but I am not sure right now.

To reiterate, I asked to be released from every single negative mental pattern so I was a pure vehicle for the divine. I know Swamiji or whoever you consider to be the divine does 50%; the other 50% comes from within and there has to be a deep, intense desire for the pattern to be reprogrammed. I have two negative mental patterns still in my subconscious. I realized name and fame is the surface limiting belief because the pattern is so much deeper. The real pattern is the need for unconditional love.

The truth is no one really believed me; I am talking about people who have known me a long time. However, strangers started believing me and I was able to throw the ball to them and they are now sharing the letter with the world. As I mentioned previously, the outcome is extremely positive. With name and fame, I know people will be professing their love to me once again. I bet some would say they always believed me and others would say they were praying. When push came to shove, there was no one who really stood by me. People are punished in this society for going against the norm. It is just a fact; I should know since I lived through it.

So, now I am trapped. All the cosmos wants me to join them; they want me to be enlightened. In fact, they are doing everything they possibly can to help me. Unfortunately, I don't have the intensity to achieve name and fame or release my fantasy about Swamiji. I am not even sure if this book will be published since I will only allow Hay Publishing to do the honors. Even though I know this book will help thousands and potentially millions of people, I am unable to release the negative mental pattern which will make this book a success.

I am sorry! The problem is I am only human and I always craved unconditional love. I guess I want that even more than helping mankind. It is shocking even for me to see the truth. I am now stuck in a body whose soul only has pure thoughts of love and compassion. I have tried to be angry or vindictive and the emotion is just not there anymore. In fact, last night was our last forum. Earlier in the day, I didn't want to share my power with people who didn't believe me. However, at 7PM, I was on the tele-conference waiting to give the participants their dream and show them the power that exists inside of them. Praying for each other for 21 days allowed each person to obtain their dream.

What do I do now? I am not sure. I have about $120 left so it isn't going to take me very far. I want to be financially stable so I could get my own place. It kills me that the kids are off this week and yet there is no place for them to go other than their dad's. Every time a person called me crazy or didn't believe me, it shattered a part of my soul. Since we are all one, it is to be expected. I will be able to repair that and relatively quickly because I know the techniques. My heart breaks for the victimized person who never met an Avatar and never learned the techniques to help them survive in society. I pray the book reaches those people's hands!

I have become almost a perfect channel for divine energy to flow through and I intend to share that with the world. I am not sure how that will be manifesting. It may be through healings. It may be through motivational speaking and trainings. It may be through the techniques I learn as a Siddha Medicine Doctor. It may just be by hanging around my energy field. It may be all of those combined! All I know, I will not let the people of the world down. I will help them achieve inner peace and higher consciousness. That is my promise.

I just have to add a few more sentences. My friend Jill just sent my letter to someone who knows Marianne Williamson. Maybe this book will be published after all! Either way, it is wonderful to know Jill did that for me!

Vanaja Ananda MA; MS

It's A Happy Ending After All

I endured an enormous amount of suffering yesterday, but that trauma cracked open one of the few seeds that still lay unruptured. I now have the intelligence to discern between illusion and reality. I recognize my intense passion is to help all beings in every dimension. Unconditional love from others is an illusion created by my cunning mind to keep me as a prisoner. Once we love ourselves unconditionally, we don't need anything from the outside world. I am complete and whole by myself. As a result, I offer that love to all beings without expecting anything in return. I do it because I see the divine in every entity. I am fulfilled when I help others appreciate their own divinity as well as all those around them.

I have evolved from a timid and frightened sheep into the lioness or queen of the forest. The lioness protects her babies against all predators. I intend to do that for all of you! When I hear the word forest, I think of the entire planet. Let's walk safely through the magnificent forest and explore the beauty of all who inhabit our earth.

I believe there is a hero in this story and it is not me. The emperor is finally having the courage to put all fear aside for the benefit of all humanity. There is no proof of this yet, but I believe this statement to be true.

After I wrote the passage about Keanu Reeves, I searched google. Within 5 minutes I knew Keanu was married and he is indeed gay. I know Keanu and I will be close friends and I am looking forward to riding on his motorcycle and dancing to the music he plays. In addition, I am looking forward to kissing, cuddling, and holding hands with a man who shares my same passion for humanity. I know making love to him will be amazing!

I guess we will all have to witness what happens to our planet in 2012 and what unfolds in the life of Vanaja Ananda. Since I love surprises, I am as excited as you to find out what lies ahead. I have a feeling it is going to be better than anything I have ever imagined!

THE END! THE END! THE END! THE END! THE END! THE END! THE END! THE END! BUT NOT THE FINAL LOL!

My Great Friend, Nachu

It is April 8th and Easter; it is now 2:45AM and I couldn't sleep. The cosmos wants me to write this, but I really didn't want to until now. How do I start? The trauma that just occurred is so much worse than even

the ostracism that I endured. The ostracism was directed at me, I knew the outcome was positive and I intentionally brought it into my life to release a mental pattern. The pain I am about to explain was the torture I felt as I watched someone who I loved so deeply suffer as I was powerless to do anything else.

I have decided to dedicate "Dreams Are Reality" to my wonderful, dear friend Nachu. He was born February 1, 1994 and his short life ended on planet earth April 6, 2012. Nachu was an inspiration to his family and his friends. Through all his pain and agony, he managed to land a full academic scholarship to the University of Miami. In fact, the day before I arrived at his house, he had a phone interview with this school. That was the day he lost sensation from his belly button down to his feet. The interviewer never even knew he was sick with a terminal illness.

Nachu is a hero! He would talk to his friends about colleges and watch movies with them. He heard about their spring vacation escapades and the senior trip to the Bahamas which began two days after I arrived. He always told them to enjoy their trips and that he would see them when they got back. When his friends would arrive, the first thing he would ask them is if they wanted a drink or food. His charismatic charm attracted people like fireflies. There was never less than 50 people in that household while I was there; they were all there for Saint Nachu. He was the perfect host even though he couldn't move out of bed. He rarely complained and just asked me to move my hands to certain areas of his body to heal. He never uttered a disrespectful word and had difficulty expressing anger. As I mentioned a long time ago, the thought that creates cancer in our body is "not being able to express oneself." The only karma Nachu possessed was directed at himself because even though I begged him to scream and let it all out, he simply couldn't do it.

Here's the story. I called Sona one day because she was on my list to tell people about upcoming events for Swamiji. The minute I spoke to her, I felt a connection. She told me about Nachu and I asked her to send me his picture. Sona also sent me a picture of the entire family. I brought those pictures to Swamiji, Braco, every saint, and every temple. I spoke to the deities, angels, Archangels and every divine being I could think of to help Nachu self heal as well as give his family members the strength to persevere through this hardship.

About one month after our first phone conversation, I met Sona face to face at Kalpaturo where Swamiji gives you anything you want. Sona had a huge picture of Nachu with her and she was the first to go up. Swamiji said he would heal Nachu. I was so relieved, but wondered why he didn't give his blessings which meant it was definitely going to happen. I wasn't sure and was concerned, but I never said anything to Sona.

A few months later, June 2011, Nachu's father died in a motorcycle accident. I couldn't believe it! My heart went out to this family and I felt I knew each one personally, including Nachu's dad, Mohit. I could feel the love generated from that family from miles away. There is no distance between space and time in the cosmos. While I thought I didn't understand what this concept meant, I realized the minute I laid eyes on Nachu, his sisters and Mohit's picture exactly what that phrase meant.

In January 2012, Nachu was in the hospital and he did pradyksha pada puja with Swamiji. I remember Swamiji asking Nachu if he wanted to live; it was shown on en-tv. Nachu told Swamiji he wanted to live over and over again. Swamiji ended the discourse immediately. Sona told me Swamiji told her privately he was going to go inside Nachu and heal him. He offered his blessings. I was so relieved to hear this, but yet I still had doubts. How is it possible for him to go inside and heal him? It sounded way too esoteric! Of course, this was before I took the Siddha Medicine class and found out the Siddhars were able to shrink to a size of an atom and travel through the body. Then a click went off. However, when I first heard this, I was skeptical and at the same time I was convinced Nachu was going to live and a miracle was happening.

Nachu started progressing slowly. He did have setbacks though in between. On March 28th, I received an email from Sona stating that Nachu lost sensation in more than half of his body. I was in a quandary because I was supposed to pick Heidi up at the airport from her trip to Paris on Saturday and it was only Wednesday. I sent an email out to everyone explaining the circumstances, asking them to pray for a miracle and requesting assistance for Heidi's arrival. MaryAnn offered to meet Heidi at the airport so I left early Thursday morning for Maryland.

I knew a miracle was going to happen. I just needed to reprogram Nachu's subconscious. The quickest way to do this was to have positive group thoughts from around the world circulating to the cosmos. I thought this would be easy since helping a boy with cancer is much more important than a book. However, I was totally wrong. I put a post on my facebook wall as well as the 100 top spiritual leaders, spiritual authors and actors. I sent emails to many spiritual groups as well. I was a pro at this since I did it many times before so I was able to do this all on Wednesday, the day before I left. The response was apathetic to say the least. I was shocked, but had no time to write more posts or emails. Here is the post . . .

EMERGENCY! PLEASE READ THE ENTIRE MESSAGE . . .

Nachu is an 18 year old boy with bone cancer. He is currently in Hospice and the prognosis is getting worse every minute. I met his mom, Sona, in person once and we became fast friends. It was as if we knew each other forever. I never met Nachu, but I feel a soul to soul connection with him. Since we are all made of energy and we are all divine, it makes perfect sense.

Nachu is fading fast because his subconscious and conscious are in alignment. Unfortunately, they both believe there is no hope and the message going out to the cosmos is death. God could only do 50% of the work and the person does the other 50%. For a miracle to happen, the person has to have the passion and desire. Right now, Nachu has neither.

I am going to Maryland tomorrow to do everything in my power to help him reprogram his subconscious. However, his conscious still needs to have the passion and desire to survive. I asked Nachu what his dream was and his response was to be happy! Could you believe that is all this 18 year old boy wants! I told him he has to believe he is healed and he said it is too difficult. He told me he needs to see a sign. I told him signs can come through dreams, visions, songs, people, anything . . . . I know this was not good enough for him.

Vanaja Ananda MA; MS

Tears are streaming down my face as I write this because only Nachu can make this miracle happen. The divine is cheering him on, but it is not enough. I thought of a way to give him a sign and I pray this will work.

I know the power of group prayer. I am asking each one of you to pray for Nachu and share this post. It will be on the Vanaja Ananda page. It will be the first post. Please tell Nachu you are praying for him. I plan to be in his room 24/7. I will let him know who is praying for him everyday. I believe this will be a sign to show him people love him and want him to fulfill his mission on this planet. His happiness will radiate to 1000's. It is important we all use the same prayer. It is below.

THIS IS THE PRAYER . . . . Thank you for all the blessings and abundance in my life. Please allow Nachu to recognize his strength and his ability to self-heal. Give Nachu the passion and intensity to fulfill his dream of happiness and enjoying every moment of every day. Every cell in Nachu's body is enjoying vibrant health. Nachu is a blessing to all of humanity and we thank you (God, cosmos, universe, Jesus, Buddha, Swamiji, source or anything you want to call the divine) for bringing Nachu to our planet. We know Nachu will be bringing love, compassion, bliss and healing to mankind!

Thank you for sharing this letter with the world and showing Nachu you care about his existence. Sona told me his name means overcoming death so I believe your prayers will help him live up to his name. God bless you all!

Vanaja

When I arrived at Sona's house, I immediately went to Nachu and told him to make a wish on the padukas. There were about 50 people in the house and I felt the negativity throughout the house. I was concerned. About an hour after healings with Nachu, I told the household about Brad Yates and asked if they would do EFT tapping because the energy will transmit to Nachu. His friends and family members agreed and we all tapped to Vibrant Health. Some of the kids were rolling their eyes during the exercise so I felt compelled to offer a lecture on the virtues of tapping and how it will benefit them. Even though everyone applauded after my speech, Nachu was embarrassed and so I decided to tread lightly for his sake.

I needed the atmosphere positive with thoughts of miracles so I asked Sona to tape a sign on the front door. The sign said "leave your shoes and mind here; miracles happen here!" Every morning I would do puja to the padukas and we put the padukas in the doorway and asked everyone to touch them and say "thank you God for Nachu's miracle. The house became more joyful and Nachu was believing in miracles. People were smiling and laughing around Nachu. Friends were staying until 11PM to 11:30PM so there was no way to watch Swamiji. I thought having friends around was even more important than Swamiji. When his friends left every evening, his sisters, mom, Ravi and cousin would gather around Nachu's bed for an hour and hold his hand or rub his arm. Afterwards, we would do a couple of meditations. If he slept, it was even better because then the words in the meditation were penetrating to his inner being.

His friends were so supportive and fun. I enjoyed them tremendously. We would talk while I was doing my healings with Nachu. His family members were incredible and I could see why Nachu chose to be born into this family; I am talking about extended family members as well including grandparents, cousins, aunts, uncles and more.

I believe it was Monday when Nachu started experiencing chest constrictions and difficulty breathing. Immediately, I knew he needed to express himself. I told him to repeat after me. "I am angry. I am furious. This disease is unfair. I am magnificent. I am powerful. I am strong. I am courageous. I am God . . . . and so on and so forth." His breathing went back to what was considered normal for him. So, there was validity to this thought pattern after all.

I knew Nachu needed to express himself so the cancer would leave permanently. He agreed to do an exercise with me. He was going to dictate and I would write whatever he needed to say to anybody in his family, including his deceased father. It was an emotional day, but he did it. He was able to express anger and resentment that had been buried for a long time. He shed tears and he told me his wish for his family. I already knew his wish for himself was to be happy and pain free. Once he was done with the last person he needed to express something to, we gathered the family together for a burning ceremony. We ripped to shreds all the written pages and burned it so the ashes would go up to the heavens and never torment him again. I told him now his healing would probably take 21 days and he told me he could do it sooner!

Almost immediately after this ceremony, he asked his family to put on "The Secret." I watched him as he absorbed every word uttered by these visionaries. I forgot to mention Nachu was brilliant with a vocabulary most people would never achieve even if they lived to 100! He was a leader in every sense of the word! I was 100% sure he was going to live and help mankind in 2012. Every core of my being believed he was going to help teens and patients with cancer. After all, he was Nachiketa which means overcoming death. If you read the story in the Upanishads, Nachiketa goes to death's door before he was called so nobody was there to greet him. He waited 3 days. When Yaman, the God of death, finally arrives, he offers Nachiketa 3 boons or miracles and Nachiketa goes back to earth.

He took a day of rest from his friends and processed everything. That night, Nachu, his grandpa and I watched Swamiji. Nachu said the energy was intense and he loved it. The next day, Wednesday, he looked great. A lot of friends came over and they started watching "The Devil's Advocate." I always encouraged comedies, however he and his friends loved blood and guts movies so I was so happy this movie at least wasn't filled with violence; it also had my favorite star in it. Halfway through the movie, Nachu's lip was becoming numb so I did some healing around his jaw area. Soon after, his jaw and teeth were aching and it was climbing to excruciating 10 out of 10 levels. All the kids went home. Nachu's pain was escalating and I knew if he screamed, it would be alleviated. I tried to get him to scream. I let out a blood curdling scream to show him what to do. However, that backfired because not only didn't he scream, but all the relatives were upset with me, especially his grandma. I came up with another plan. During the exercise a couple of days before, we spoke to his inner child. I thought we could do that again and ask his inner child to scream. He just told me he was too tired and wanted to be put to sleep. I would have pushed it, but I knew the relatives would pounce on me so I sat around the bed with all the family members watching him in silence. I felt totally powerless.

I told Nachu I would go with him to Hospice and I had every intention of going. I grabbed my computer so I had the meditations we needed. They only allowed one person on the ambulance and of course that was Sona. I thought I could go with someone else, but they drove off so fast without me. Then Gauri, Nachu's sister was going to take me, but one of the other relatives forbid her from taking me. I didn't want to cause the family any more anxiety, so I decided to meditate and keep the house positive. I knew while he was at Hospice, all thoughts would be negative. I figured the minute he came home, I would change that mood around once again.

On Thursday, I was told the medicine is working and Nachu would be home at 2PM the next day. I was so excited. I meditated, meditated and meditated some more preparing my body for his return. On Friday morning, I didn't want to wake up at 4:30AM and so I didn't start puja till 5:30AM. I woke up with an unsettling feeling that I couldn't shake. This was the day Nachu was coming home, but something was wrong. I found out a couple of hours later that Nachu wasn't coming home. I still believed on a conscious level that Nachu was going to live. However, my subconscious knew the truth and probably revealed it to me while I slept and that is why I was unhappy when I woke up.

When I heard Nachu wasn't coming home, I went into a panic. I sent an email to everybody begging them to write a message to Nachu on the Caring Bridge guestbook. I knew that would be the only way to counteract the negativity by about 100 people. I needed more than 100 people writing and thanking God for Nachu's miracle. I plastered the email on all 3 of my facebook sites. Here is what it said . . .

Please read below and if there was ever a time in your life that you honestly loved me, please fulfill my wish. I have no time to go on facebook or email. In fact, right now I abhor these two vehicles of communication. When Nachu is here, I am by his side every minute except for bathroom breaks and I eat once a day. We start after I am done with puja and meditation and we are up until 1:30AM every morning. That is why there are no new posts on facebook or email until yesterday when he wasn't here. This time I need your prayers for me!

I HAVE LOST MY FAITH IN THE GOODNESS OF HUMANITY! I AM BEGGING YOU TO HELP ME SO I COULD HELP A PERSON I LOVE SO MUCH! Nachu comes home at 2PM today. For the last two days, I

Vanaja Ananda MA; MS

have been meditating every minute that I have been awake and praying to the divine to help me restore my faith in humanity. So far, I am still angry at the injustices society has placed upon an innocent being whose sole purpose was to bring love, peace and compassion to this planet. I wanted to help you recognize the amazing changes our planet was experiencing in 2012 which is going to bring us to the fourth and fifth dimension, yet you would rather judge than listen. I may be able to understand you live in constant fear and this happening is way beyond anybody's logic. However, what I don't understand is how humanity doesn't want to help an 18 year old boy with cancer by writing on his Caring Bridge site. That would take about 5 minutes of your time! What has the human race come to? I am finding it difficult to forgive humanity right now. I need to know that there is a chance for humanity. I need a sign and that sign would be for people to write to a boy who I didn't know in person until last week, but yet I love beyond belief. Please let me continue to bring him thoughts of love within my healing powers instead of anger and disappointment. While everyone has my unconditional love, my faith is shattered. Please help me restore it so Nachu could fulfill his mission on earth. All the angels, Archangels, Masters, Ascended Masters and saints have shown me enough clues to know that Nachu survives. I want him to believe in the goodness of mankind and I don't want any of my feelings entering his bio-memory! http://www.caringbridge.org/visit/nachubhatagnar

And this is written on his caring bridge site. Right now, I don't have internet connection so I am missing the first paragraph, but as soon as I do I will paste it here . . .

The first time I spoke to Sona, Nachu's mom, was via telephone. She told me about Nachu's bout with cancer over a year ago. I started praying for him immediately. I brought his picture to a variety of saints and I also brought his entire families' photos with me. I prayed a miracle would happen and that his family would be able to endure the trauma involved with this sickness.

The minute I met Nachu, I felt like I have known him my entire life. I believe it is a soul to soul connection and I love him so much. Nachu is the epitome of a saint himself. He is always kind, sweet, loyal and honest. When I arrived at his house last Thursday, Nachu was surrounded by about 50 people. His friends and relatives are phenomenal and they do everything in their power to make Nachu comfortable every moment of every day. Everybody who comes in contact with Nachu loves him. His personality is amazing and he smiles often even though he deals with pain. He loves helping others and this trait is revealed in every action he performs.

I know Nachu is going to survive this terrible ordeal. There have been so many signs from Archangels, Angels, Ascended Masters, Avatars and all divine beings that Nachu has a huge mission to fulfill on this planet. 2012 is the year of transformation and Nachu has power, creativity and strength beyond belief. He is a blessing to mankind.

Two days ago before the excruciating pain in his jaw commenced and he was rushed to the Hospice Hospital, Nachu said he wanted to expedite his healing. I told him he will probably heal himself in 21 days and he told me he could do it sooner. It is now day 4. Please help me show Nachu the strength he possesses inside of him by writing him a message in his guestbook and choosing a prayer from below. Group prayer is a message to the divine that we are working together with the sole purpose of offering love for another being. When pure love is eminent, the cosmos will move mountains to fulfill our wishes He is almost over the hurdle and the remainder of the race will be much easier. Help him climb over the top by showing

Vanaja Ananda MA, MS

him you care even if you don't know him. We are all one and love is the key.

Please believe that miracles do happen and they are happening right now. Please say "THANK YOU GOD FOR NACHU'S MIRACLE AND SPEEDY RECOVERY" every time you think of Nachu.

There is another prayer you may like better. A few days ago, Nachu and I were doing an exercise that enabled him to express himself. The belief in our subconscious related to cancer is not being able to express oneself. The first person Nachu spoke about was his grandma who he called Dadi. He adored his grandma and he mentioned the perfect sign for him would be to see his Dadi in his dream. So here is another prayer "THANK YOU GOD FOR ALLOWING NACHU TO SEE HIS DADI IN HIS DREAMS."

Thank you everyone for taking the time to write a special message to Nachu. This will be a keepsake for him for the rest of his life and he has a long life ahead of him on planet earth. I know he will be an inspiration to teens as well as patients with cancer! His prom is a month away; we would love to attach a picture of Nachu and his date to show you that your wonderful prayers and positive thoughts worked. God bless you all!

All day long I meditated to the miracle prayer which was given to me a couple of weeks ago. Here is the website and you will absolutely love it. It is from the Jewish tradition and is extremely powerful. http://wwww.trypbro.com/TYBRO/The.Miracle.Prayer.html?utm.source=EliteEmail&utm.campaign=Tenth%20Anniversary&utm.medium=email

At around 6PM, I decided to do some tapping. Sona kept telling me the doctor said Nachu was dying, but consciously I still believed a miracle was coming. I thought maybe he would die and be reborn; many people have had near death experiences. Since it was Good Friday, I thought Nachu might die, but he would be resurrected today on Easter. Every time I checked Caring Bridge, there were less than a dozen messages. I was starting to feel defeated.

I chose Brad Yates Fear and Panic video to tap to. I tapped non stop for an hour using Nachu's name in place of my own. I then changed to Brad Yates Some Things Are Out of My Control. I did this for a half hour. I finally ended with Brad Yates Surrendering to God. I think at that point I knew the truth because he says even death in that video. I believe that was the first time reality set in on a conscious level, but still I chose to deny it. I still believed miracles could happen. What I didn't realize is that Nachu wanted to die and everybody was praying for his death as well. One person believing in a miracle simply wasn't enough.

After tapping, I felt much more relaxed and went back to the miracle prayer, but this time I prayed for Nachu to see his Dadi. I still thought he would see her in his dreams, not death. In fact, there was a live meditation with Jacqui at 11PM and she was channeling Serapis Bey who helps with regeneration and resurrection. I knew once we made it to midnight, Nachu would be fine. We had to get through Good Friday. Jacqui started the meditation at 11:30PM because she was explaining who Serapis Bey was. At 11:36PM the phone rang and I knew at that point I lost. Nachu was dead and nothing I could do would bring him back.

When Nachu's grandpa told me, I was in a state of shock and had no reaction. All of a sudden, I wanted to go home. I didn't want to be there one more minute because I couldn't stand the pain. I packed as quickly as I could and was about to go, but Nachu's grandparents begged me to leave in the morning. I left early because I couldn't face anyone. I told everyone a miracle was going to happen and it didn't. I got everyone's hopes up and then allowed them to come crashing down. I loved this family and yet I took them on an emotional roller coaster. I am not sure I could forgive myself for this. Sona said I helped their family, but I don't feel like I did.

Earlier tonight I fell asleep and I saw Swamiji. He held me in his arms and I cried uncontrollably. Then Nachu came and we hugged each other. Swamiji's form expanded and he held each of us securely. Then came a lady with long white hair and Mohit. They both hugged Nachu and the four of us sat on Swamiji's lap while his arms surrounded us. I know the lady was Dadi. Dadi, Nachu and Mohit were laughing and so happy; I was still crying. They jumped off of Swamiji's lap and holding hands floated backwards into space. I cried some more while Swamiji held me and then I woke up. I know Nachu is extremely happy, free from pain and disease;

he is now with other loved ones from his family and they are all guardian angels for his family on earth.

There are many heroes in this ordeal. Of course, it goes without saying that Saint Nachu is the number one hero! But, there are others too. His mom, Sona stood strong for the entire family and friends. She would hug every one of Nachu's friends and make sure there was a ton of food for her guests. She would sleep about 2 hours each night and spend the rest of the time in Nachu's presence. When any of Nachu's friends shed a tear, she would offer them words of solace. She held onto the belief that a miracle was going to occur until the end.

Radha is the youngest of the three siblings. She absolutely adored her big brother. Radha waited on Nachu hand and foot. She would make him special treats and reminisce with him about their childhood years. Radha is a beautiful soul. When her father died, she lost trust in people. I was starting to gain her trust and then I was whisked away. I want her to know that I love her and I am here for her. I told her she could travel with me to orphanages and I want her to know to keep to my word so whenever she wants to come, she is welcome. My home is always open to her. I am blessing Radha to release the wall separating her from loving and trusting another human. Please have the courage Radha to knock down "The Rock of Gibraltar" like I did. I will help you.

Gauri is an amazing soul and one year older that Radha. She always has a beautiful smile and gives fantastic hugs. She is a great hostess as well. I am concerned she feels she has to please others; she reminds me of my angel Raquel in so many ways. Gauri gave me special chocolates that her friend's mother made for her. I will always remember and appreciate that gesture. I want Gauri to know I love her too and she could travel with me also if she wants; my home is open to her as well. I bless Gauri with releasing the need to please people and only do what her heart really wants. I want her to love herself and not care what others think.

Myonk is Nachu's cousin. He would meditate and chant for 5 hours every single day. He would change Nachu's diapers and sit by his bed whenever he had the opportunity; friends were usually in those positions most of the day and evening. Myonk would talk to Nachu and read stories to him. He would do physical therapy exercises with Nachu's legs. He has a heart of gold. Myonk is an upcoming star and his dream is to be on the show "Good Wives." I bless Myonk to be on that show. So, if anybody

Vanaja Ananda MA; MS

knows the producers of Good Wives, tell them about Myonk please. He will definitely be an asset and attract many viewers; the ratings will soar!

Sona deserves happiness in her life and I believe he was sent by Mohit. His name is Ravi and he sat by Nachu's side every evening, brushed back his hair and spoke words of love. It was a beautiful scene to witness. Nachu loved Ravi. When I asked him why he loved Ravi, he said "Ravi's heart is so pure and he is wonderful." Nachu's last wish was for everyone in his family to accept and love Ravi so there is no more conflict within the household. I believe Ravi will be a great role model for the girls if they allow him into their hearts and I pray that this occurs. This family needs happiness and joy. I know Mohit would only send the best person to his beloved family!

I bless this entire family, and that includes grandparents, aunts, uncles, cousins, friends and anybody who supported this family through their tragedies, to have tons of abundance in every way! Thank you for allowing me to be part of your beautiful community even if it was only for a week! I will never forget the week that my faith in humanity was totally restored by family and friends who offered unconditional love to a phenomenal soul!

I miss you so much my wonderful, magnificent, awe-inspiring, and courageous friend. I am so glad you are finally receiving the peace and happiness you deserve! I love you so much Nachu!

I came back to my house yesterday because I wanted to love something that wouldn't judge me and that was the house that I lived in for 17 years. I knew beyond a doubt that even though I treated this house poorly, it still loved me and accepted me for who I am. I needed to be in this deity to obtain the peace I needed so desperately,

After I left Maryland, I went to Heidi's, packed all my belongings and left her a note of eternal gratitude for opening up her home to me in times of need. I texted Duane to see if I could renege on our deal and come back home. He didn't respond immediately so I went to the beach and walked for two hours. During that walk, Duane told me there was no internet, heat or hot water. I didn't care and so I arrived at my house at 4:30PM. Before I arrived, I asked him if he could buy me a pizza so I had food sustenance for a few days. He said he would.

I had no money at all. A couple of weeks ago, I tried to donate $1 so I could be on Neal Donald Walsh's blog, but the debit card was denied. I am assuming the bank took the $30 I had left for their disgusting monthly charges. I had $15 cash left a couple of weeks ago and when I saw Duane at

Raquel's induction ceremony into the honor society, I asked him to borrow $100. I was planning to go to Washington DC for the Peace Ceremony and needed the money for gas and tolls. Even though MaryAnn was going too, I knew I needed to travel separately because I was planning to leave after Raquel's concert on the 17th. Little did I know, I would be using that gas and toll money for a trip to Maryland.

Duane and Kyle were at the house when I arrived. Although I was thrilled to see them, I wanted to be alone in the house. Duane gave me $50 to get pizza. So far, I haven't gotten any food and every food item is out of the house except two boxes of Matzoh which I have been munching on. Ironically yesterday was the first day of Passover. I may need to save that money for gas and tolls. I really want to participate in the 21 day Peace Meditation, but I am not sure the heads of the organization will let me due to the anger with all my emails. If I am not allowed to participate, I will have to go to Shamadu's, Michele's, Marcy's or Shelly's. Either choice involves money gas and tolls.

Even though I wanted to rest in solitude for a few days in the house I love, it is freezing here and I cannot sleep. To make matters worse, Duane apparently fell through the attic into our bedroom so the bedroom ceiling has a huge hole and a draft. My bedroom has always been my sanctuary and I choose to stay in this room. I guess I won't be getting my few days of peaceful retreat unless Duane brings me a heater.

I am not worried because I know with 100% certainty the divine always provides. So even though it seems bleak, I am convinced the situation will improve quickly. In fact, a couple of days ago Dave sent me an email about job opportunities for all coming very, very soon. Here is what is happening starting this month. Oh, I forgot I have no internet connection so here is the site . . . http://the2012scenario.com/2012/04/gregg-prescott-imminent-mass-arrests-of-globalists-bankers-and-political-elite/.

I posted it on all 3 of my facebook pages as well, but the only person who wanted to share the site was Ishtar. I met Ishtar through facebook when I started my Dreams Are Reality pages. He truly believed what I had to share. Not only that, he designed a cover for Dreams Are Reality. He designed it because he told me "in India people are taught to believe we are all brothers and sisters and should help each other whenever we can." Ishtar told me he knew I was going to be famous, but he didn't expect anything in return. I told him he would be famous as well because he would receive the credit and compensation he deserved. Ishtar sent a design and I didn't have a chance to really look at it because that was the day I was posting about Nachu; the Wednesday Sona told me to come quickly to Maryland. I am sure the design is perfect and that is the cover I choose for Dreams Are Reality because it was produced by a beautiful soul who only knew my energy through a few short conversations on facebook. Thank you Ishtar for believing in me; may you and your family be blessed with tons of abundance in every way!

EPILOGUE

A lot has happened since I last ended this book. There is a guided imagery tonight on May 20, 2012. There will be a solar eclipse and people will be praying around the world for the negativity in our etheric and astral realms to be released. If 144,000 people are doing this meditation, then we will be moving into the 4th and 5th dimension relatively soon. There is a designated time for everybody around the world to begin the visualization so everyone will be synchronized to the exact moment when the shadow of the Moon touches the mountaintop of Mount Shasta.

When the Moon eclipses the Sun in front of the Pleiades, a colony of stars, a light will emanate from the Galactic Sun directly through the Pleiades towards the Earth. This beam of light will burn through all obstacles on the etheric and astral planes. In short, fears, worries, greed, and other non-physical, detrimental forms will be dissolved so the divine light can emerge around the planet. We will be inviting the divine entities into our world to bring love, peace and compassion. This was so beautifully orchestrated and I had no idea this was the way our planet would be saved. As you could see for yourself, our civilization was transformed through the power of 144,000 people praying together! As a result of this magnificent change, I am now adding to the front cover "and all the people on this planet who joined together as one to bring our civilization back to its utopian beginnings."

Even though this monumental time in history is cause for celebration, there will be a lot of uncertainty, confusion and fear amongst society because corrupt politicians, banksters and corporation leaders will be removed from their positions and replaced with citizens of integrity, honesty and morals. People who don't understand the significance of what is transpiring will be bombarded with media sensationalism that will create fear and deep depression. Dreams Are Reality will help people comprehend what is truly happening to our planet in 2012 and even though it is incredulous, they will recognize ways to cope with their disbelief. This is the year for enlightenment and if it is your deep desire, you will achieve it. The quickest and most effective means to obtain this state of euphoria is to follow the techniques throughout this book. When one person exudes joy, hundreds around him receive this blessing as well.

I would like to end with an excerpt I posted on the "Dreams Are Reality Book" Facebook site. It is titled "Dreams Are Born From A Seed." As you are reading the passage, picture yourself as the seed rupturing and then helping other seeds rupture along with you. After this post, I will show you the last channeling from Greg Giles about what to expect in 2012.

DREAMS ARE BORN FROM A SEED . . . . When the seed is watered and nourished, it grows into a beautiful tree. The tree offers fruit and flowers for insects and animals to feast. Crevices and holes in the tree become shelter for small animals. Flying birds rest on the branches in between flights. Shade is supplied by the enormous branches and leaves. Children climb the sturdy trunk and build strong neuronal pathways as they explore the bark of the tree and swing from its branches. Those who see the tree as divine will experience healing energy when they are touching it. The roots of the tree are grounded securely in the earth so its strong trunk allows it to stand tall.

The tree of knowledge tells all the other seeds that are trapped inside their shell how to break free and join him in the forest. The tree guides the other seedlings and offers them the courage to rupture. Once that occurs, they become just as strong and tall as the first tree. One tree is not enough for all the creatures in the forest. Then there would be a "survival of the fittest" because each animal, bird, insect and so on and so forth would fight each other in order to have the blessings from that one tree. There need to be many trees in a forest for the world to maintain its existence! The universe is full of abundance . . . let's share the richness with all! Make Your Dream A Reality and Help Mankind In The Process!

What To Expect in 2012
http://2012portal.blogspot.ca/2012/04/plan-2012-normal-0-microsoftinternetexp.html
Plan 2012
LIBERATION OF PLANET EARTH
Phase 1: The Event (3-7 days)
Mass arrests of the Illuminati

- Military sweep
- 1 day viral and mass media info distribution
- 1 day arrests
- Up to 3 days shutdown
- 5 to 6 days conviction process

Phase 2: Restructuring (3-6 months)

- New financial system backed by precious metals and commodities introduced
- Federal Reserve dismantled, US Treasury prints gold backed money
- Basket of currencies (6 or more) base of world financial system
- Worldwide debt forgiveness
- Bank debts cancelled (credit cards, loans, mortgages)
- Banks must be re-licensed, no interest (usury)
- Multinational companies split and nationalized
- Redistribution of world's wealth begins
- Prosperity funds released
- Humanitarian and environmental projects funded
- Free energy technology and advanced medicines released
- Government UFO involvement disclosure
- International criminal court tribunal of Illuminati
- Statutory laws invalidated, return to Common Law
- Interim national governments and then elections
- UN restructured as head of Provisional government

- Disengagement of warring parties, military forces recalled permanently from active duty and restructured into peace keeping force, nuclear weaponry disarmed

Phase 3: First Contact (1-3 months)

- Contact with selected private individuals
- Re-education of humanity, including our history not told: Atlantis and Lemuria
- Global releases over TV and internet
- Increasing number of spacecraft make themselves known, culminating in a massive flyover when tens of thousands of ships will take part as final proof that other civilizations are out there
- Two week contemplation period
- First contact: Public contact at UN—Electric surge into Earth Light body—Galactic / Cosmic synchronization / Tachyonic alignment

After First Contact

- Interaction with Galactic Federation and Ascended Masters
- Start of technology transfers and educational programs
- Beginning of pollution cleansing and renewal of ecosystem
- Start of full consciousness training (Ascension chambers)
- Reunion with Confederation Fleet and Inner Earth

I just heard there will be a Lunar Eclipse on June 5th and there will be a special event in Kauai, Hawaii on August 11th-16th. Kauai is considered the "Garden of Eden" on earth. The Renaissance of Planet Earth is quickly approaching. The exact date is yet to be determined, but by the end of 2012 earth will be transformed into a new world and it happened because of you!

AFTERWORD

I knew prosperity wasn't coming until Dreams Are Reality was published because that was my intense desire. It was essential that people actually witness the abundance of the cosmos firsthand through me. Then, people will realize dreams aren't for a select group of the population; anyone can obtain anything he wants once he reprograms the limiting beliefs holding him back.

So, when I was staying at my house with no food, no hot water, and no internet, I knew I had to earn money quickly. I had three interviews the week after Easter and I didn't care what the job was. I just needed to be paid! The first interview was for an assistant to a physical therapist. The physical therapist said I was overqualified, but he wanted Wellness Kinesiology and would pay $100 for the session. I scheduled an appointment with him. At the next interview, the Director told me I would despise the job because it was a telemarketing position. However, she wanted me to conduct parenting workshops for her client base. I was guided to the third interview by my friend, Liza. The job entailed helping a stroke patient. I met the people and we immediately liked each other.

I went to work for Jack and Jill. I planned to play cards and games with Jill, go for walks on the Boardwalk and do some healing. However, the job was a blessing because I was able to use many techniques in this book.

Jack liked quantum physics. In fact, he had more books on the subject than I did. His inner being was craving the knowledge of his existence, but his external being was objecting. Did I mention Jack is an attorney and he needs irrefutable evidence? Even though he heard testimonial after testimonial about Braco's healing powers, Jack told me he would like to cross examine every person who spoke about the miracles that occurred as a result of Braco's gaze. I found Jack's skepticism extremely entertaining and similar to my own many years ago.

Jill was new to the quantum physics arena, but she learned quickly. Jill was extremely depressed when I arrived. She was devastated and angry for the unfairness of her current situation. Moreover, she was furious people abandoned her during her time of need. She would often say "miracles happen to other people, but not to me."

I will not go into any personal details, but from a physiological perspective Jill's left side of her body had minimal functioning capabilities. This is known as hemiplegia. It is ironic that my Master's Thesis was a case study about a Cerebral Palsy child who was hemiplegic. Jill's neuro-muscular impairment was exacerbated by her depressed emotional state. Specifically, she constantly thought about committing suicide. Prior to this illness, she would joke about getting a stroke. Please be careful what your thoughts are. Even as a joke, the belief becomes ingrained in our bio-memory and becomes a reality.

Jill went from visions of leaving the planet to enjoying life and laughing constantly. In fact, she said "my depression is totally gone; it flew away". She decided which relationships were detrimental to her well being. As a result, these people quickly disappeared from her life. Moreover, Jill realized she was pushing beautiful souls out of her life due to fear and panic. Once she allowed the walls to crash, she made strong bonds with loved ones and added new friends into her circle. People and animals were attracted by her energy. Her cat, Lovey, would barely approach Jill a month ago and now she comes easily, purring and offering lots of love, healing and companionship.

Her relationship with Jack moved toward divine love. A month ago, she blamed Jack for all the heartache in her life. Now, she adores him and focuses on his wonderful attributes of which there are many. Jill is currently planning a Caribbean vacation for their anniversary in December.

Before the debilitating illness, Jill was active. She jogged three times per week and did yoga a few times per week as well. Since her stroke in August 2011, she rarely moved from the bed. She refused to do exercises with her limbs when I first arrived. There was always an excuse. She worked arduously on her emotional healing so physical exercises weren't a priority although I was concerned the muscles would atrophy. I encouraged her to walk as much as possible.

One day, Jill and I went out for lunch. As we were walking into the restaurant, we bumped into her physical therapist from a couple of years ago when Jill had hip surgery. Mary's energy was great and it was evident she genuinely cared about her patients. The following week, Jill started physical therapy sessions with Mary. Jill worked hard and the results were transparent. At the third session, Mary complimented her for the vast positive changes. In fact, Mary literally bowed down to Jill in reverence. I smiled profusely.

I was ecstatic that Jill finally recognized her inner strength so the following morning I told her she could do whatever she wanted that day. Prior to that day, I would constantly give her choices, but the schedule was filled with meditations, healings, chantings and more with few breaks. Guess what we did that day? Absolutely nothing! I almost fell asleep. I was annoyed, but I didn't judge or say a word.

The next day I explained to Jill what I believe transpired the previous day. Jill felt she wasn't worthy of praise and she panicked when Mary commended her for her accomplishments. Jill was comfortable feeling inadequate and was petrified to believe she was not only worthy, but an amazing soul who was extremely competent. I told her she was sabotaging her recovery.

She was quiet for about 10 minutes and then she had a huge breakthrough. We sat outside in the sun waiting for her niece. Her niece was caught in Friday traffic, so we met her at the Diner. Jill walked from the middle of the parking lot, up 10 steps and into the restaurant. She didn't want the wheelchair and didn't ask to be dropped at the doorstep. She walked back to the car in triumph as well. This leap happened last Friday and it is only Tuesday, June 12th.

Yesterday, we listened to "The Vortex" by Esther and Jerry Hicks. I forgot about this collection of CD's, but recently I brought them out after a 2 year rest. Jilll loves these audios. When I arrived today, she told me she was going to purchase the CD's and give them to people who brought her to this state of high consciousness. Jill was referring to people she wanted out of her life, but she still cared about them and wanted them to achieve peace and fulfillment. Jill went beyond her revenge, anger and fear and wanted to help a being in need of love and support. I agree with Mary and I bow down to Jill as well.

Jill is truly an inspiration. Once again, I met a person with perseverance, drive and will power. Her creative juices enabled Jill to make gorgeous jewelry in the past. Soon, she plans to design her own jewelry line filled with healing crystals and one-of-a-kind artistic gems. I am so excited for her!

Jack and Jill are a glorious couple and I am elated we are friends. They have opened their home to me and they treat me like one of the family. I love them both so much!

I would be remiss if I didn't speak briefly about "The Musgatova Method" and "The Vortex" so you could add them to your stockpile of approaches. "The Musgatova Method" is a Tactile Integration technique founded by Dr. Svetlana Musgatova. She used this form of neuro-stimulation with burn victims in Russia. There was a school bus explosion and the students were severely burned. Dr. Musgatova activated all the layers of the skin through this massage therapy. As a result, the children began healing and releasing their fear. I learned this method directly from Dr. Musgatova when she traveled to New York. The class was outstanding and I recommend it highly. Her website is www.musgatovamethod.com.

"The Vortex" is a book about the "Law of Attraction." While I didn't read the book, a friend gave me 3 of the audios. In those audios, Esther answers questions about the universe. This series is an excellent vehicle to alleviate any fears of the unknown. You could read about Esther, Jerry and Abraham, the name they use for divine energy at www.abraham-hicks.com.

There are many strategies interspersed throughout this book. Using a myriad of sources will bring you to an awakened reality quickly. Usually the combination of methods will trigger an epiphany in the soul. That is what happened to Jill.

This Friday, June 15th, I am invited to teach En Kriya, Swamiji's peace meditation, to the Tao group. I was flabbergasted and elated. Tao followers learn about Buddha and Confucius. I have been to a few Tao classes and I plan to receive when the Tao Masters come to New Jersey. Their teachings are about love, peace, compassion and oneness. It was truly validated to me that this close knit group accepts other traditions and realizes we are all one no matter what faith we practice. I applaud them for merging the Hindu tradition with the Buddhist philosophy. I pray this group sets the prototype for all faiths joining together to promote love and peace. By the way, today is Buddha's birthday and I wish him a fabulous birthday! I was told he has a fat belly because he stores everyone's karmas. I absolutely love him!

Last week, Wendy gave me the "I Ching." It reminds me of "Living Enlightenment." I love it! I feel blessed Wendy bought this book for me and I plan to treasure it. I want to learn every faith and culture wherever I travel. I hope people and beings will have the patience to teach me. I also want to learn the language of the animals, plants and entities from other dimensions. I really believe I will! I will be the next Dr. Doolittle who teleports across the universe! OK Spock… it is time to make room for me and the rest of the world.

Today, June 14th, we went to see Amma Karunamayi. Jill decided to leave her wheelchair at home. She managed to walk all the way up the wide path into the temple. She was in excruciating pain and my heart went out to her. She never complained, but tears coursed down her face at intermittent intervals.

I guess Amma Karunimayi felt her angst because we were led to a front row seat and Amma walked directly in front of us as she traveled to her chair on the stage. The hilarious part of this beautiful scene was that I was holding a roll of toilet paper between my hands in prayer position as Amma passed. The videographer was recording her procession. Since I wasn't able to find tissues for Jill, I grabbed the toilet paper. The problem is I forgot to put it down. We laughed about that scenario all the way home.

At darshan, Amma told me to mix her sacred ash with mustard oil and apply the solution to Jill's hand and foot. Amma said the limbs will be back to normal. I was thrilled to hear this. Jack immediately went out to search for the mustard oil. He is still searching!

Jill was courageous and her fearlessness has paid off. She finally understands "the truth" and she phrases it so eloquently. Unfortunately, neither one of us remembers the words that came out of her mouth! Jack and Jill both have hearts of gold!

Jack reminded me about singing crystal bowls. Jill and I will be going to the concert next week at a place close to their house. More important, I want to tell you about T Love because she was also instrumental in my spiritual growth. T Love is a Reiki Master and conducts sound healing therapy through crystal bowl music. The vibration and frequency at which the crystal bowls resonate heals our body at a cellular level and penetrates our inner core. After these concerts, I felt rejuvenated and at peace. Visit T Love's site at www.quantum-wellness-center.com.

Rebecca is a channeler who brings in Mother Azna. Mother Azna is the divine feminine and she could be considered anybody you wish…Mother

Mary, Mother Theresa, Devi, Lakshmi, source, existential energy and so on. Mother Azna teaches Heart Point Technique and inserts a ray into your heart chakra to help you manifest your heart's desire. Go to www. rebeccamarina.com to read about Rebecca and Mother Azna.

The Jothi Light works at a cellular level. This meditation is magnificent and during the regeneration process, new cells are formed. During this process, the old and deformed cell is replaced with a healthy and vibrant cell. As a result, we naturally evolve into higher consciousness. Masha in New Jersey conducts these retreats and meditations. To find out more about Jothi Light please visit http://pranashakty.org.

I watched an excellent film on you tube last week I want to share with you. The movie, Thrive, is a phenomenal movie that should be in theatres. Foster Gamble's documentary weaves extraterrestrial findings, energy sources, The Federal Reserve, banking corruption, and the birth of a new world.

There is a World Congress in Kauai, Hawaii you may be guided to attend in August. Patricia Cota-Robles explains it beautifully so I share her letter below. Apparently our DNA is changing from carbon based to crystalline solar based. Please view the incredible video on you tube as well as last year's opening and closing ceremony; visit www.eraofpeace. org for details.

The 26th Annual
World Congress On Illumination

August 11-16, 2012
Kauai Marriott Resort, Kalapaki Beach
Kauai, Hawai

Humanity rode into 2012 on a wave of Unity Consciousness beyond anything we have ever experienced. Now our new Planetary CAUSE of Divine Love, which was cocreated in 2011 through the unified efforts of Heaven and Earth, is destined to become the order of the New Day on Planet Earth. With many miracles taking place this year, the Earth and all her Life will enter a renaissance of Love.

This transformation will not occur by happenstance, it will manifest through the conscious efforts of you and me and dedicated people all over the world. After all, we are cocreating this Earthly experience. In order to accomplish this mighty feat, the Company of Heaven is calling all of us to a higher service. Listen to your inner guidance and respond to this vital Heart Call from your I AM Presence.

Contrary to what we are seeing in the media, Humanity has reached a critical mass of awakened consciousness. The chaos we observe around the world is a critical factor in Earth's purging process. The obsolete, fear-based archetypes that have caused appalling pain and suffering for Humanity must collapse. This process is clearing the way, so that an Awakened Humanity can cocreate the patterns of perfection for the New Earth.

The people responsible for the atrocities we witness around the world consist of a minuscule fraction of the 7-billion people evolving on this planet. These wayward sisters and brothers of ours have absolutely NO power over the Light.

In Truth, every single day there are literally billions of people who turn their attention to a Higher Power and ask for Divine Intervention in their lives and the lives of their loved ones. These prayers are always heard, and they are always answered. As a result of Humanity's heartfelt pleas, the floodgates of Heaven have opened, and the Beings of Light in the Realms of Illumined Truth have come through the veil to meet us halfway.

For the past 25 years we have been anticipating the year 2012. There is a lot of speculation and misinformation circulating about what will happen during this auspicious year. Most of the sharings are fear-based and predicting things like devastating cataclysmic earth changes and the end of the world. Nothing could be further from the Truth.

We have already entered the initial impulse of the Shift of the Ages, and we have begun our ascent up the Spiral of Evolution into the 5th-Dimensional Realms of God's Infinite Light. Now it is up to all of us to fine-tune this natural evolutionary process, so that our global transformation will occur gently with the least amount of outer-world stress.

Humanity's ability to cocreate a new Planetary CAUSE of Divine Love in 2011, and our ability to expand that Divine Love into the order of the New Day on Planet Earth in 2012, has been greatly enhanced by the Love and Light flooding the planet from our sisters and brothers in the Company of Heaven and throughout our Solar System. One of the most powerful factors in this celestial assistance has come from our sister planet Venus.

Venus has always been considered the planet of Love. This is not just romantic hyperbole. Venus actually does reflect the full gathered momentum of our Father-Mother God's Divine Love to all of the planets in our Solar System.

Every 104 years Venus' service of bathing the Earth with Divine Love is greatly amplified through an event known as the Venus Transit. During this transit Venus passes between the Earth and the Sun, an event that lasts for 6-7 hours. As Venus crosses the face of the Sun frequencies of Solar Light exponentially expand Venus' ability to radiate Love to the Earth. This increased influx of Divine Love is anchored in the core of purity within every electron of precious Life energy on Earth.

The Venus Transit occurs in two parts. After the first transit the Love of Venus builds in momentum within every particle of Life on Earth. This prepares every facet of Life on Earth for the amplified influx of Divine Love that will bathe the planet during the second phase of the transit. The second part of the Venus Transit happens exactly 8 years minus two days later.

The first phase of the Venus Transit which we are now in the midst of took place on June 8, 2004. Since that time, the Love from Venus has been building in momentum softening the hearts and minds of Humanity and greatly enhancing the awakening that is taking place around the world.

On June 6, 2012, we will experience the second phase of the Venus Transit. Due to the unparalleled awakening that has taken place on Earth since June 8, 2004, this influx of Light will catapult Humanity and our new Planetary CAUSE of Divine Love into position for an event that will establish a renaissance of Love on Earth. With the God Victorious success of this impending event, Humanity will shift into a higher state of consciousness, a consciousness of Divine Love that will manifest as the order of the New Day for Planet Earth.

This unprecedented event will take place during the 25th anniversary of Harmonic Convergence, August 11-16, 2012. This will be a critical step of preparation before the influx of Light that will bathe the Earth during the December 21, 2012 Solstice.

It is difficult for us to truly grasp the magnitude of what this will mean for the Earth and all her Life. But the Beings of Light have said that from that moment forth, the physical manifestation of the patterns of perfection for the New Earth will begin to externalize as a tangible reality. This will be the Heaven on Earth of our own creation through our I AM Presence. These patterns for the New Earth will reflect Humanity's Oneness and the Reverence for ALL Life.

The Divine Plan

In order to accomplish this monumental facet of the Divine Plan, we are being asked by our Father-Mother God and the Company of Heaven to unite our hearts, heads, and hands during the global event that will take place August 11-16, 2012. There will be many diverse ways in which we can weave our Light into this Divine Plan. Pay close attention to the opportunities that are presented to you. Ask your I AM Presence for guidance, and ask this wondrous aspect of your own Divinity to pave the way, so that you will be able to fulfill your heart's calling.

As you may know, the Hawaiian Islands are remnants of the continent of Lemuria. The initial impulse of Humanity's fall from Grace took place on Lemuria aeons ago. Since Harmonic Convergence in August 1987, the Hawaiian Islands have played a critical role in reversing the adverse effects of Humanity's fall from Grace and the healing of Mother Earth. Many of the people embodied at this time have links to Lemuria. They realize that they are here now to heal the atrocities that resulted on that continent when Humanity fell into the abyss of separation and duality.

The Island of Kauai is known as the Garden Isle. This island contains within its etheric records the Immaculate Concept or Divine Blueprint for the body of Mother Earth. This is the original pristine beauty that Mother Earth expressed prior to the fall. It is the verdant splendor that we have always referred to as the Garden of Eden.

Kauai's etheric records also contain the archetypes for the Divine Potential of what Mother Earth will express when she Ascends into her rightful place on the 5th-Dimensional Spiral of Evolution and dons the seamless garment of her new Solar Reality.

For the facet of the miraculous Divine Plan that will take place August 11-16, 2012, our Father-Mother God and the Company of Heaven have asked us to organize a gathering of dedicated people from all over the world who will be willing to work with the Company of Heaven and to serve as surrogates on behalf of ALL Humanity. Together, these selfless volunteers will cocreate a mighty transformer through which the Light of God will flow to catapult Humanity and our new Planetary CAUSE of Divine Love into a frequency of Light that will establish a renaissance of Love for all Life on this blessed planet.

Then, through the I AM Presence of every man woman and child, Humanity will shift into a higher state of consciousness establishing Divine Love as the order of the New Day on Planet Earth.

This gathering will take place August 11-16, 2012, within the embrace and exquisite beauty of Kauai in the Hawaiian Islands. The vehicle that will be used for this gathering will be the 26th Annual World Congress on Illumination.

Listen to your heart; a Clarion Call is now reverberating from the Heart of our Father-Mother God invoking your assistance in this holy endeavor. Respond according to your inner guidance. Know that whenever you volunteer to serve as an Instrument of God on behalf of Humanity and ALL Life evolving on Earth, the floodgates of Heaven open to support you and to help pave the way for your participation.

It is critical that Lightworkers from around the world be physically present for this important facet of the unfolding Divine Plan. All of the Lightworkers who have been prepared to serve in this wondrous way on behalf of Humanity and all Life on this sweet Earth will know who they are through the inner promptings of their heart. Trust your inner guidance. Your Light is needed NOW!

In addition to those who are inspired to be physically present in Kauai, there will be people who will join in consciousness from points of Light around the world. These dedicated souls will project the Light flowing through their Heart Flames into the Portal of Light where selfless volunteers are physically gathered in Kauai, Hawaii. Thus our unified efforts will expand a thousand times a thousandfold.

Every person will be in his or her right and perfect place. No facet of this Divine Plan is any more important than another. What IS important, is that we each respond to whatever our I AM Presence is guiding us to do. We must Trust and KNOW that if we are being guided to be physically present on the Island of Kauai, then our I AM Presence and the Company of Heaven will assist us in paving the way. This is true whether we need assistance with time, energy, money, or courage to accomplish this facet of our Divine Mission.

The Company of Heaven has asked us to organize this monumental event in a beautiful, healing venue, so the selfless volunteers who make the sacrifice to serve in this way will truly experience a glimpse of Heaven on Earth. I want to assure you that this will be a life-transforming experience for you. In wondrous ways, your life will never be the same.

If you feel the heart call to participate in the 26th Annual World Congress on Illumination, please read the following pages very carefully, and follow the simple instructions.

If you do not feel the heart call to be physically present in Kauai, know that this is a global event and you can weave your magnificent Light into our Chalice of Light from wherever you are on the face of the Earth.

God Bless YOU, for your willingness to be the Open Door for the influx of Light that will lift Humanity's consciousness and establish a renaissance of Love for all Life on this blessed planet.

The Beings of Light will be guiding us step by step through the months leading up to the event in August. I will be sharing the information through my free e-mail articles which you can sign up to receive on our website www.eraofpeace.org.

In addition to the guidance we will be receiving from the Company of Heaven, each of our I AM Presences will be guiding us through our own unique preparation.

Ask for assistance, and remain in a state of Listening Grace at all times. This is an amazing opportunity for each of us to add to the Light of the world.

Today, June 19th, was an extremely challenging day. For the past few days, Jill has been regressing. Anger, fear, discontentment, and hopelessness have surfaced. It is not uncommon for emotions to crescendo after seeing an Avatar face-to-face. Whatever is troubling the soul usually appears like a viper so it could be destroyed. Sometimes, people want to escape from the mirage of terrifying emotions and others will face it head on. Jill has wanted to escape and I couldn't let this happen. I needed her to delve into the source and I encouraged her to feel angry, hatred, fear, sadness or any other emotion for 15 minutes. It was difficult for her, but she did the best she could. I fed her some words to use. By the end, she was exhausted and furious at me! She tried to get me to quit, but I only offered her unconditional love with no commiseration. I feel this may send her on the road to a speedy recovery or it might backfire….she may recoil into a shell. I am praying she will once again overcome her fear. I feel her torment and my heart breaks, but I know I have to be tough to help her through this roadblock. Only time will tell if Jill's recovery is expedited or prolonged. Either way, I know she will be a blessing to humanity and she will heal herself! I bless Jack and Jill to have a great relationship and excellent health.

Tonight my mala (rudraksha bead necklace) broke. A year ago, 3 malas broke in one week. They all had pictures of Swamiji and they were energized by him. When the third mala broke, I understood it was time to release Swamiji's form. I put on my original mala that contained the rudraksha beads without Swamiji's picture. I never took the mala off. In fact, I had a mala on for 3 years. I wore it to bed, in the shower, and in the ocean. It was a part of my very being. When my mala broke tonight, I realized it was a sign. I no longer need the security of that necklace on my personage. I finally am able to release my attachment to Swamiji. I absolutely adore him, but I no longer need him. It is a magnificent feeling! I love everything and everyone, especially myself unconditionally. People have gotten angry at me and then they love me again. I accept people for who they are. People live in a state of fear and they harbor ill feelings as a result. I will continue to send my love and bless them to release any blockages preventing them from reaching eternal peace. We are all one and we are all a magnificent child of the universe. Solely, we are a microcosm in the universe just floating around, but together we become unified into one beautiful soul that is capable of creating our utopian society. Open your heart and let the love expand. Follow your dreams and your passions. Radiate joy and transmit that excitement and enthusiasm to all those in your presence. You chose to be on this planet right now for a reason and that reason is becoming clear. Celebrate your courage and heroism. You all deserve it.

I have added new entities to my prayer this last month. I want to share it with you now. I am deeply grateful to all these beings and I embrace the light they all shine upon every man, woman, child, animal, plant, inanimate object and electron on this planet. I look forward to meeting and hugging the aliens from other dimensions. Traveling on their spaceships will be loads of fun! Thank you divine beings in every dimension and the universe! I love you all!

I am grateful for all the blessings and abundance in my life. Thank you Swamiji, Lakshmi, Shiva, Devi, Ganesh, Kali, Durga, Saraswathi, Parvati, Patanjali, Krishna, Brahma, Vishnu, Shankara, Usui, Banyan Tree, Bhakta, Bikram, Buddha, Jesus Christ, Vanaja, Champ, Shamadu, Dheera, Reverend Janice, Pastor Augustine, Amma Karunamayi, Ammaji, Mother

Meera, Braco, Sai Baba, Osho, Babaji, all the deities, Archangel Michael, Raphael, Gabriel, Uriel, Metatron, Sandolphon, Jophiel, Haniel, Raziel, Zadkiel, Aziel, Angel Daniel, Crystal, Chantall, Aurora, Maya, Isabella, Fairy Kayla, Nemah, all the dragons, all the snakes, all the gnomes, all the salamanders, the house and the lawn at the house, the padukas, money in any form, Dreams Are Reality, Kailish, Arunachala, Kauai, Malaysia, Bididi Ashram, Mother Theresa, Mother Mary, Serapis Bay, King Solomon, Lady Isis, Lady Azna, John of God, Padre Pio, Confucius, Kwon Yin, Guanine, Agoris, Merlin, Saint Germain, Joan of Arc, Arcturian Healing Team, Ashtar Command, Dr. Lorphan, Galactic Federation, Menokshee, Nandi, Hanuman, Nachu, Mohit, Malaysian Masters, Siddhars, all Celestial and Terrestial beings, Vanaja in every dimension, Ashwini and Ashwini twins, Mother Nature, the sun, the moon, all the planets, all Ascended Masters, all of mankind and all existential energy. Thank you for your divine blessings and for pouring your love onto this planet and allowing everyone to open their heart chakras. Love and compassion are back on earth to stay!

CONCLUSION

At one point, Lena asked me why I wasn't self publishing if the information was crucial to release to the public. At the moment of her inquiry, I believed people had to pray together for the publishing to occur. Shortly after I made that statement, I received emails from several sources directing people to pray for world peace during the Solar Eclipse and Venus Transit. These emails demonstrated to me that Lightworkers in countries around the world were organizing group prayer meditations in order to eliminate negativity and invite divine beings to our planet. I forwarded these emails and posted them to my facebook pages.

My ego told me I was the one who needed to disclose this information. In reality, Lightworkers have known about the transformation for many years. Thank God I only knew since February 2012. The divine knows me too well. If I knew 8 or even 4 years ago, I don't think this book would have been written. Patience is not my virtue although I have gotten much better with my waiting abilities.

Once I was convinced Lightworkers were disseminating the information in a friendlier way, I was at ease. I decided to self publish through Balboa Press which is a subsidiary of Hay House. Dreams Are Reality should be available in approximately one month. All this information needs to reach the public as quickly as possible and my ego needs to be slashed. Right now, who publishes this book is irrelevant.

I have been attempting to edit this book for the past few weeks. Since I am a perfectionist, I feel this book will never be published. I have found numerous grammatical errors. I have spelled words like tattoo incorrectly and inserted then when I meant than. An English professor

280

would probably give me a C if this manuscript was graded based on punctuation and grammar.

It is July 7, 2012 and I decided I am sending this book to print unedited. I will just be adding the Afterword and Conclusion sections. I feel if I change even one word, you would question whether I edited other parts of the book. It is imperative you know this book was written unedited and it is crucial this book is available to people when the transformation starts to occur.

You will find the contents fascinating and helpful. You will find it captivating to observe the writing style changes as my mind transformed from the beginning to the end of the book. Hopefully, you will be able to ignore minor mistakes and focus on the crux of the book. I am sending this to Balboa on Monday, July 9th. Let's see how long it actually takes to come out in print.

LETTERS

This was the first letter on my Dreams Are Reality Book site to share with the world...

> To All the Beautiful Souls on this Planet,
>
> I finished the book "Dreams are Reality." I have attached passages for your perusal. This manuscript needs to be in the hands of Louise Hay at Hay Publishing on February 29, 2012. Louise Hay is a renowned global author and her publishing company was chosen for two reasons. First, she speaks about the power of thoughts and positive affirmations in all of her books. In fact, her reference guide explains how negative mental patterns create disease and that is the premise of my book. I have learned techniques to help people release negative mental patterns so they could self-heal quickly. All is revealed in the book. Second, Louise Hay is spiritual so she understands that everyone is Divine.
>
> The gravity of the earth is decreasing and as a result people will have fewer thoughts; it has already started. Those who are achieving inner peace through meditation and yoga will be happy with this transition. However, the majority of the population will be distraught, depressed and suicidal. "Dreams

Are Reality" will help these people move to higher consciousness rapidly.

I started this book on January 19th and my intuition says the manuscript will be at Hay House on February 29th. This may sound ludicrous, but I have seen miracles occur before when the impossible became real. In 2000, I and a few other individuals were instrumental in creating enough media and political noise to get a bill fast tracked through the legislation. This bill enabled organizations renting from churches in New Jersey the ability to continue their businesses. Archives in newspapers and network news broadcasts will validate this statement. Moreover, this happened in one month.

I also wrote a 180 page proposal for a potential elementary charter school in less than 3 months. The New Jersey Board of Education liked the curriculum and we passed all interviews until the final interview; at that point True Potential was denied funding.

I know the strength of thoughts especially when many people have the same intensity. A friend reminded me about the book "Six Degrees of Separation" by John Guare. The idea behind this book is that we are approximately six steps away from any person on earth. He says networking is the key because it provides a chain to connect two people in six steps or less.

I am asking you to read the excerpts. If you believe what is written in those pages are true, please send this letter and the attachment to your friends and colleagues. Right now, I am solo, but with the help of all of you, we could help create a planet of love, peace, grace, compassion, bliss and healing.

Thank you for taking the time to read this. In 1776, Dickinson wrote "United We Stand, Divided We Fall." These seven words became the motto for America. Please help Dreams Are Reality become the motto for the entire world.

Vanaja Ananda.

This was the post that was emailed to spiritual leaders around the globe. It was also posted to 100's of facebook and twitter sites!

MIRACLES HAPPEN EVERYDAY...I need your help for a miracle to happen today! I just finished a book titled Dreams Are Reality. I have learned how to reprogram negative thought patterns buried in the subconscious and all the secrets are revealed in the book so you could obtain any desire you want.

I chose certain sites to share this message because I believe the people reading this paragraph have been guided to it by the divine. I want this book to be published by Hay House exclusively because I know Louise Hay knows the power of positive affirmations.

Here's how you can help. Please pray "Dreams Are Reality" is published by Hay House. That is all. If you feel moved, please share the site with others. When people pray together in passion for a cause, the universe will move mountains to fulfill your wishes.

I want to thank you in advance for making my dream a reality. My dream is to bring love, peace, compassion, grace, bliss and healing to the world. God bless all you beautiful souls! http://www.facebook.com/pages/Dreams-Are-Reality-Book/406139436068366

This is the first letter I wrote to Louise Hay. I was hesitant to show it to you, but it is important for you to understand the state of my mind at that time. I believed the transformation was occurring on February 29th. When I read this now, I am amused. Who writes letters like this and actually sends it? I raise my hand...

February 19, 2012

Louise L. Hay
Hay House, Inc.
Carlsbad, CA 92018-5100

Dear Louise,

I am writing to you today because I have a bestselling book. I am soon to be a renowned global author. I have reached a level of higher consciousness where I recognize the truth, and I know you understand exactly what I mean. I chose Hay House Publishing because so many signs have pointed toward you. The divine wants you to publish this book.

This book may cause controversy, however the truth always prevails so I am not concerned. This year, 2012, is the year of huge transformation among our citizens. The earth is changing and as a result people are going to be in depression if they don't understand what is happening and techniques to release them from the torture. You know the power of positive affirmations. You are even included in my book as a source to help mankind achieve inner peace.

The book I am writing will be finished on or before February 29th. It is a book about my life and the buried negative mental patterns in my subconscious. It teaches effective strategies and techniques to overcome these beliefs that are embedded within our bio memory. It talks about my guru, Ascended Masters, Archangels and the divine in all of us. I speak about the power of thoughts and how we are able to manifest anything we want because the cosmos the is full of abundance. The best part is the end. I want people to watch my life transform right in front of their eyes since many manifestations are about to occur quickly.

Right now, I have $200 left. When my bank statement comes, I can prove it. There is a little under $100 in the bank and I have $100 in my purse. I have no job and I have been staying with a friend since January 16, 2012; I started writing this book 2 days later on the 18th. Abundance in every way is about to be showered on me because it is the cosmic law. I have a couple of mental patterns left and they are quickly dissolving because I know the secret. The secret is shared to the entire world in this book.

I feel this book is being downloaded from the cosmos as I am just a conduit for the divine like everyone on this planet. I was going to send this to you when I was finished, but now I feel urgency. I need you to record the date and time of this email. Starting tonight at 8:30PM EST an auspicious celebration in the Vedic tradition commences. This event lasts 24 hours. I am not sure what is going to happen during this festival, but I feel strong energy coursing through my body and riches may be appearing from the divine quicker than I think. There is no time or distance in the universe.

I plan to send an email to my friend Heidi tonight. I will tell her which chapter I have completed in the book at 7PM. Although, I may be revising grammatical errors, I promise I will not make any significant changes to the content from the beginning to the point where I stopped at 7PM. Heidi promised to save the email. In case auspicious things start occurring in my life, it is important for people to realize up until this point, I was a pauper with no idea how I was going to support myself and my children.

Even though I had doubts in the past, there are no doubts now. I am positive that *all* my dreams will be a reality. They are all documented in the book and I plan to create more dreams along the way.

I know, beyond a shadow of a doubt, that I will soon be a billionaire. I am going to use that money to help so many people and fulfill my dreams. In case I don't get to the end in time, I want people to also know I am going to use the money for materialistic purposes as well. I am going to have a home on the beach and a personal shopper since I love clothes, but don't enjoy shopping. Anything I want, I will get and people will just have to accept that fact. However, my big mission is to bring as many people as I can to higher consciousness. I will help all of mankind from any religion, race or creed. I will offer scholarships for those who truly can't afford my services or my guru's, but also have the intensity and determination to transform. I plan to change the educational paradigm because it is failing our children. I plan to heal children with neurological disorders. I plan to sell my curriculums to both preschools and elementary schools around the world. I plan to visit orphans around the world and show them the divine loves them and they are not alone. Our house is in foreclosure; I plan to nourish that house back to health so that my ex husband and my kids are back in the home they love. More important, I want to show people that I am no different than them. They have the same power. I want to show them how they could access that power so we could transform the world together. Even though we are individuals, we are all one. All religions are all the same because we are all created from the same energy source.

Everyone came to this earth as a blank slate and societal norms tarnished our innocence and beauty. Through my book, I show people how to love themselves first and then transpose the internal adoration to an unconditional love for every being on this planet and in other dimensions as well.

I look forward to hearing from you and feel blessed we are all connected; when one succeeds, hundreds succeed and when thousands succeed, millions succeed! Many miracles have already happened and more are about to explode; not just for me but for the entire world. There are enlightened beings all over this planet helping people as we speak. Many are mentioned in my book. Let's bring our planet back to a civilization of peace, love, grace, compassion, bliss and healing.

Thank you for understanding the contents of this letter without further explanation and before you even read the book. It is imperative we get this book published quickly and circulating throughout the world. I know your publishing company is the vehicle to help the divine with its vast mission.

Best Regards,
Vanaja

Here is the second letter dated almost a month after the first letter...much calmer.

March 8, 2012

Ms. Louise Hay
Hay House, Inc.
P.O. Box 5100
Carlsbad, California 92018-5100

Dear Louise Hay,

If you are reading this letter, then I know people have finally joined together in unity and our world will soon be a place of peace, love, compassion, grace, bliss and healing. I am thrilled! I have been trying to show people the power they possess inside when thoughts are reprogrammed. More important, I was teaching them about the strength of collective consciousness when people pray for a cause together. In this case, the cause is to help mankind.

I have written a book titled "Dreams Are Reality." This book describes in detail the negative emotional patterns trapped in my subconscious and the techniques I used to reprogram these limiting beliefs. Of course, among the techniques is your book "Heal Your Body" which I always carry in my purse. Dreams Are Reality refers to similarities between various religions and the meaning behind the phrase "everyone is divine and we are all one." I speak about angels, Ascended Masters and enlightened beings currently on the planet available to help anyone who asks. In addition, I explain neuroscience concepts and how they relate to our thought patterns, specifically the fight or flight mode.

Furthermore, the story unfolds to demonstrate the love by a disciple for her Avatar. The trust, faith and surrendering to the divine was the inspiration to pursue the dream to help mankind against all adversity and ostracism from society. This love is so beyond any lust; it is pure unconditional love. That love has transmitted to the world.

The best part is the ending because everybody stands together as one and puts other people's fears above their own by sharing a letter from beings in other dimensions. When this occurred, we sent the message to the divine that we are ready for the transformation into the 4th and 5th dimension!

I have attached the original letter that went out to all the beautiful souls on this planet. I also attached the passages that were included with that letter. Please let me know when you would like to see the manuscript which will help people overcome the fear and shock they may be experiencing in 2012. The answers to help people reprogram their negative thoughts are all in Dreams Are Reality.

Have a wonderful day! Thank you for having a beautiful soul and showing me the power of positive affirmations. I am eternally grateful. I can be reached at xxx-xxx-xxxx or via email at xxxxxxxxxxxx. I look forward to hearing from you!

Best Regards,
Vanaja Ananda

ABOUT THE AUTHOR

 It is difficult for Vanaja to remember a time when she was not intrigued by human emotions, self-esteem and stress. She was convinced negative beliefs began in the early childhood years. In an attempt to gain an understanding of the central nervous system, Vanaja undertook a program in neuroscience and education and graduated with a Master of Science from The Teachers College at Columbia University. Also, she has a Master of Arts in Early Childhood Education from Kean University.

While pursuing her degrees, she owned and operated an early childhood learning center full time and an alternative healing center for people seeking to achieve their true potential. Vanaja is a Reiki Master and Nithya Healer. In addition, her specialties include Neurofeedback, Wellness Kinesiology, Tactile Integration, memory retention techniques and other cutting edge programs.

Her spiritual journey began in 2009 at a class in India with an enlightened Master. That program transformed Vanaja's life and there was a major shift physically, emotionally and spiritually. This awakening was extremely powerful and she wants to share her findings with the world.

Vanaja lives in New Jersey and loves nature. She loves dancing, movies, nature walks, and reading. She enjoys being spontaneous and playful. She finds joy in everything she does and offers unconditional love to all. The simple things in life excite Vanaja. She adores her two children, Kyle and Raquel.